ReFocus: The Films of Steve McQueen

ReFocus: The International Directors Series

Series Editors: Robert Singer, Gary D. Rhodes and Stefanie Van de Peer

Board of advisors:
Lizelle Bisschoff (Glasgow University)
Stephanie Hemelryck Donald (University of Lincoln)
Anna Misiak (Falmouth University)
Des O'Rawe (Queen's University Belfast)

ReFocus is a series of contemporary methodological and theoretical approaches to the interdisciplinary analyses and interpretations of international film directors, from the celebrated to the ignored, in direct relationship to their respective culture – its myths, values and historical precepts – and the broader parameters of international film history and theory.

Titles in the series include:

ReFocus: The Films of Susanne Bier Edited by Missy Molloy, Mimi Nielsen and Meryl Shriver-Rice
ReFocus: The Films of Francis Veber Keith Corson
ReFocus: The Films of Xavier Dolan Edited by Andrée Lafontaine
ReFocus: The Films of Pedro Costa Nuno Barradas Jorge
ReFocus: The Films of Sohrab Shahid Saless Edited by Azadeh Fatehrad
ReFocus: The Films of Pablo Larraín Edited by Laura Hatry
ReFocus: The Films of Michel Gondry Edited by Marcelline Block and Jennifer Kirby
ReFocus: The Films of Rachid Bouchareb Edited by Michael Gott and Leslie Kealhofer-Kemp
ReFocus: The Films of Andrei Tarkovsky Edited by Sergey Toymentsev
ReFocus: The Films of Paul Leni Edited by Erica Tortolani and Martin F. Norden
ReFocus: The Films of Rakhshan Banietemad Edited by Maryam Ghorbankarimi
ReFocus: The Films of Jocelyn Saab Edited by Mathilde Rouxel and Stefanie Van de Peer
ReFocus: The Films of François Ozon Edited by Loïc Bourdeau
ReFocus: The Films of Teuvo Tulio Henry Bacon, Kimmo Laine and Jaakko Seppälä
ReFocus: The Films of João Pedro Rodrigues and João Rui Guerra da Mata Edited by José Duarte and Filipa Rosário
ReFocus: The Films of Lucrecia Martel Edited by Natalia Christofoletti Barrenha, Julia Kratje and Paul Merchant
ReFocus: The Films of Shyam Benegal Edited by Sneha Kar Chaudhuri and Ramit Samaddar
ReFocus: The Films of Denis Villeneuve Edited by Jeri English and Marie Pascal
ReFocus: The Films of Antoinetta Angelidi Edited by Penny Bouska and Sotiris Petridis
ReFocus: The Films of Ken Russell Edited by Matthew Melia
ReFocus: The Films of Kim Ki-young Edited by Chung-kang Kim
ReFocus: The Films of Jane Campion Edited by Alexia L. Bowler and Adele Jones
ReFocus: The Films of Alejandro Jodorowsky Edited by Michael Newell Witte
ReFocus: The Films of Nuri Bilge Ceylan Edited by Gönül Dönmez-Colin
ReFocus: The Films of Claire Denis Edited by Peter Sloane
ReFocus: The Films of Yim Soon-rye Edited by Molly Kim
ReFocus: The Films of Steve McQueen Edited by Thomas Austin

edinburghuniversitypress.com/series/refocint

ReFocus:
The Films of Steve McQueen

Thomas Austin

Edinburgh University Press is one of the leading university presses in the UK. We publish academic books and journals in our selected subject areas across the humanities and social sciences, combining cutting-edge scholarship with high editorial and production values to produce academic works of lasting importance. For more information visit our website: edinburghuniversitypress.com

© editorial matter and organisation Thomas Austin, 2023, 2025
© the chapters their several authors 2023, 2025

Grateful acknowledgement is made to the sources listed in the List of Figures for permission to reproduce material previously published elsewhere. Every effort has been made to trace the copyright holders, but if any have been inadvertently overlooked, the publisher will be pleased to make the necessary arrangements at the first opportunity.

Edinburgh University Press Ltd
13 Infirmary Street,
Edinburgh, EH1 1LT

First published in hardback by Edinburgh University Press 2023

Typeset in 11/13 Ehrhardt MT by
IDSUK (DataConnection) Ltd

A CIP record for this book is available from the British Library

ISBN 978 1 3995 1093 6 (hardback)
ISBN 978 1 3995 1094 3 (paperback)
ISBN 978 1 3995 1095 0 (webready PDF)
ISBN 978 1 3995 1096 7 (epub)

The right of Thomas Austin to be identified as the editor of this work has been asserted in accordance with the Copyright, Designs and Patents Act 1988, and the Copyright and Related Rights Regulations 2003 (SI No. 2498).

Contents

List of Figures	vii
Notes on Contributors	ix
Acknowledgements	xi
Introduction: Why Steve McQueen Matters *Thomas Austin*	1

Part 1

1	From *Exodus* to *Small Axe*: Steve McQueen's Filmic World of Two Halves *Elisabetta Fabrizi*	17
2	Surplus Liveness and Black Male Performance in *Girls*, *Tricky* *James Harvey*	30
3	Eye Witness: Memorialising Humanity in Steve McQueen's *Hunger* *Eugene McNamee*	41
4	Shame and the City: Subverting Neoliberal, New York Singleton Culture in *Shame* *Niall Richardson*	59
5	If it is to be done, how?: Considering a Robeson Biopic *Shana L. Redmond*	73
6	The Slave Narrative and Filmic Aesthetics: Steve McQueen, Solomon Northup and Colonial Violence *Philip Kaisary*	78
7	Working for/working with/working against – *Widows* and the Politics and Poetics of Genre *Matthias Grotkopp*	96

Part 2

8 Is *Small Axe* Cinema or Television and does it Matter? Discourses of Authorship and Production in the Publicity for *Small Axe* 113
   Christine Geraghty

9 *Small Axe* and/as Cinematic Television 128
   Hannah Andrews

10 Love in a Cold Climate: *Lovers Rock* 144
   Thomas Austin

11 A Different Kind of Dread: Dub, Ecstasy and Collective Memory in *Lovers Rock* 158
   Kwame Phillips

12 The Burden of Expectation: Where are the Women in Steve McQueen's *Small Axe* Films? 172
   Patricia Francis

13 *Boy with Flag* and Black British Experience in *Handsworth Songs* and *Red, White and Blue* 185
   Thomas Austin

14 *Small Axe* is a Start: An interview with Bernard Coard 194
   Thomas Austin

Films and Television Programmes 199
Bibliography 201
Index 220

Figures

0.1 Steve McQueen, *Charlotte*, 2004 (still). 16 mm colour film, no sound, 5 minutes 42 seconds, continuous projection. © Steve McQueen. Courtesy the artist, Thomas Dane Gallery and Marian Goodman Gallery   2
0.2 Denise Gooding and Wayne Haynes in *Uprising* (2021). BBC ONE   3
1.1 Steve McQueen, *Bear*, 1993. 16 mm black-and-white film transferred to video, continuous projection, no sound, 10 minutes 35 seconds. Exhibition View, 'Steve McQueen', 16 March–1 September 2013, Schaulager, Muenchenstein/Basel 2013. © Steve McQueen. Courtesy the artist, Thomas Dane Gallery and Marian Goodman Gallery. Photo Tom Bisig, Basel   20
1.2 Steve McQueen, *Exodus*, 1992–7. Super 8 mm colour film transferred to video, no sound, 1 minute 5 seconds. © Steve McQueen. Courtesy the artist, Thomas Dane Gallery and Marian Goodman Gallery   27
2.1 Steve McQueen, *Girls, Tricky*, 2001 (still). Colour video transferred to digital file, sound, 14 minutes 47 seconds. © Steve McQueen. Courtesy the artist, Thomas Dane Gallery and Marian Goodman Gallery   34
4.1 Brandon's deathly white face represented in an out-of-focus shot so that it resembles the ghoulish mask of Michael Myers. Fox Searchlight, Film4, UK Film Council   66
4.2 Halloween lighting emphasises the sense of dystopia and makes David's pick-up of Sissy seem very sinister. Fox Searchlight, Film4, UK Film Council   69
7.1 Veronica at the crossroads. New Regency Productions, See-Saw Films, Film4, Lammas Park   97

7.2	Obama posters in the background of Marcus's murder. New Regency Productions, See-Saw Films, Film4, Lammas Park	103
9.1	Kingsley (Kenyah Sandy) bathes, a moment of affective intensity in *Education*. BBC ONE	134
9.2	Leroy (John Boyega) a small figure in the foreground as he is scrutinised by an interview panel. BBC ONE	136
9.3	Leroy (John Boyega) as a silhouette, robbed of individuality and agency in his placement between two incompatible worlds. BBC ONE	136
10.1	Martha and Franklyn in *Lovers Rock*. BBC ONE	150
10.2	Steve McQueen, *Just Above My Head*, 1996 (still). 16 mm black-and-white film, transferred to video, no sound, 9 minutes 35 seconds, continuous projection. © Steve McQueen. Courtesy the artist, Thomas Dane Gallery and Marian Goodman Gallery	151
11.1	*Lovers Rock Dub* screenshot	170
13.1	*Boy with Flag, Winford in Handsworth Park, 1970* by Vanley Burke	186
13.2	*I Am Not Your Negro*. Velvet Film, Artémis Productions, Close Up Films, 2016	190

Notes on Contributors

Hannah Andrews is Associate Professor in Film and Media at the University of Lincoln. She is Senior Editor at *Critical Studies in Television* and is the author of *Television and British Cinema: Convergence and Divergence since 1990* (2014) and *Biographical Television Drama* (2021). Her current book project is *TV and Caricature*, due in 2024.

Thomas Austin is Professor of Film Studies at the University of Sussex. This is his seventh book.

Elisabetta Fabrizi is a curator and academic based in Newcastle. As Head of Exhibitions at the British Film Institute, Curator of Artists Films at Tyneside Cinema and Curator at BALTIC Centre of Contemporary Art, she has gained extensive experience of curating and commissioning artists' moving image, across galleries and cinemas. She holds a PhD on the curation of the moving image from Newcastle University.

Patricia Francis is a doctoral candidate at Nottingham Trent University, a filmmaker and Royal Television Society Award nominee. Her films include *Many Rivers to Cross* (2013), *Making Waves* (2015) and *The Art of Oppression* (2021). Patricia's practice-based research explores women's activism through documentary art film.

Christine Geraghty is Honorary Professorial Fellow at the University of Glasgow. Publications include *Women and Soap Opera* (1991) and *Now a Major Motion Picture: Film Adaptations of Literature and Drama* (2008). Her most recent research examines diverse casting in British period drama. She is an editor of the *Journal of British Cinema and Television* and is Book Reviews editor for *Critical Studies in Television*.

Matthias Grotkopp is Assistant Professor of Digital Film Studies at Cinepoetics – Center for Advanced Film Studies, and the Seminar for Film Studies at Freie Universität Berlin. He is the author of *Cinematic Poetics of Guilt. Audiovisual Accusation as a Mode of Commonality* (2021). He supervises the project 'Intervening World Projections: Audiovisuality of Climate Change' funded by the German Research Council.

James Harvey is Lecturer in Film and Media at the University of Hertfordshire. He is the editor of the collection, *Nationalism in Contemporary Western European Cinema* (2018), and the author of *Jacques Rancière and the Politics of Art Cinema* (2018).

Philip Kaisary is the author of *The Haitian Revolution in the Literary Imagination: Radical Horizons, Conservative Constraints* (2014) and *From Havana to Hollywood: Slave Resistance in the Cinematic Imaginary* (forthcoming). His writing has appeared in *Atlantic Studies*, *Law & Humanities*, *MELUS* and *Slavery & Abolition*. He is an Associate Professor at Carleton University, Ottawa, Canada, where he teaches legal, literary and cultural studies.

Eugene McNamee is Professor of Law at Ulster University Law School. His research interests include law, culture and humanities themes that relate to constitutionalism.

Kwame M. Phillips is Senior Lecturer in Media Practices at the Winchester School of Art, University of Southampton. He is the co-author of '"The people who keep on going": a radical listening party' in *The Futures of Black Radicalism*, and co-creator of the multisensorial sound art work 'Kabusha Radio Remix'. Phillips's work focuses on resilience, race and social justice using multimodal and experimental methodologies.

A writer and scholar, **Shana L. Redmond** is the author of *Anthem: Social Movements and the Sound of Solidarity in the African Diaspora* (2014) and *Everything Man: The Form and Function of Paul Robeson* (2020), which received numerous awards, including a 2021 American Book Award. She is Professor of English and Comparative Literature at the Center for the Study of Ethnicity & Race at Columbia University (New York) and, in 2022–3, President of the American Studies Association.

Niall Richardson convenes the MA in Gender and Media at the University of Sussex. He is the author of the monographs *The Queer Cinema of Derek Jarman* (2009), *Transgressive Bodies* (2010), *Ageing Femininity on Screen* (2018) and *Trans Representation in Contemporary Popular Cinema* (2022).

Acknowledgements

Thanks to: all those who wrote chapters for this book; Philip Kaisary and Eugene McNamee, who very kindly allowed me to republish their articles; Bernard Coard for being such a generous interviewee; Clive Nwonka, Rinella Cere, Louise Cope and all those who attended the Annual Contemporary Directors Symposium on McQueen at the University of Sussex in September 2021; Gillian Leslie and Sam Johnson at Edinburgh University Press and the ReFocus series editors Robert Singer, Stefanie Van de Peer and Gary D. Rhodes for all their hard work, support and enthusiasm; Alicia Canter for her brilliant photograph of McQueen; Vanley Burke, Leila Hassan Howe, Sarah Lee, Robert Yates, Gavin Mensah-Coker, Medeni Fordham; Georgia Spickett-Jones and Rosa Gubay at the Thomas Dane Gallery; the School of Media, Arts and Humanities at the University of Sussex for research leave and funding; finally Guy, Noah, Stella and most of all my number one, Charlotte.

Chapter three, 'Eye Witness: Memorialising Humanity in Steve McQueen's *Hunger*', by Eugene McNamee, was first published in *International Journal of Law in Context* 5: 3, 281–4 (2009) by Cambridge University Press.

Chapter five, 'The Slave Narrative and Filmic Aesthetics: Steve McQueen, Solomon Northup and Colonial Violence', by Philip Kaisary, was first published in *MELUS* 42: 2, 92–114 (2017) by Oxford University Press.

Chapter twelve, '*Boy with Flag* and Black British Experience in *Handsworth Songs* and *Red, White and Blue*', by Thomas Austin, was first published in *Senses of Cinema* 98 (2021) online.

In memory of my mum, Sue Austin, 14.4.1944–26.12.2019

INTRODUCTION

Why Steve McQueen Matters

Thomas Austin

In 2013 the companion publication to a major exhibition spanning twenty years of works by Steve McQueen at Schaulager, Switzerland, quoted him: 'The eye is the only part of the body that is all about the inside as such. Like an open wound' (Stäheli 2013: 133). One of the pieces in that show, *Charlotte* (2004), is a silent, looped 16 mm film of just under 6 minutes. Shot in red and black, the eye of actress Charlotte Rampling is framed in extreme close-up. Slowly, from screen right, McQueen's finger approaches the eye, until it finally touches, pokes and prods it, and the eye blinks repeatedly in response. (See Figure 0.1.) The following summary captures how the vulnerability of Rampling's eye generates acute discomfort for viewers: 'The cropped image keeps going in and out of focus. In analogy to the camera eye, the lens of the actress's eye must continually adjust to the approaching finger. [. . .] Viewers cannot help sharing the almost unbearable sense of vulnerability that wavers between excitement and menace' ('*Charlotte*' 2013: 170). In her influential study of the horror film genre, Carol Clover wrote: 'Horror privileges eyes because, more crucially than any other kind of cinema, it is about eyes. More particularly, it is about eyes watching horror [. . .] we take it in the eye' (Clover 1992: 167, 202). With its threatening red hues, McQueen's *Charlotte* certainly invokes the horror genre, and perhaps pornography too, while the eye in peril recalls an iconic sequence from Buñuel's *Un Chien Andalou* (1929). But *Charlotte* also reminds us that all visual art enters viewers' consciousness via the eye, and that this constitutes both an opportunity and a responsibility for the artist. Relatedly, visual art carries another potential threat, that of truth-telling. The late Jean Fisher wrote: 'If one accepts that art, rather than existing in some detached aesthetic realm, is part of life, then its efficacy lies in its capacity to disclose the unacknowledged forces that govern our reality' (2013: 74). Such understandings have shaped McQueen's career, and his mainstream output as much as his gallery work.

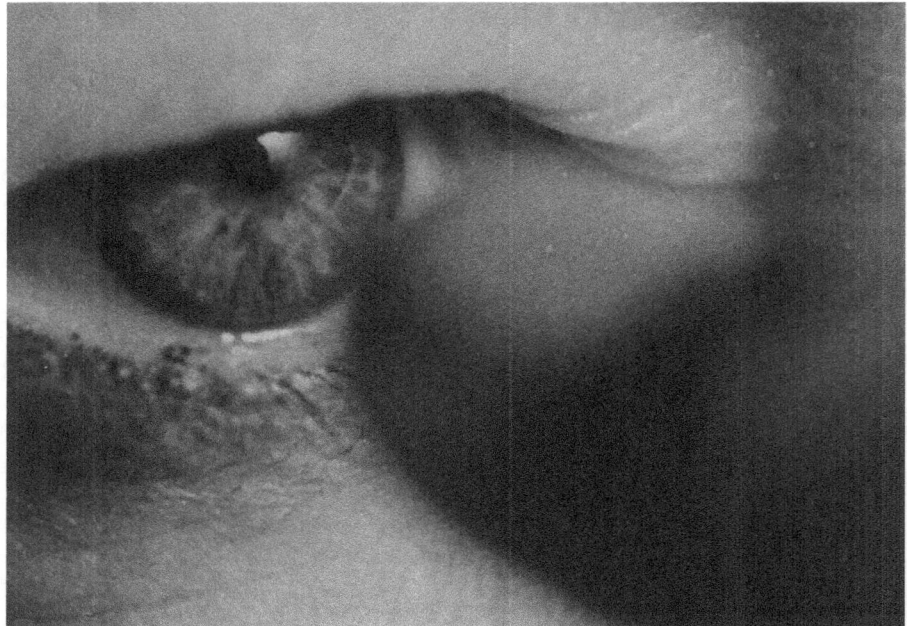

Figure 0.1. Steve McQueen, *Charlotte*, 2004 (still) 16 mm colour film, no sound, 5 minutes 42 seconds, continuous projection. © Steve McQueen. Courtesy the artist, Thomas Dane Gallery and Marian Goodman Gallery.

In *Blame*, the central episode of *Uprising* (BBC ONE, 2021), McQueen and James Rogan's three-part television documentary about the 1981 New Cross Fire in which thirteen young Black people died, editor Brett Irwin inserts extreme close-ups of interviewees' eyes four times in the first two and a half minutes.[1] (See Figure 0.2.) If *Charlotte* stages Rampling's somatic response to an external stimulus, *Blame* focuses on bodies in close-up as corporeal indices of internal stimuli, particularly the emotional impacts of recalling a night of trauma and loss. In doing so, it adheres to the logic of what I have called the *surface-depth hermeneutic* (Austin 2016b: 421). Evident across fiction films and documentaries, as well as photography, this visual regime presents bodily surfaces as texts to be deciphered, legible cues to the inner depths of the person on screen.[2] 'Perhaps more than any other image in cinema, the closeup of the human face is a surface that conventionally implies intimate access to, and knowledge of, the "truth" of the human subject' (Austin 2016b: 422).[3] The emotional and psychological interiority of fire survivors Sandra Ruddock, Wayne Haynes and Denise Gooding, and the latter's mother Ena Gooding, is crucial to the cumulative power of *Uprising*, and the *Blame* episode in particular. An implicit promise to divulge inner truths is encoded in close-ups of their eyes, but is not mobilised in the

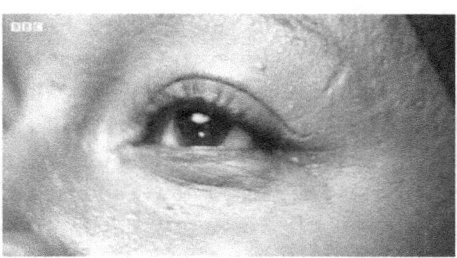 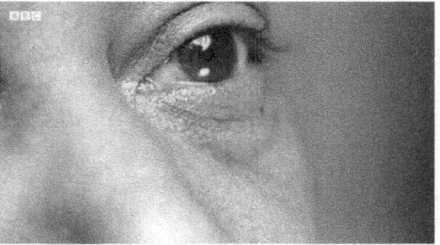

Figure 0.2. Denise Gooding and Wayne Haynes in *Uprising* (2021), BBC ONE.

other interviews in the same episode, with Black activists or the white fire investigator and various police officers. The documentary builds from this visualisation of Black pain towards a systemic critique of white structures of power in policing, politics and the media, whose responses to the New Cross Fire ranged from callous indifference to open racism.

What both *Charlotte* and *Uprising* share, despite their evident differences, are two elements that have characterised much of McQueen's work over the decades. First, physicality, in particular an abiding exploration of the power of haptic imagery and how it can contribute to an immersive experience for viewers. This often serves a critical engagement with race, and manifests his understanding of the corporeal and sensorial dimensions of racialisation. As Sachi Sekimoto and Christopher Brown have written: 'Race is not a static object that circulates within social discourse and practice; race is charged with emotion, affective energy, communal affiliation, moral orientation, gut reaction, bodily rhythms, and multisensorial memories' (2022: 6).[4] McQueen's multisensorial filmmaking celebrates Black cultures, including the rituals and textures of food, language, music and fashion.[5] He repeatedly challenges the racist disciplining of Black sensory experience, since 'oppression functions by depriving individuals of their sensorial authority and ownership of their own perceptual experience' (Sekimoto and Brown 2022: 14). But he also explores the impacts of power on white bodies too, most notably in his first feature film, *Hunger* (2008), which is analysed by Eugene McNamee in chapter three.

Secondly, *Charlotte* and *Uprising* manifest a self-reflexivity about image-making per se, what Darby English (2013: 40) has called 'the feeling of madeness'. This is more or less overt in *Charlotte*, which incorporates a projector as part of the installation, but it is also implicit in *Uprising*'s self-conscious determination to claim space for a re-examination of 'momentous events in our nation's history', as McQueen has put it.[6]

The ambition to tell marginalised or previously unheard stories, especially those of Black people in Britain, also shapes the landmark television series *Small Axe* (2020), which is discussed extensively across seven chapters in the second half of this book. Released on BBC ONE television in the UK and streamed via Amazon Prime Video in the US, the *Small Axe* pentalogy was one of the most important Anglophone audio-visual events of 2020. Coinciding with a year of Black Lives Matter protests across the world in the wake of the murder of George Floyd in Minneapolis, the series brought hitherto neglected stories of Black Britain to peak-time mainstream television, and within reach of more than 100 million Amazon Prime subscribers (Travers 2021). In conversation with the historian David Olusoga, McQueen has stressed the importance of both the Black Lives Matter movement and the Covid-19 global pandemic in shaping its reception.[7]

> Olusoga: I think people will presume these films were rushed into existence in response to the murder of George Floyd.
> McQueen: You could never make these films in that time. We were in the middle of it when this unfortunate thing happened with George Floyd. [. . .] the catalyst [for the wide exposure of the ensuing protests] was Covid-19, this pandemic. [. . .] kids out on the street . . . People all over the world were sat at home because of the pandemic, looking at the TV, it was undeniable. How many times [before] has a Black person been murdered with a camera on them? (Olusoga 2020: 32)

Small Axe also showcased Black creative talent in filmmaking, acting and music. Olusoga (2020: 26) comments that the series 'raises difficult questions not just about the history of British racism. It also stands as an indictment of the UK film and television industry and its failure to value Black stories and harness Black talent.' Furthermore, if, as Nadine El-Enany argues, 'the abstraction of day-to-day life in Britain from its colonial history means that immigration law and policy [. . .] are not seen as ongoing expressions of empire' (2020: 2, cited in Naidoo 2021: 18), then this dramatisation of the recent history of the West Indian diaspora in London counters the dominant tendency of post-Imperial disavowal in UK media, politics and education.

A BLACK MAN IN WHITE SPACE

McQueen faced discrimination and disparagement at an institutionally racist secondary school but went on to build an extraordinarily successful career in the visual arts, becoming an artist of global significance.[8] He won the prestigious Turner Prize for contemporary art in 1999, the best motion picture Oscar in 2014 for *12 Years a Slave* (2013) and was knighted in 2022.[9] In the process, he repeatedly overcame structural barriers as a Black man entering white space.[10] To achieve this level of success, autonomy and influence in the UK and Hollywood media industries as a Black Briton is unprecedented. McQueen's gender has certainly been an important contributing factor here. It is also vital to acknowledge the work of significant pioneers of Black British image-making in the decades before his emergence.[11] These include, among others, Trinidad-born Horace Ové, whose groundbreaking *Pressure* (1975) was the first feature film to be made by a Black Briton;[12] Melenik Shabazz, whose *Burning an Illusion* (1981) was the second such film; Isaac Julien, Maureen Blackwood and the Sankofa Film and Video Collective (formed in 1983); and John Akomfrah and the Black Audio Film Collective (formed in 1982).[13] In order to briefly resituate McQueen within something of this context, I present in chapter thirteen a comparison of the visual styles and political strategies of Akomfrah and McQueen, grounded in an analysis of their differing remediations of a photograph by Vanley Burke in, respectively, *Handsworth Songs* (1986) and the *Small Axe* episode *Red, White and Blue*.

Despite his presentation in media discourse as an exceptional figure, McQueen is also, and necessarily, a team player. His collaboration with former BBC Films producer Tracey Scoffield, a founding director of Turbine Studios, began with *Small Axe*, a series that was ten years in the making.[14] (In chapter eight, Christine Geraghty explores Scoffield's role in the making of *Small Axe* 'as an intermediary who can manage the film/television differences and is committed to getting McQueen's vision through the television processes and onto the screen'.) The pair prioritised employing BAME crew on the production whenever possible, and also established a training scheme for BAME workers (see Geraghty's chapter; Thorpe and O'Hagan 2020). McQueen used his profile and institutional leverage to co-develop television productions that extended some of the topics of *Small Axe* into documentary formats, again working with Scoffield as executive producer, along with James Rogan and Soleta Rogan of Rogan Productions. He was an executive producer on *Black Power: A British Story of Resistance* (BBC TWO, March 2021, directed by George Amponsah) and on *Subnormal: A British Scandal* (BBC ONE, May 2021, directed by Lyttanya Shannon). The latter documentary is on the dumping of Black children in schools for the 'educationally subnormal', a topic which was the focus of the fifth *Small Axe* drama, *Education*. (Both *Education* and *Subnormal* are discussed further in chapter 14.) McQueen also worked with Scoffield and Rogan Productions on the documentary trilogy *Uprising* (discussed above), which he co-directed with James Rogan.[15]

It is important to note that McQueen continues to work across a range of diverse forms with their particular implied audiences. His career is not simply an inevitable, teleological 'progression' from gallery work to the broader address of independent cinema with *Hunger* and *Shame* (2011), then Hollywood with *12 Years a Slave* and *Widows* (2018), followed by BBC television and Amazon Prime with *Small Axe*. (At the time of writing, his most recent new gallery work is *Sunshine State*, which premiered at Milan in April 2022.)[16] The diversity of these works also corroborates the veracity of Fisher's statement on McQueen: 'Although [he] emerges from the socio-political and historical configurations of British culture and its imperial legacy, his work is certainly not reducible to it' (Fisher 2013: 73). Indeed, as late as 2017 Ashley Clark admitted to 'a slight ruefulness' that McQueen was 'not yet making films about Black British life'.[17] Of course, that has changed dramatically with *Small Axe* followed by *Uprising*, *Black Power* and *Subnormal*.

In the interview with Olusoga (2020: 29), McQueen said of *Small Axe*:

> Sometimes . . . I want the burden. I hope that by doing it, one can inspire other people to do other things. . . . To push on to the next generation. [. . .] You get a lot of white people saying, 'Oh Steve, the burden of this.' It's like, "The burden of what?' We have to talk about this. What would I do otherwise? Write love songs? These stories are so rich. I feel the opposite. I feel blessed.

The chapters gathered here consider how McQueen has negotiated this burdensome blessing, alongside many other concerns and interests pursued across nearly thirty years. Looking back from *Small Axe* and *Uprising* to McQueen's early video work in the 1990s and his subsequent move into filmmaking, this book explores key continuities as well as moments of change across his career so far. How has he navigated multiple audio-visual formats and varied institutional settings? What might be considered his salient aesthetic and political achievements, as well as his weaknesses?

WHITE ON BLACK, BLACK ON WHITE

The majority of chapters in this book are written by white people, including myself. This might accord with perspectives that have characterised McQueen as 'a white darling', that is as a Black artist whose work has been widely recognised, praised and awarded by white cultural gatekeepers and institutions.[18] But, just as importantly, it also attests to the relative paucity of Black academics in film and television studies, particularly in the UK.[19] Moreover, the freedom of white academics to write about Black filmmakers and topics is a privilege that should be interrogated as a tacit marker of asymmetrical power relations, rather than simply taken for granted. The act of white writing about McQueen should not be apologised for, but neither should its politics be elided, since it is a raced, and classed, entitlement that is not available to all. To think otherwise would be to ignore Bourdieu's reminder, following Weber, that every elite has 'a theodicy of [its] own privilege' (1998: 43).

McQueen himself has consistently refused to be confined to Black subjects and collaborators. In a 2012 interview to promote his second feature, *Shame*, he asserted:

> Yes, it's all about white folks [. . .] [But] The majority of my art films have black protagonists. So I'm free to do anything I can do. Rock 'n' roll, blues, classical, whatever. My next picture is going to be predominantly black people, and the one after. I grew up in a society where – fortunately, in Britain – I didn't live in a segregated area. So I make movies about whatever I want to make movies about. (James 2012: 38)[20]

Such freedom is not easily granted to Black creatives, and might be considered another manifestation of the discourse of exceptionalism which often circulates around McQueen, one in which he himself has participated at times. (See further discussion of this exceptionalist narrative in chapter eight by Christine Geraghty.)

In his introduction to the edited collection *Black on White: Black Writers on What it Means to be White*, white American professor David Roediger writes:

> few [white] Americans have ever considered the idea that African Americans are extremely knowledgeable about whites and whiteness. [. . .] [But] From folktales onward African Americans have been among the nation's keenest students of white consciousness and white behavior. [. . .] As [James] Baldwin argued, '. . . a vast amount of the energy that goes into what we call the Negro problem is produced by the white man's desire not to be judged by those who are not white'. (Roediger 1998: 4, 6, citing Baldwin 1985)

McQueen should be acknowledged alongside the Black writers and artists celebrated by Roediger as a filmmaker whose work has not only investigated multiple dimensions of Black experience, but has also repeatedly explored the meanings of whiteness, in both British and American contexts. Some of these insights are examined in Niall Richardson's examination of *Shame* in chapter four and Matthias Grotkopp's discussion of *Widows* in chapter seven. A further instance I would like to briefly draw attention to here is the way in which white British upper-middle-class taste is skewered in the Small Axe episode *Alex Wheatle*, a coming-of-age narrative based on the life of the eponymous Black British writer. In a flashback, the fifteen-year-old Wheatle listens to a car radio as he is driven away from Shirley Oaks, Croydon, the brutal white-run children's home where he grew up, to a hostel in Brixton. The public-school tones of broadcaster Roy Plomley introduce the writer Roald Dahl as his guest on BBC Radio Four's *Desert Island Discs*. Dahl states his love of 'very great music, like a Beethoven quartet', but as he does so the broadcast fades out and is replaced by *Everyday Wondering*, a reggae song by Johnny Clarke. At the same time, the leafy lanes of Shirley give way to a slow-motion point of view shot figuring the teenager's first impressions of Brixton. This concise gesture combines a refusal of the institutionally sanctioned cultural taste of privately educated white men with a celebration of Wheatle's discovery of a 'very great music' of his own, reggae. The drama goes on to chart his emergent sense of belonging via the street talk and reggae music of Brixton in the late 1970s and early 1980s.[21]

McQueen's oeuvre not only spans inquiries into Black and white experience at the level of primary content. His aesthetic influences also derive from both Black and white artistic traditions. To take just the most obvious examples, he has reworked a canonical white text, Buster Keaton's 1928 silent classic *Steamboat Bill Jr.*, in his short film *Deadpan* (1997), along with the popular but less critically sanctioned UK television series *Widows* (1983–5) in his 2018 film of the same name. And he has also engaged with Black cultural antecedents, from his adaptation of Solomon Northup's 1853 slave narrative *12 Years a Slave* to his deployment of reggae music, most notably in the *Small Axe* dramas *Lovers Rock* and *Alex Wheatle*.[22] McQueen's output can thus be understood as 'double-voiced', in that it draws on 'a two-toned heritage' and also speaks to both Black and white audiences, in much the same way that Henry Louis Gates Jr. has characterised African-American literature (1988: xxiii).

THE SHAPE OF THIS BOOK

The Films of Steve McQueen is an interdisciplinary collection of responses to the multiplicity of McQueen's artistic universe. Necessarily, the chapters assembled here employ diverse critical methodologies and formats to scrutinise his work. They variously probe political, institutional and discursive contexts, and offer textual analyses shaped by considerations of race, gender, aesthetics, music and social memory. The book is structured chronologically and in two parts, the first of which centres on McQueen's gallery installations and the feature films *Hunger, Shame, 12 Years a Slave* and *Widows*. Chapter one also looks forward from McQueen's artworks to the *Small Axe* pentalogy. The second part of the book addresses multiple dimensions of *Small Axe*, but also reaches back to trace some connections with McQueen's earlier gallery work, as in chapter ten.

In chapter one Elisabetta Fabrizi examines how an 'interest in creating the conditions for viewers to become aware of their own presence is at the core of McQueen's oeuvre', in both gallery works and films. She tracks how McQueen 'has adapted the framing strategies employed in the gallery to develop a highly personal and potent cinematic language' that hinges on the coexistence of realism and abstraction. James Harvey's close reading of the installation *Girls, Tricky* (2001) in chapter two mobilises related questions by comparing it to earlier works where McQueen also 'displays a concern for deconstructing classical modes of bodily representation'. For Harvey, 'The relationship between stillness and movement here, embodied at different times by McQueen's camera and Tricky's performance, works to undermine the film technology's ability to fully capture the Black male performer.'

Eugene McNamee employs a differently political methodology in chapter three in order to contextualise and explore *Hunger*, McQueen's first feature, which centres on the hunger strike and death of Irish Republican Army officer Bobby Sands in the Maze Prison in 1981. McNamee writes that in *Hunger* 'the idea of humanity as nobility and resilience in the face of extreme physical situations to the point of death is offered to the public as a form of memorialisation that [. . .] even if it cannot avoid political interpretation, manages to avoid political partisanship and cliché'.

Chapter four is Niall Richardson's 'Shame and the City: Subverting Neoliberal, New York Singleton Culture in *Shame*'. Richardson posits *Shame* as a nightmarish reworking of Manhattan as a sexual utopia, the glamorous 'backdrop for countless rom-coms and musicals'. He suggests that, through a combination of McQueen's distinct visual aesthetics and a dystopian revision of genre conventions, '*Shame* refuses to represent sex "addiction" as a pathology, or the result of trauma, but instead codes it as the *inevitable* consequence of neoliberal, pornographied society.'

In chapter five Shana Redmond considers McQueen's abiding interest in the life and career of singer-actor-activist (and more besides) Paul Robeson. Redmond both responds to and looks beyond McQueen's 2012 gallery installation *End Credits*, which staged redacted FBI surveillance reports on Robeson, speculating about a (once rumoured) McQueen biopic of Robeson. She argues that the life of this 'Black giant' was 'messy and complicated and vast, exceeding the big screen'. Could McQueen capture the impossibility of such an idea, by delivering a Robeson biopic that would inevitably challenge the genre's simplistic investments in the singularity of an individual, much as Robeson himself did through his manifold achievements?

McQueen's next feature after *Shame*, the widely lauded *12 Years a Slave*, won an Oscar for best motion picture, along with two others (best actress in a supporting role to Lupita Nyong'o and best adapted screenplay to John Ridley). However, like its two predecessors, the film also met with some criticism, and Philip Kaisary offers an important critique in chapter six. He writes: 'the film's extremely moving visual and aural poetics deepen its problematic occlusion of slavery's "systematicity"'. Key to this problem are changes made in the adaptation of Solomon Northup's 1853 narrative, which is 'stripped of its accounts of black agency and rebellion'. Another omission is Northup's detailed descriptions of the production of sugar and cotton in Louisiana: 'This emphasis on the production of a commodity for the market as a mode of explanation for plantation slavery is absent in the McQueen version, which instead conceives of slavery as either paternalistic or barbarous based merely on the contrasting personalities of individual slave owners.' Finally, the 'gorgeous cinematography' of the film ultimately 'reproduces the colonial gaze of the tropics as paradisiacal', a perspective diametrically opposed to that of the people enslaved there.[23]

In chapter seven Matthias Grotkopp focuses on *Widows*, a heist film that surprised some reviewers and audiences with its unapologetic generic foundation. Attending to *Widows*' mise-en-scène, Grotkopp argues that 'These surface features are important both for the allegorization of the heist with the craft of filmmaking but also with reference to a world in which appearances of race and gender are matters of life and death.' Dramaturgical structure and dialogue also present the widows' heist as 'an action within a world ruled by masculinity and racism as means to wield power'.

Christine Geraghty opens part two of the book by asking 'Is *Small Axe* cinema or television?' Her analysis includes how *Small Axe* was discussed and reviewed in the UK magazine *Sight and Sound* as primarily a collection of films, rather than a television series. Geraghty explores McQueen's public comments, which oscillate between defining *Small Axe* as television or as five distinct cinema films. She notes his omission of any 'detailed discussion about the input of the BBC' in making *Small Axe*, and states, 'at a time when the BBC is under threat, McQueen's reticence about this crucial aspect of British screen production is striking'. Finally, Geraghty emphasises the significance of executive producer Tracey Scoffield as a key 'intermediary between television and film', between the BBC and McQueen as a filmmaker and artist.

In chapter nine Hannah Andrews also interrogates the status of *Small Axe*, asking 'what it means for *Small Axe* to be conceptualised as "cinematic television"'. She pursues an answer via four vectors of inquiry: aesthetics, affect, address and access. In terms of audience address, she notes throughout *Small Axe* a switching from foreground to background which encodes a Black gaze that is 'not only trained to scan the background for traces of [social and cultural] recognition but also for signals of risk'. Andrews argues that 'An access-led understanding of cinematic television may conceive of *Small Axe* as cinema *through* television, at the levels of production and reception.' Indeed, 'While the imagery, composition, and construction of affect in the *Small Axe* films may be "cinematic", their political significance [. . .] is profoundly televisual.'

In her book *The Sonic Color Line*, Jennifer Lynn Stoever argues that listening is 'an indispensable mode of literacy, imagination, and memory, both personal and historical' (2016: 52). She notes, however, that 'Without ever consciously expressing the sentiment, white Americans often feel entitled to respect for their [aural] sensibilities, sensitivities, and tastes, and to their implicit, sometimes violent, control over the soundscape of an ostensibly "free," "open," and "public" space' (2016: 2). This commonly assumed white privilege which simplifies and devalues Black sounds and musics, regulating and disciplining them as variants of 'noise', is prevalent in the UK as well as the US, but is vigorously contested in the *Small Axe* episode *Lovers Rock*. Here McQueen celebrates a house party in early 1980s West London as a joyful assertion of community and identity in the face of prevalent racism. In chapter ten I consider the gender politics of both lovers' rock as a sub-genre of reggae and *Lovers Rock* as a drama. I also scrutinise the film's aesthetics, including the ramifications of McQueen's redeployment of a framing device first used in his short *Just Above My Head* (1996).

Kwame Phillips takes a different angle towards *Lovers Rock* in chapter eleven, initially by focusing on the 'Kunta Kinte Dub' dance scene at the end of the party. Phillips argues that 'as depicted in *Lovers Rock*, dub provides an ephemeral space for ecstatic liberation from racial trauma'. He then asks, 'what would a dub cinematic version of *Lovers Rock* look like?' The resulting project, *Lovers Rock Dub: An Experiment in Visual Reverberation*, condenses the 70-minute runtime of *Lovers Rock* to 17 minutes of 'manipulated, mixed, remixed, reordered, resequenced footage', which uses dub music as an inspiration 'to explore the "lingering and tugging resonances, echoes, hauntings, associations [and] traces" of diasporic memory' (Vidali and Phillips 2020: 69).

In chapter twelve, Patricia Francis develops a feminist critique of *Small Axe*. She argues that, although the series 'offered wonderful insights into aspects of the lived experiences of Black Britons', in the process of constructing it around Black male protagonists 'McQueen risks reinforcing traditional, patriarchal and racist conceptions'. Francis writes that 'Black women are seen in multiple roles across the *Small Axe* films [. . .] but the emphasis is on the women as carers, nurturers, and sexual beings'.

Vanley Burke's photograph *Boy with Flag, Winford in Handsworth Park, 1970* appears in both the *Small Axe* episode *Red, White and Blue* and in Black Audio Film Collective's seminal 1986 film *Handsworth Songs*. In chapter thirteen I ask, what parallels and contrasts are evident across these two deployments of Burke's image? What do they tell us about the aesthetic and political strategies of two of the most important directors in British filmmaking, John Akomfrah and Steve McQueen?

Chapter fourteen is based on my interview with renowned Grenadian activist, politician and author Bernard Coard. Our discussion revisits his seminal 1971 work on institutional racism in British education, *How the West Indian Child is Made Educationally Sub Normal in the British School System*. Coard talks about his response to the dramatisation of the scandal he uncovered in the *Small Axe* episode *Education*, his involvement in the spinoff documentary *Subnormal* and his critique of the current state of UK education.

NOTES

1. The trilogy traces links between the fire, the subsequent Black People's Day of Action and the Brixton uprising that same year. IMDb credits McQueen and Rogan as joint directors of *Uprising*, and executive producers, along with seven others.
2. Metaphors of exteriority and interiority, surface and depth, are somewhat reductive figurations of the complex interfaces between body and mind. Elizabeth Grosz (1994: 22) augments these with an alternative paradigm, the Möbius strip, which she argues is better suited to developing an understanding of 'embodied subjectivity' and 'psychical corporeality'.
3. See also Doane (2003: 90): 'It is barely possible to see a close-up of a face without asking: what is he/she thinking, feeling, suffering? What is happening beyond what I can see?'
4. My own critical approach to McQueen is influenced by Sekimoto and Brown's argument that 'Race is real *because* it is socially (and perceptually) constructed' (2022: 3, italics in original).
5. McQueen is thus not only interested in what James Baldwin termed 'the rage of the disesteemed' (1998: 121). On the importance of food in *Small Axe*, see Robinson 2020; Travers 2021.
6. '[T]he New Cross Fire passed into history as a tragic footnote, but that event and its aftermath can now be seen as momentous events in our nation's history' (McQueen in Morgan 2022).
7. For further discussion of the series' critical reception, see chapter eight by Christine Geraghty.
8. McQueen told David Olusoga, 'I was cast aside really, and the journey of my life was drawn in the sand when I was 14 years old' (McQueen in Olusoga 2020: 29). In an online discussion of the BBC ONE documentary *Subnormal*, which explores the earlier scandal of children of West Indian origin being sent to schools for the 'educationally subnormal', a topic also addressed in the *Small Axe* episode *Education*, McQueen stated: '[I]t was very painful for me because to bring this story up, even in *Education* [. . .] in some ways there was [. . .] a deep shame [about] what happened to me at school. [. . .] That would have been my path. And Kingsley, the character in *Education*, would have been me' ('BFI at Home' 2021). See also Aitkenhead 2014.
9. In his 2012 book, published ten years before McQueen was knighted, Eddie Chambers (2012: 54) writes: '[A] feature on Steve McQueen in *The Independent* of 15 July 2008 [. . .] reported that McQueen was "dismissive of the OBE he was awarded in 2002, saying he only accepted it for the sake of his parents, who were proud of him, and that it doesn't mean anything to him." McQueen was awarded first an OBE, then a CBE, several years later.' Chambers (2012: 55) notes writer Benjamin Zephaniah's refusal of an OBE in 2003: 'Zephaniah perceived a none-too-subtle strategy of appropriation and neutralization to be at work in that letter from the Prime Minister's office – a strategy in which Black writers (and others, including Black artists) were packaged, promoted, and, above all, used as colourful motifs of New Labour's era of fairness, justice, and creativity.'
10. To suggest this is not to assume that all McQueen's projects have been successful. For instance, his *Codes of Conduct*, intended as a six-episode mini-series, was cancelled by HBO in 2016. A pilot episode was shot but never screened. See Travers 2018. On the

11. social, political and psychological dimensions of white space, see Anderson 2022; Sekimoto and Brown 2022: 63–4, 111–12.
11. In chapter eight Christine Geraghty queries McQueen's reluctance to do so explicitly.
12. Completed in 1975, *Pressure* was not released until 1978. The lengthy delay was due to 'the racist assumption that the film might provoke riots' made by both Scotland Yard and the Race Relations Board (Young 1996: 142, cited in Mayer 2021: 116).
13. For overviews of this terrain, see Chambers 2012; Malik 2021: 21–40. It is striking how male dominated the list is, although this is not surprising given the persistent gender bias in the UK media sector.
14. See The Royal Television Society 2021, available at <https://www.youtube.com/watch?v=xVLLWR1aeNo>
15. The Black activist Leila Hassan Howe, one of the interviewees in *Uprising*, comments: 'I never met Steve McQueen. [. . .] Most of the journalism was down to James Rogan' (Austin 2021).
16. 'The double channel, four-screen installation emits the sound of the artist's voice telling a story [about racism encountered by his father while working as a fruit picker in Florida], spliced and fragmented and paired with visuals from the 1920s black and white film *The Jazz Singer* about a musician who performs in blackface' (Abrams 2022; see also Simmons 2022). McQueen's *Year 3* photography exhibition of 3,128 specially commissioned school class photographs, 'depicting two-thirds of [London]'s entire population of seven-to-eight-year olds', ran at Tate Britain from 2019 to 2020. See <https://www.tate.org.uk/press/press-releases/steve-mcqueen-year-3> McQueen has described the project as 'a love letter to London' and 'almost a time capsule for now'. Paul Gilroy calls it 'a challenge, a provocation'. 'By putting up this proliferation of difference, it says "well, what is different? [. . .] What is so different that it would make you frightened or anxious?"' ('Steve McQueen', 2022). In late 2017 McQueen filmed the ruined Grenfell Tower from a helicopter. The resulting film, *Grenfell* (2019), was exhibited at the Serpentine Gallery, London, from April to May 2023.
17. Black Film British Cinema Conference panel discussion, 19 May 2017, later published as Martin, Nwonka, Koksal and Clark 2021: 83.
18. The phrase is from Howe, in Austin 2021. McQueen's reception among white commentators and audiences may also have been shaped by what the African-American music critic Nelson George has called a white 'romance of blackness' (George 1988, cited in Roediger 1998: 225). bell hooks's caution is also pertinent here: 'Whether or not desire for contact with the Other, for connection rooted in the longing for pleasure, can act as a critical intervention challenging and subverting racist domination, inviting and enabling critical resistance, is an unrealized political possibility' (hooks 1992: 367).
19. While precise statistics are hard to find for these disciplines, a 2020 report by the Higher Education Statistics Agency showed that in the British HE sector fewer than 1 per cent of professors identified as Black (Adams 2020). In addition, 'of the almost 20,000 UKRI scholarships for PhD students awarded between 2016 and 2018, only 1.2% were awarded to Black or Black mixed-race students' (Williams, Bath, Arday and Lewis 2019, cited in Joseph-Salisbury and Connelly 2021: 23).
20. Compare similar remarks made by Horace Ové, Trinidad-born director of *Pressure*: 'There is a kind of trap that you can fall into – a ghetto situation which says that a black filmmaker can only make films about black people or black militancy whereas a white filmmaker has complete freedom to go about and make films on any subject anywhere in the world. [. . .] To us, the idea that black people can't understand white is a joke' (*Sunday Times* 1978). 'We know you, we have to study you in order to 'survive'' (Paskin 1987).

21. Wheatle's later writing for teenagers was itself a marked departure from the white perspective and characters of Dahl.
22. In 2012 McQueen listed one Black film, Spike Lee's *Do the Right Thing*, in his ten favourite films. The other nine were: *The Battle of Algiers, Beau Travail, Couch, Zero de Conduite, La Règle du Jeu, Le Mépris, Once Upon a Time in America, Tokyo Story* and *The Wages of Fear*. <https://www2.bfi.org.uk/films-tv-people/sightandsoundpoll2012/voter/1176>, last accessed 28 October 2022.
23. Elsewhere, Kaisary (2019) has compared *12 Years a Slave* unfavourably with the Cuban film *El Otro Francisco* (1974).

PART I

CHAPTER 1

From *Exodus* to *Small Axe*: Steve McQueen's Filmic World of Two Halves

Elisabetta Fabrizi

Since the start of Steve McQueen's career as an artist in the early 1990s, cinema has gone through epochal changes. It has gone digital; it has both populated our computer screens and reached centre stage in the art gallery. Contemporary art has gone from being a relatively small market to increasing 2,000-fold; likewise, moving image installations have gone from being unmarketable to passing the $1,000,000 mark at auction. McQueen has skilfully navigated and utilised such changes, first establishing himself as one of his generation's leading contemporary art personalities and then as a successful film director. Despite his world acclaim as an Oscar-winning filmmaker, his career in the art world has continued to develop alongside (but clearly distinct from) that in cinema and (more recently) television.

This duality is not in itself uncommon, as contemporary artists have often attempted to build parallel careers in cinema and vice versa. What makes McQueen's career unique is that he has succeeded in reaching the critical and commercial apex of both sectors. In terms of the art world, he was awarded a Turner Prize in 1999 and was the first moving image artist (and the first Black artist) to represent Britain at the Venice Bienniale (2009). While gaining prestigious art accolades and exhibiting in some of the most important art institutions in the world, his gallery work has also been commercially represented by leading private galleries. This, in turn, played a meaningful role in securing the place of his art in some of the best collections in the world (MOMA, Tate and Metropolitan Museum of Art, to name a few). Equally, McQueen's feature film work has transcended the restricted audiences that generally characterise artists' films, gaining world cinema distribution and reaching mass audiences. This capacity of mixing intellectual and generalist cinema audiences, state-funded and privately owned art networks, is a feat that has escaped the very many artists who have ventured into industry filmmaking, as well as the countless directors engaging with the art world. Only Julian Schnabel – a very successful visual artist turned Oscar-winning director – with films such as *Before the Night Falls* (2000) and *The Diving Bell and the Butterfly* (2007) has approached the level of audience and critical success in both the art world and cinema that Steve McQueen enjoys. For Schnabel – a painter – the distinction between his artworks and his films has been an easier one to maintain, while for McQueen – predominantly, although not exclusively, a video artist – this has been more challenging. Perhaps this is why McQueen has strenuously worked to create a clear separation between his visual art and cinematographic work, a topic he has often stressed in interviews. Considering his installations as separate from his narrative films, he has rejected the idea that they may have acted as a mere training ground for his later cinema work. Instead, he has underlined the fact that although his goal stays the same, his video installations are not *short films* but *artworks*, and even if in them he uses the medium of celluloid or video, he employs a different language than that used in his films (McQueen and Riley 2018).

This approach is reflected in the way McQueen creates works that exist and circulate in liminal yet separate spaces of cultural production but share the same urgency of exposing that which is not acknowledged by society. While McQueen's cinematographic work is 'unlimited', and readily available for viewing (in cinemas, television, streaming services), his artworks can only be seen in selected contemporary art contexts and acquired through commercial art galleries. However, the rules structuring the cinema field and that of contemporary art are different and so are the rules governing the production, distribution, exhibition and sale of the works. From early in his career, McQueen has demonstrated a skilled approach to navigating such unspoken regulations, as evidenced by his capacity to exploit the possibilities available to him in both the publicly funded and the private sector of the contemporary art field.

Although the moving image is now routinely part of the art market, this was only just beginning to happen in early nineties Britain, when the young Steve McQueen was making his entry into the creative sector. In the UK, unlike in the United States, that was still a time in which moving image artists were working predominantly outside of an art market still grappling with the difficulty of selling film and video, owing to their essence as infinitely reproducible media. McQueen is part of a generation that contributed to shifting the restricted field of artists' moving image practices closer to the market by embracing the limited edition. He, like colleagues such as Tacita Dean, was able to demonstrate that film and video in the gallery could be profitable and worthy of private (as well as public) financial support.

McQueen secured representation of his moving image work at an early stage (1996), working with leading private galleries in London (initially with

Anthony Reynolds Gallery then with Thomas Dane Gallery) and New York (Marian Goodman Gallery, by then already one of the most influential commercial galleries in the world). Through such representation and his exploitation of the limited edition model for the sale of film and video, by the mid-nineties McQueen's moving image artworks were already being collected by wealthy private individuals and leading public museums alike. This cemented the artist's position in the art world early in his career and aided the creation of the springboard from which he could experiment with feature filmmaking.

WHO'S FRAMING WHOM?

Despite McQueen's success in developing his practice along two distinct tracks, an analysis of his work across platforms demonstrates a common intent to place the viewer in an active, knowing space. One powerful example is found in *Mangrove*, episode one of the five that make up the *Small Axe* BBC series (2020), in a sequence portraying a violent police raid on the Mangrove restaurant in Notting Hill. McQueen ends the dramatic sequence with a shot that lingers on the floor of the diner's kitchen. The take is still, mostly silent, and the camera is positioned on the ground, at an uncomfortable angle. As a result, the viewers' bodily self-awareness is elicited: the image composition, camera placement and extended length force the spectators to feel as if they are restrained against the floor alongside Frank Crichlow (Shaun Parkes), the innocent Trinidadian immigrant owner of the restaurant. The viewers' self-awareness is augmented, and with it, their ability to focus on their thoughts and feelings. The silence, dramatic camera angle and duration (1 minute 24 seconds) create the conditions for viewers to take stock and emerge from the emotive grip of the story to become aware of the numerous interpretations that can be placed upon an image.

This interest in creating the conditions for viewers to become aware of their own presence is at the core of McQueen's oeuvre, a founding characteristic of his feature films as much as his gallery works, the genesis of which can be traced back to *Bear* (1993), McQueen's earliest moving image gallery installation. (See Figure 1.1.) Five minutes into the artwork we see a long sequence of two naked men (McQueen and Vernon Douglas) shot from a low, awkward angle. Looking up, we watch the men gripping each other and the two entangled bodies moving above the camera, forming a barrier from which we cannot escape, forcing us to scrutinise their most intimate parts. Just like in the *Mangrove* restaurant scene, we are placed on the floor where we are given the role of vulnerable voyeurs who can physically sense the risk of violence portrayed in the footage. This sequence demonstrates that, despite being the first moving image work completed and exhibited by McQueen, *Bear* is an accomplished

Figure 1.1. Steve McQueen, *Bear*, 1993. 16 mm black-and-white film transferred to video, continuous projection, no sound, 10 minutes 35 seconds. Exhibition view, 'Steve McQueen', 16 March–1 September 2013, Schaulager, Muenchenstein/Basel 2013. © Steve McQueen. Courtesy the artist, Thomas Dane Gallery and Marian Goodman Gallery. Photo Tom Bisig, Basel.

example of the artist's aim to place viewers in a position to watch themselves watching and to challenge a unilateral reading of reality. It is a 10 minute, silent 16 mm black-and-white film transferred to video which is characterised by precise physical image-making and by an aesthetic of early cinema that is closely related to McQueen's other installations from the nineties, most notably *Five Easy Pieces* (1995), *Stage* (1996), *Just Above My Head* (1996), *Deadpan* (1997), *Something Old, Something New, Something Borrowed, Something Blue* (1998) and *Cold Breath* (1999).

Bear also shares a number of similarities with *Hunger* (2008), McQueen's first feature film, including the concentration on the naked body and the continuous manipulation of the viewers' psychological position. *Bear* elicits confusion: we are not sure whether the performers are in a boxing ring or in a darkroom, whether they are lovers, brothers or simply fighters. Furthermore, the aesthetic of silent cinema clashes with the presence of the Black body, so rarely portrayed by the first filmmakers. We are at times led to feel like accomplices in the flirting game, or objective witnesses of the violent event unfolding; sometimes we feel as if we are participating in the game, and other times as if we are crushed by it. Oscillating from tenderness to violence and back, it is an installation that exploits film's capacity to elicit physicality. Equally, *Hunger* is permeated by a visual structure aimed at creating tangibility in the moving image in order to complicate the interpretation of the narrative, where closeness, bodily exposure and violence are wrapped together. When we find ourselves in the confined space of a police van with young Riot Prison Officer Stephen Graves (Ben Peel) getting ready to tame a revolt in Northern Ireland's Maze Prison, his face barely emerges from the darkness, while a frontal handheld camera close-up forces us to share the man's nervous, worried wait. We are catapulted into the van right after being placed in close contact with the naked bodies of IRA political prisoners, including Bobby Sands (Michael Fassbender). There, as in *Bear*, we are side by side and confronted with their unclothed bodies which, through their most basic functions (nakedness, feeding, urine, excrement) they offer as the ultimate resistance to the ruling powers. When, in a coordinated protest, they start to violently smash their cells' furniture, the sequence alternates between quick edits of shots filmed within the rooms and from the outside looking in (through the sliding peepholes used by the prison guards). We feel vulnerable when inside the cell (objects are being thrown in the direction of the camera's eye) and safe when behind a peephole. In this way McQueen uses film language to position us in an in-between psychological space, continuously and frenetically shifting from a position of power to one of desperate defiance.

Thus, what unites *Bear* with McQueen's directorial work is not only the capacity of eliciting a bodily response to the subject (Kim 2020: 9) but also the primary role given to the viewers' awareness of their own presence in front of the portrayal of violence and resistance. However, *Bear* is an artwork shot on film made for gallery exhibition which the artist has described as sculpture born out of a desire 'to be in the canvas as opposed to just painting it' (McQueen and Comer 2014). As such, the piece is the earliest example of the importance of the gallery space in McQueen's work, with the installation form being as much part of the experimentation as the footage itself. The single-channel video is projected floor to ceiling (7 m × 4 m × 3 m) on the back wall of an enclosed space that has been painted black, creating 'a kind of blanket effect' (Horlock 1999: 7) in which the dimensions make the figures sculptural and monumental – larger than life. The work is shown on a loop so that visitors can enter at any point, and no seats are provided as ambulation is encouraged, using the floor as a reflecting surface that doubles the projected image and allows the audience's bodies to coexist with those in the footage.

The same installation scheme is repeated in *Deadpan* (1997), a work in which the artist further develops the relationship between sculpture, film and installation. The work continues *Bear*'s address of the invisibility of the Black body in cinema and the sculptural exploration of race, violence and endurance, but it does so with an insistence on the play between vertical and horizontal lines both within and outside the film itself. The 4 minute work (16 mm black-and-white film transferred to video) sees McQueen performing alone, recreating the hurricane scene from Buster Keaton's film *Steamboat Bill, Jr.* (1928) in which the strong winds cause the facade of a house to fall around the protagonist (Bill, played by Keaton). McQueen takes Keaton's place and uses multiple camera angles, repetitions and the larger-than-human proportions of the projection (projected on the entire wall) to place us alongside his own physically perilous position. As we fear for the artist's safety, he remains stoic, apparently unafraid of the impending fall, after which, unlike Keaton, he remains still and imperturbable among the pieces of the broken building. Not a mere tribute to early cinema but an examination of it, the artist uses the projected image in the gallery space to challenge us to reassess familiar images, objects and actions. This is a common feature of McQueen's generation of artists active from the early nineties, who made the most of new projection and video synchronising technologies that allow the normalisation of the moving image in a gallery context.

Throughout his art career, McQueen has experimented with the number and type of screens and with the gallery space to critically scrutinise accepted cinematic norms: in *Drumroll* (1998) he used the three-channel projection; in *Pursuit* (2005) the single-screen projection is repeated multiple times via infinity mirrors; *Ashes* (2002–15) is a double-sided projection; *Charlotte* (2004) and *Mees, After Evening Dip, New Year's Day, 2002* (2005) are projected small scale on celluloid (16 mm). In each of these examples, the installation is a bespoke creation that frames the artwork as much as the onlooker, because, as Newman writes, in McQueen's gallery work 'political ramifications do not stop at the level of content but encompass lighting, editing, shots and installation' (Newman 1999: 24). Although in the work we find a level of storytelling, they induce contemplation by isolating a moment (*Deadpan*), an action (*Bear, Cold Breath, Charlotte*), a place (*Static*, 2009) or an event (*Ashes*; *Caribs' Leap*, 2002). These isolated elements are then dissected using the tools found in the liminal space between the cinema and the gallery.

Unable to control the presentation of his feature films in cinemas, televisions or computer screens, McQueen has adapted the framing strategies employed in the gallery to develop a highly personal and potent cinematic language. Instead of expanding the conceptual analysis of the real through abstraction and condensation (a common trait of feature-length artists' films), he has chosen to retain it and insert it within a traditional approach to the script. This is most evident in his Hollywood films, *12 Years a Slave* (2013) and *Widows* (2018), as well as in his television work for the BBC, such as the aforementioned *Mangrove*. The extensive use of screens, frames and walls is exemplified by *Shame* (2011), where they are tools for conveying the characters' inner feelings of entrapment. Brandon (Michael Fassbender) and Sissy (Carey Mulligan) inhabit spaces in which their (often naked) bodies are continuously reflected and confined, similar to those in *Five Easy Pieces* (1995), a work which McQueen has acknowledged as an important one in the development of his career (McQueen 2019: 396). At the start of the film, Brandon's naked figure goes from one room to the other in his apartment, moving through door frames and in front of windows as if he was part of synchronised multiscreen video projections, allowing him to shift across screens but never escape the installation loop.

In *Mangrove*, we find one of the most eloquent examples of framing strategies in the whole of McQueen's career, one that contributes to understanding the influence of his early gallery work on all of his output, including that made with prime-time television audiences in mind. As activist Darcus Howe (Malachi Kirby) is in the courtroom making his argument in an attempt to defend himself from the accusation of inciting to riot, he looks through a piece of cardboard cut in the shape of the slit of the police observation van being discussed. The sequence that follows is shot with the cardboard held still by Darcus right in the centre of the frame, while the camera moves; the result is that as it pans across the courtroom, the space of the tribunal is literally framed by the acts of film recording and of us watching through a very partial perspective. At this point McQueen shifts our position by showing Darcus turning around to face the camera with the slit in front of his face, becoming the one simultaneously being framed and framing us. As Darcus turns around again, another cut takes us to a shot of the jury members in which the cardboard is superimposed on the camera eye. The image of the group is narrow, horizontal and surrounded by white, making it look like it is floating. As we try to put the scene in focus, we see ourselves watching reality through the cinematic device, one that frames everybody and everything, including us. Although the function of the shot is diegetic, its abstract form is unusual for a court drama – literally, a peephole view which looks like a projection in a gallery – and leads us to stop to make sense of what we are seeing. When artistic insertions like the cardboard in *Mangrove* are taken alone, they appear at odds with the rest of the footage. But when they are taken in context, they merge with the flow of the narrative and are therefore ultimately perceived as integral to the plot. These devices bring an element of abstraction into a realist context and subtly suspend time, echoing the process of McQueen's installations.

However, on occasion, McQueen goes a step further and includes durational sections in his feature films that, if taken out of the narrative context, could operate as stand-alone artworks. One such occasion is found when in *Hunger* a prison guard enters a cell to clean faeces off the walls. The camera zooms in on the dirty surface and follows the dripping water jets as if it was analysing Richard Long's mud work *White Water Circle* (1994) for an art documentary. With this shot, McQueen transforms what in the plot are the traces of physical resistance left behind by prisoners into performative mark-making worth recording before they are permanently erased from collective memory. A white monochrome shot is also at the centre of the sequence of the final moments of Bobby Sands's life. As he is motionless, lying on the prison hospital bed dying of hunger, and only able to stare at the ceiling, a tracking shot slowly follows the cracks in the white paint, closing in on the materiality of the surface. The line in the monochrome surface acts as a path which eventually leads Bobby to an image of his younger self staring at him. As in McQueen's early gallery works, the absence of sound is crucial to reinforcing the viewer's perception of watching themselves watching the film.

As seen in these examples, McQueen's works are characterised by a play of the opposites that make up what we see. In the gallery, this is achieved through the combination of in-footage composition and screens (or their reflection), while in the feature films this often takes the form of a diptych. *Widows* (2018) is a particularly clear example of such an approach, as it is a film that makes the continuous play of black and white elements its stylistic trademark (evidenced in the choice of actors, costumes, sets and even pets, all inhabiting the same spaces and yet remaining clearly separate). Images such as Veronica (Viola Davis) desperately trying to make sense of the dramatic events unfolding in the film are typical of how diptychs in McQueen's films frequently bring abstraction and realism side by side, associated but not joined. In the shot, the right side shows the despairing actress, against a white background, wearing black; the left side is undefined, white and grainy; the two parts are delimited by a faint, grey, thin vertical line (a wall). Whenever Veronica moves her arm and head so that they enter the space of the left half of the shot, they too become unreadable, losing their human form. Although the scene is realistic within the events told, and functions to move the plot along, it also carries an abstracting, psychological element that brings together what Demos (in relation to McQueen's *Western Deep*, 2002) has defined as 'indeterminacy and bare life' (Demos 2013 : 34).

EVERYTHING IS POLITICAL VS THE POLITICS OF EVERYTHING

The 'bare life' approach to the moving image plays an important role in McQueen's films, but it may appear at odds with the early gallery work considered in this text so far. Nevertheless, analysing his contemporary art career to date, we note that he progressively brought together the language typical of his work from the 1990s (black-and-white, silent video installations employing a highly aestheticised structuralist language) with a realist approach. We note that from 1993 to 1996 all of McQueen's work is in a style similar to *Bear*, but that from 1997 the artist's practice becomes more multifaceted: he starts to use colour (*Exodus* and *Catch*, both 1997; *Drumroll*, 1998; *Prey*, 1999), photography (*Barrage*, 1998), sculpture (*Untitled-Wall* and *White Elephant*, both 1998), sound (*Soane, Echo, System I* and *II*, both 1999), print (*Pink Nails*, 1999) and slide projections (*Current*, 1999). He does this while continuing to make his trademark black-and-white works (*Deadpan*, 1997, and *Something Old, Something New, Something Borrowed, Something Blue*, 1998). The early 2000s mark a change, with the artist bringing the documentary approach centre stage in his practice (*7th November* and *Girls, Tricky*, (both 2001), and *Caribs' Leap/Western Deep* (2002)). The latter is of particular interest in the context of our discussion, and comprises two works, the two-screen *Caribs' Leap* and the single-screen *Western Deep*, both commissioned for *documenta 11* in Kassel. The context in which they were made is of relevance as this very influential exhibition was curated by Nigerian art historian and writer Okwui Enwezor – the first non-European art director of *documenta* – who created what is considered the first truly global, postcolonial *documenta* exhibition, and a group show which contributed to bringing documentary practices to the forefront of contemporary art discourse. The two installations were shown as one work, although in separate rooms, and it is worth noting that, uncommonly for McQueen's work up to that point, they were both shot by cinematographers with very recognisable styles and well-established careers in arthouse cinema. *Caribs' Leap* (shot by Jarman, Von Trier and Wenders's cinematographer Robby Müller, who, also in 2002, shot McQueen's gallery work *Ashes*) consists of a poetic and abstract work of a continuously falling man (12 minutes 6 seconds, 35 mm film transferred to video). Projected on a hanging screen, it is exhibited alongside a monitor showing documentary footage (28 minutes 53 seconds, Super 8 mm transferred to video) capturing contemporary life on the beachfront and docks of the Caribbean island of Grenada, where McQueen's mother was born. Together, the two parts of the installation memorialise the 1651 event (*Caribs' Leap*) when, following the defeat by French colonial forces, local Carib resistance fighters chose to jump off a 40-metre cliff rather than accept the colonialist powers. Meanwhile, *Western Deep* (24 minutes, Super 8 mm colour film transferred to video) was screened in a cinema-like space (a first for McQueen) and was entirely shot with a handheld Super-8 camera in South Africa's TauTona gold mine (the world's deepest at 3.5 km underground).

Although only in his early 30s, this was already McQueen's second participation at *documenta* (*Catch* was shown at *documenta 10* in 1997). However, in *Western Deep* we see evidence of how Enwezor's curatorial framework foregrounding artistic documentary approaches (among which the moving image had a central role) provided the artist with the confidence to develop the factual strand of his practice in new directions. The work is essentially a documentary exploration of the inhumane conditions of the goldmine's workforce, but it unites McQueen's abstract, condensed approach to the filmic language with gritty realism to make the body 'the subject but also the target' (Bailey 2012: 184). Choosing the title *Western Deep* (as the gold mine was formerly known), McQueen referenced the apartheid era; once he gained access, he recorded the workers operating in temperatures that averaged 80 degrees Celsius and under air pressure 920 times higher than normal. To film the piece, McQueen employed Sean Bobbitt, whose work in Michael Winterbottom's *Wonderland* (1999) he had admired for the use of sped-up 8 mm footage. Although he had collaborated with cinematographers before (including Noski Nevill, who shot *Bear* with a 16 mm Eclair, and Müller), McQueen has talked about *Western Deep* as the first work in which he did not hold the camera himself, and therefore the first time he fully directed (Searle 2012: 202). The artwork was also a turning point in installation terms, as at *documenta 11* it was projected in a seated gallery and with starting times, in what McQueen's installation specifications for the work indicate as 'cinema-like conditions'. *Western Deep*, shot mostly in darkness, includes moments that recall *Bear* and *Deadpan* (repetitions, manipulation of speed, the focus on the body, the play between darkness and light), brought together with realist images of the hardship endured by the workers. As in these installations as well as in *Hunger*, this is a work about the body as site of political resistance. In both *Western Deep* and *Hunger* we see men emerging from gates, let through by men in uniform and inhabiting spaces – the prison building and the mine – that have similar constraining structures. In *Western Deep*, on our way into the depths of the gold mine, through locked gates and pitch-black tunnels, our only appeal to life is a feeble torchlight. In *Hunger* McQueen appears to echo the same sentiment, when Father Dominic Moran (Liam Cunningham), on his way into the prison to meet Bobby, also has to go through locked gates and traverse a corridor steeped in black shadows, only occasionally broken by dim rays of light.

Together with *Bear*, the other progenitor of the hybrid language found in *Western Deep* is *Exodus* (1992–7), the first work that McQueen ever shot on film (in 1992). While this in itself is relevant, what makes *Exodus* of particular interest is that the 8 mm, 65-second colour silent film is very different from the works made by McQueen in the early to mid-nineties. (See Figure 1.2.) The artwork is unscripted, in colour and employs a documentary aesthetic of *cinéma vérité* that could not be further from that employed in *Bear*, made only a year later. A student initially interested in painting and sculpture, McQueen credits the then Head of Art Jon Thompson at Goldsmiths (where McQueen studied Fine Art, 1990–3) for encouraging him to explore film and for suggesting 'to always carry a camera round with you all the time and just look through the lens' (Searle 2012: 193). With *Exodus* McQueen did just that: the film records a found event, the moment when walking along Brick Lane and carrying his Super 8 camera, he

Figure 1.2. Steve McQueen, *Exodus*, 1992–7. Super 8 mm colour film transferred to video, no sound, 1 minute 5 seconds. © Steve McQueen. Courtesy the artist, Thomas Dane Gallery and Marian Goodman Gallery.

came across two West Indian men carrying potted palms along the busy London street. The artist follows the men in the crowd, trying to keep them in sight and using the tall plants to keep track of their whereabouts until they board a double-decker bus and disappear from sight. McQueen's realist tendencies, evident in this work, nevertheless remained dormant, as after shooting the footage, he did not use it, putting it away for three years because he 'did not know what it was' (Searle 2012: 194). This is hardly surprising for a young student who had embarked on studies at art school with the intention of becoming a painter under the influence of artists such as Willem de Kooning, Edward Burra and Jean-Michel Basquiat.

When *Exodus* was finally exhibited in 1997, it was as part of McQueen's first solo show in New York, in the high-profile context of the Marian Goodman Gallery. Through its installation, the artist reiterated that it was a profoundly different piece from his other artworks at the time. *Exodus* was displayed on a monitor on a plinth, in a lit gallery, bringing the footage closer to the televisual experience of the everyday. Watching the work with the knowledge of McQueen's most recent work, one could imagine the two men in Brick Lane getting off the bus in Notting Hill to meet friends at the Mangrove restaurant. Because *Exodus* was the very first use of film by McQueen and was shot as an impromptu sketch, its analysis can act as a magnifying glass on the interconnections between the onset of McQueen's gallery career and his present-day filmmaking. With the hindsight afforded by time, the artwork acquires new meaning, revealing itself not only as the first experiment on film of an artist's illustrious career but also as the first iteration of a long and multifaceted creative development; one that would lead McQueen to gain the power needed to make *Small Axe* and bring the disappearing stories of men such as those filmed in *Exodus* into the focus of national television audiences.

A FILMIC WORLD OF TWO HALVES

Although television sets often appear in McQueen's films, art very seldom does. In *Widows* we find the exception when father and son corrupt politicians Tom and Jack Mulligan (Robert Duvall and Colin Farrell) discuss whether a newly acquired $50,000 contemporary art painting is really art or wallpaper. This tension can be seen reflected in the realism/abstraction duality that we find in McQueen's work, one in which the two halves are joined by common objectives and yet divided by conflicting methods. The same duality and dilemma are also apparent in the way the artist approaches the distinct fields of contemporary art and of cinema, which, as in a diptych, are liminal yet kept clearly separate. McQueen's creative output functions in two opposing manners: he has created feature-length films, but also music videos (Kanye West's *All Day/I Feel Like That*, 2015) and promotional material (*Mr Burberry*, 2016; *Bleu de Chanel*, 2018) that behave as mass media, commercial products that are easily available on a number of platforms (cinema, television, streaming platforms, and so on). Anyone can watch them by paying a small amount or for free; no single person can decide to own the works beyond the copyright holders, as the films' copies are unlimited. On the other hand, the art market is based on authenticity and uniqueness, and McQueen's (moving image) artworks are therefore sold as limited editions (normally of four plus an artist's copy) and can only be accessed in the appropriate installation form in exhibitions approved by the artist. The artworks, therefore, address a restricted audience (that of contemporary art visitors who are able and have the financial means to travel to the worldwide exhibitions). Furthermore, they are only sold through powerful commercial galleries and exclusively to highly select clients, who, commonly, for an artist of McQueen's stature, would be either leading public museums or major private collectors.

The two systems may seem incompatible with work engaged with questions of race and structural societal inequalities. This was the attitude of past generations of British political and experimental filmmakers (most notably those at the London Film-Makers Co-op) who rejected the art system for its non-democratic uniqueness, seen as the polar opposite of an inclusive stance aimed at bringing about real change. However, McQueen is a true representative of the artists of his generation, in that he navigates these different institutions – and the inescapable framing inherent in each of them – with ease. McQueen, like in *Bear*, and like many of his contemporaries, charges ahead at us, exploiting all the avenues available to him to challenge the spectators' social and political understanding of the lived experience of marginalised individuals. As his practice exists along distinct lines as both art installation and feature film, the artist uses the duality described above to avoid simplifications or overtly political stances and achieve consensus among the critics, the audience and the markets. When everything is political, the political becomes embedded in real life (like wallpaper or television), and then all that is left for the artist to do is what art asks of men: 'the art is to be infiltrated into the broader and wider surroundings' (Searle 2012: 202), however contradictory this may seem. *Red, White and Blue* (2020), episode three of the *Small Axe* series, connects this demand to historical events in telling the real story of Leroy Logan (John Boyega), a Black policeman in a predominantly white and racist police force. Here, and in all his work across media and fields, McQueen brings together extreme positions to show us that along the dividing line of the diptych of life is a conflicted border that can nevertheless be used as both a space of resistance and of interconnection between bodies that inhabit the same humanity. This is the essence of McQueen's work, radical and poetically beautiful while seeming flawlessly embedded in the system(s) and its contradictions.

CHAPTER 2

Surplus Liveness and Black Male Performance in *Girls, Tricky*

James Harvey

In March 2001, newly founded online fashion magazine *SHOWStudio* commissioned recently awarded Turner Prize recipient Steve McQueen to interview a person of his choice. McQueen chose trip-hop artist Adrian Thaws, aka Tricky – who, according to the magazine, is McQueen's favourite musician. In the interview, McQueen initiates a sprawling discussion around the music industry, fame, race and cultural differences between Britain (where they are both from) and the US (where Tricky had recently moved). While disavowing the interviewer label early on, McQueen does not shy away from applying his own readings of Tricky's artistic tendencies: he has 'already changed music once'; he is 'like Miles Davis'; he has a very 'feminine situation' which gives him 'a certain tenderness'. Despite its rambling conversational nature, the interview gives a clear sense of McQueen's admiration for Tricky, which appears to be based on his refusal to fit into any predetermined category. This clearly resonates with McQueen, who has previously expressed his own dissatisfaction with the limitations of generic categories. In an interview for the exhibition book accompanying McQueen's 2020 Tate exhibition, Hamza Walker posits McQueen's work within structural film and political cinema traditions. He dispassionately refutes both claims, preferring instead to align his work with the creation of an environment (Walker and McQueen 2020: 108). He goes further, confirming that the medium itself is never a priority and that there is no distinction between his artworks and his narrative cinema; that the priority is just 'responding to what is in front of you'. This chapter engages with McQueen's second meeting with Tricky on these very terms, attempting to understand the forms of his *response to what is in front* of him – that is, a Black male performer at work, recording music – and to disentangle some of the resonant aesthetic and cultural debates instigated by the resulting film,

Girls, Tricky (2001). In so doing, I encounter a determined portrayal of the Black performing body on-screen, surrounded by recording technologies, in a way that invokes theoretical discourses around race and cinematic realism. *Girls, Tricky* provides a revealing albeit minor rendition of McQueen's authorial response to these discourses within the realms of creative production.

THE BLACK MALE PERFORMING BODY ON-SCREEN

Girls, Tricky is the result of a second meeting between McQueen and Tricky. After the *SHOWStudio* interview, McQueen was offered the opportunity to collaborate with the musician further, taking his video camera for four days during the production of Tricky's fifth album, *Blowback*. In the tight confines of the recording studio, McQueen was granted maximum intimacy, gaining a privileged bodily proximity to the artist as he sings at the microphone. The resulting film is a fifteen-minute documentation of intensity and emotion. We witness the accumulation of energy into a trance-like state, as Tricky spits across the frame, his body shuddering under the flailing sentiments of the written lyrics. His voice rises from gravelly low tones to high-pitched screams, with little regard for the cadences of the instrumental accompaniment. There is an improvisational quality to what Tricky does vocally that clashes with the structures of mainstream music production. McQueen appears to capture some of this contradiction in his own attempts to frame the action – we shift between mid-shots of Tricky's upper body; a shaking camera; and steady focus on the recording space vacated by Tricky, as he moves in and out of shot.

In this summative exposition of the action of *Girls, Tricky*, one perhaps already gets a sense of how the film relies on McQueen's familiar aesthetic style. Shuttling between austere stasis and spontaneous movement, the camera aligns itself with both the body of the performer and the immediate space around that body, achieving a perceptual alignment between spectator and the on-screen subject. This is above all an affective project, utilising video as an attempt to translate the sensory qualities of Tricky's music into a visual style. But the conceptual implication of this approach, it might be argued, begins to engage the politico-aesthetic dimensions of Black male performance. Alessandra Raengo has argued that cinema has historically fetishised Black performers, attributing to these bodies an 'ability to reconcile the cinematic apparatus with the aspiration of the moving image to move in a life-like manner' and a reliance on the 'black voice' to 'resolve the problem of sound/image synchronization' inherent to early cinematic images (Raengo 2016: 194). Raengo's reference point here is McQueen's *Deadpan*, in which he restages Buster Keaton's stunt from *Steamboat Bill, Jr.*, where the artist stands motionless as the façade of a house repeatedly collapses onto him, capturing him in its empty window frame. Raengo's reference to the depthless representation of Black characters in early Hollywood follows James Snead's critique of film history's 'almost metaphysical stasis' with regard to Black subjects, who are 'seen as eternal, unchanging, unchangeable' (Snead 1994: 2). Taking Snead's critique to McQueen's quotation of Keaton, Raengo attends to *Deadpan*'s ability to foreground cinema's historical reification of subjects determined by racial frames, as well as its prominent role in these racial constructions.

In its formative years, cinema objectified and thus dehumanised Black bodies, with both material and ontological consequences. As Alice Maurice explains in *The Cinema and Its Shadow: Race and Technology in Early Cinema*, the indexical marker of race becomes 'a significant rhetorical tool for the cinema's claims to presence, authenticity, and meaning' (Maurice 2013: 4). Fatimah Tobing Rony has made a similar point in the context of documentary film, referring to Félix Regnault's pioneering use of film in anthropology. Film was viewed to function as an index of racial measuring through its ability to capture movement. Its anthropological achievement provided a 'supreme and unconscious indicator of evolutionary development' (Rony 1996: 35). Raengo contributes to such arguments on film history's racial indexing, highlighting film history's preoccupation with 'innate overabundance of performativity and affectability' in representations of Black bodies. With *Deadpan*, she argues, McQueen provides a potential challenge to this through the Black performing body's ability to act as a 'repository of a surplus liveness' (Raengo 2016: 194). McQueen's 'performance of suspension' challenges the racialised conventions of an early cinematic reference point. As with earlier works, including *Bear*, *Just Above My Head* and *Cold Breath*, McQueen's own body plays a central role. Broaching the subjection of Black bodies in the artist film context, foregrounding in order to subvert the Black body's association with kinetic excess is shown to contain a potential to subvert the disciplinary procedures of a racist visual language.

Loaded with the history of cinematic representations before them, the sounds and images of Black performers have been reified around thought-less conventions. These conventions are routinely motivated by qualities of excess – the notion of having *more than* is needed in the public sphere. Nicole Fleetwood has broached this topic in relation to the 'excess flesh' of Black female artists and public figures, which she describes as 'an enactment of visibility that seizes upon the scopic desires to discipline the black female body through a normative gaze that anticipates its rehearsed performance of abjection' (Fleetwood 2011: 112). Michelle Ann Stephens takes a psychoanalytic approach to the 'radically relational and intersubjective context' of Black male performance, which is negotiated within a libidinal economy of sameness/difference, masculinity/ femininity, Blackness/whiteness (Stephens 2014: 12). Sites of performance often host intersectional meeting points between bodies 'subject to symbolic and imaginary capture in racializing discourse and imagery (race as a social construction) and a bodily subject whose sensory and relational (re-)presentation of self (race as an inscription on the flesh)' (2014: 4). In *Deadpan*, McQueen becomes performer, focalising himself in the frame to rehearse a modernist politics of the image regarding the necessary self-reflexivity of the filmmaker as a marker of filmic artifice. This is one of the key ways he challenges the limits of the filmic medium itself. But rather than return to this well-trodden argument against McQueen's better judgement, I will instead return to his self-avowed phenomenological priority – that is, *respond to what is in front of us*. With *Girls, Tricky*, we are encouraged to take seriously the occupation of screen space by the body; to theorise with (rather than despite) the proximity of lens to flesh; and to prioritise these qualities in any analysis of McQueen's work.

PROXIMITY AND EMPATHY

The issue of proximity is a central one for McQueen. He has previously described the perceptual conditions of his film installations as intended 'to induce a "kind of blanket effect" in which "you are very much involved with what is going on"' (Mulcaire 1998: 10). In Okwui Enwezor's terms, the spectator becomes *reanimated* through this aesthetic; as he 'plunges them into the depths of the film installation . . . their bodies seem to have been seized by, displaced into, the illusionistic realm of filmic fantasy' (Enwezor 2012: 24). This immersive placement of the spectator in the scene is often paradoxically challenged through the changing position of the camera. We regularly shift between tight proximity to the body and a restrictive stasis, aligned instead with the limiting parameters of an interior, the body escaping the frame as we focus on some inanimate object. Tricky's movement inside and outside the frame exemplifies this.

The opening moments begin with a tight close-up of Tricky's head, right of frame, as he prepares at the microphone, raising his arm to reveal his shirtless torso. 'I've got the skunk,' he says, before inhaling deeply and then reciting the lyric, 'I've never seen my dad boy'. Besides the brief glimpse of burning ash at the end of his joint, the only light source comes through the window separating the control room and the studio, highlighting little more than the sweat on his cheek, until his face turns towards the camera so we get a better look at him, his eyes closed as he meditates over the lyrics. (See Figure 2.1.) The handheld camera rocks slightly during these moments and remains unsteady until, abruptly, the backing band ceases playing for a moment; it restarts before Tricky begins his vocal. The camera becomes still now, as he whispers the opening lines ('Girls. Boys. Girls. Boys'). As the drums kick in, he begins to move in time to the rhythm, raising his voice ('Girls wish you never had boys,

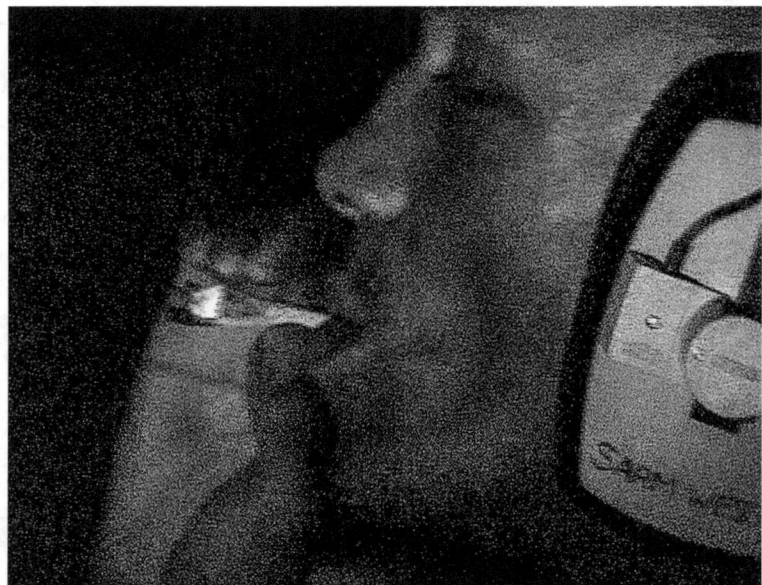

Figure 2.1. Steve McQueen, *Girls, Tricky*, 2001 (still) colour video transferred to digital file, sound, 14 minutes 47 seconds. © Steve McQueen. Courtesy the artist, Thomas Dane Gallery and Marian Goodman Gallery.

they grow up to be bad boys'). As his head begins to bob, the camera follows, carefully in time to Tricky's movement. The verse continues and the instrumental intensifies; Tricky moves clockwise round the microphone, so that his back now faces the camera. All we see is the back of his head and the top of his shoulders. This works both to obstruct the setting and abstract the body of the performer. By removing the expressive faculties of the face from the field of vision, and in turn desynchronising the sound from the on-screen action, the film's obstructing of a clear field of vision challenges the fetishistic association of Black performance with indexicality, through McQueen's contriving of a space for the performance of surplus liveness.

T. J. Demos's analysis of *Western Deep* is instructive on the camera's proximity to Tricky here. Demos claims McQueen achieves a proximity which 'is both closeness and distance . . . allows audience and image to touch, thus engendering an empathic culture between forms of difference that nevertheless maintain their separateness' (Demos 2005: 88). Despite the vast difference between the settings (one set in the deepest gold mine in the world, the other in a recording studio in Notting Hill), the formal concern for upturning aesthetic conventions around Black bodies bridges the two films. McQueen and long-term collaborator Sean Bobbitt's venturing into the Tau Tona mines is an audacious, reckless feat of artistic representation. On one level, the film could be seen to document impossible labour conditions and bring these to the attention of a Western audience. In his curatorial statement for Documenta 11, where *Western Deep* premiered, Okwui Enwezor positioned the film in the context of postcoloniality, which he explains 'shatters the narrow focus of Western global optics'; 'the postcolonial today', Enwezor claims, 'is a world of perhaps proximities . . . a world of nearness, not an elsewhere' (Enwezor 2015). *Western Deep*'s visualisation of the marginal, labouring bodies of postcolonial South Africa demands a response from its spectator, engaging proximity on its most literal, that is physical, terms.

Girls, Tricky is similarly concerned with using proximity to formally counter historical problems around the aestheticisation of Black bodies, but it does so specifically in a space of artistic production. Dwelling momentarily on this difference between the forms of labour (mining and singing) shown on-screen might be useful. Tricky is privileged enough to enjoy the benefits of wealth and fame, and to carry out his work in a comfortable and technologically sophisticated setting. The room is probably air-conditioned; the sweat on his skin is secreted through his own volition. And yet he perhaps embodies what E. Patrick Johnson terms, 'ways in which blackness exceeds the performative . . . the ways in which "living of blackness" becomes a material way of knowing' (Johnson 2003: 8). Despite the dramatic contrast to the postcolonial bodies of *Western Deep*, Tricky's recitation of his own personal experience – growing up to be bad boys; never having seen his dad – connects his musical performance to ideologically motivated and racially oriented social debates around absent fathers and youth criminality. In interviews, he has articulated clearly his upbringing, having seen his mother die at a young age, being raised by his grandmother and surrounded by the violence of his family members. Challenging sociological narratives around absent male role models, Tricky is equally keen to express his 'kinship with women' (Jonze 2019). This perhaps finds its way into his mode of performing against masculine tropes and his willingness to use his body as a mode of subversive engagement with identity, exhibited for instance in his past uses of cross-dressing during live performance. *Girls, Tricky* foregrounds this corporeality through the claustrophobic placement of the camera and lack of supplementary light source, highlighting the limits of filmic representation. The Black performing body no longer meets the realist demands of the video technology and instead thwarts the indexical relationship of film to an unmediated reality.

One of the main upshots of McQueen's highly proximous visual style is a less clear image. We are often *too close* to take it all in. It is not quite the case then, that the whole figurative nature of *Girls, Tricky* is threatened by the fragmentation of close-ups or the abstraction of motion. I was able to perceive more or less everything that was happening. But the clarity of the action is not aided by the camera's closeness to the body. Proximity itself does not work in favour of perception, but rather against it. What Demos describes as a new 'empathic culture' engendered by 'allowing audience and image to touch' (Demos 2005: 88) is perhaps undermined on the grounds that the visual intelligibility of the subject is impeded.

This analysis does not recognise the subject's formation *as* image though. *Girls, Tricky* invokes Demos's earlier recognition of the way an empathic culture both recognises and maintains difference. Challenging the potentially essentialised reading of postcolonial subjects in *Western Deep*, Demos describes the way 'the represented subject [is] continually thrown into disarray' (Demos 2015: 69). He also notes how the film's lighting 'precludes access to anything like a full account of the mining conditions, or an ostensibly truthful depiction of its laborers, which might claim to capture a subject in some illusory totality' (2015: 85–6). Despite his references to Deleuzian and posthuman frameworks in his analysis, Demos stops short of arguing for a *becoming* of the labouring subjects of *Western Deep*. Rather, McQueen's aesthetic complicates any such attempts at mounting totality – prior to or resulting from filmic representation. In the recording studio of *Girls, Tricky*, however, a notable difference emerges due to the intimacy with its subject.

THE FILMIC BODY

From first-hand experience, I would argue that being too close to see does not impact on the affective experience of *Girls, Tricky*. When I first viewed the film, it was in a dark, crowded room, at the Tate Modern exhibition in 2020. We had just come out of lockdown and the anxiety of other spectators' proximity was enough to put me on edge. The rising intensity of the instrumental, the voice, the movement of both body and camera, left my head spinning for some time after. It was the last thing I saw at the exhibition – and not by choice; I was just exhausted by the experience. McQueen is surely appreciative of the installation's excitement, bodily mobility and interactivity, contrasted with the cinema space. One is at least as aware of an encounter with the architecture of the screening space, as they are the screen itself and the content of the video played on the screen. While this general tendency has been widely explored with regard to film and video installation in museums and galleries (Balsom 2013; Bishop 2005; Connolly 2009; Mondloch 2010), I want to argue that *Girls, Tricky* invites a particular regard for the singularity of its subject, through an intensified closeness with the performer's body.

In the image and in the off-screen space, the Tricky of *Girls, Tricky* becomes a *filmic body*, channelling Vivian Sobchack's description of film as an 'empirical and functional subject-object' (Sobchack 1992: 133). A seminal text in the return of phenomenology in Film Studies, Sobchack's commitment to the embodied activity of film viewing provides a productive lens on McQueen's filmic work, which itself appears to emerge contemporaneously with Sobchack's, as an ideological critique of screen representation that simultaneously flags the limitations of ocularcentrism. Laura U. Marks argued on similar terms, that such 'haptic visuality' might even be conceived as a privileged mode of diasporic, intercultural cinema (Marks 2000: 22). What is defined as a phenomenological account of the film experience attains a political dimension in Marks's analysis, in a way that aligns with McQueen's cinema. Tricky's body utilises the technologies at his disposal to perform a kind of agency that pushes at the boundaries which would otherwise limit his performance. The knowability and, with reference to Snead's reading, the unchangeability of the Black performing body is further challenged when Tricky begins to step out of frame. The microphone (located as centrally as the subject himself) takes on a greater significance as the central pivot of the action – the thing around which Tricky performs to and with. If there are grounds to question the association of proximity with empathy, we might ask how this vital proximity between the on-screen subject and object affects the response. We might know Tricky through the public persona constructed through other media forms, but McQueen's Tricky comes to us as a product of a very particularised environment – that of the music studio and its highly engineered machinery of recording. The microphone is, in this sense, an appendage of the artist. It is this appendage that allows him to have a voice. When he leaves the frame, this appendage remains. We might question whether the microphone is a part of, more than a replacement for, Tricky's own body in the image.

McQueen has explored this nexus between bodies, objects, technology and space in other films. In *Drumroll*, he attached three video cameras inside an oil drum, recording its journey as it rolled through New York City. Screened as a triptych of each camera's footage, the resulting film installation produces an interconnecting filmic body – the sum of McQueen's presence on-screen (pushing the drum overhead); the streets passing by in the footage; and off-screen, the exhibition space of the spectator's viewing. A perceptual alignment – an 'empathic culture' in Demos's terms – occurs between the recording, the viewer and the object itself, here. In *Prey*, we hear the sound of tap dancing playing from an on-screen reel-to-reel tape recorder, which is filmed against the backdrop of grass; the recorder is then shown being dragged away into the sky by a balloon to which it is attached. And in the monochrome *Five Easy Pieces*, McQueen's camera dissects the rhythmic bodily movements of five dancers. From the formal experimentation of photography and early cinema to the sentiment underlying Bob Rafelson's American New Wave film of the same name, *Five Easy Pieces* hails film history and its aesthetic means of screening the body. In each of these works, McQueen displays a concern for deconstructing classical modes of bodily representation – that is, through spatial and temporal continuity; synchronous sound and action; and easily discernible psychical states (Thompson 1985).

Tricky's body utilises the technologies at his disposal to perform a kind of agency that pushes at the boundaries which would otherwise limit his performance. McQueen's foregrounding of technologies (either on-screen or jarringly acknowledged off-screen through formal strangeness) appears to invoke the integral role played by objects in the construction of a subjective presence – that is, an 'empirical and functional subject-object'. This occurs in *Girls, Tricky* through the relationship between body and microphone. But it is perhaps most pronounced through the use of naturalistic sound. In its rejection of standard processes of audio editing, we instead hear the *unwanted* sounds of the recording booth: the microphone surface, the clunking of equipment, the distant sound of drums rehearsing in the background prior to the performance. This is all extraneous to the essential elements of the recording itself, but it achieves prominence here, blending with the grain of Tricky's voice and, most poignantly, with the deeply sensory role of his breath on the soundtrack. Cinematic realism is founded on hierarchies of sound and vision dedicated to the suppression of such elements.

Raengo's analysis locates a determined opposition to the historical association of Blackness with the realist image in McQueen's subversion of surplus liveness. 'A perfectly integrated image', she explains, 'is one where the black body fosters the sense of a coincidence between the profilmic and the photographic image' (Raengo 2016: 192). While engaged in a historical analysis of early Hollywood cinema, Raengo is also in dialogue with classical ontological film theory, one of the core tenets of which might be summarised in André Bazin's claim that the 'aesthetic qualities of photography are to be sought in its power to lay bare the realities' (Bazin 1960: 8). The 'standard reading' (Morgan 2006: 458) of Bazin holds that photographic realism is a product of the technology's indexical relation to the material world and that, in turn, cinema can heighten our 'perceptual realism' (2006: 456) through preferred formal techniques. Where for Raengo then, McQueen's 'performance of suspension functions archivally as a recuperative gesture of the conundrum of agency manifested in early photographic technologies' (Raengo 2016: 201–2), I wish to go further. This highly self-reflexive recuperation of agency is evident in both suspension and animation – between stillness and movement, the profilmic and the out-of-frame, the human and the non-human. As these binaries interact in the spaces in and around *Girls, Tricky*, neither stillness nor liveness is privileged. Rather, each is contingent on the other for its effects.

While Raengo notes *Deadpan*'s response to a *longue durée* of Black integration into cinematic realism through a 'willed immobility' (2016: 192), *Girls, Tricky* is led by the subject's own improvisational corporeality – staging then challenging notions of Black performativity. McQueen's role behind the camera is receptive to Tricky's interruptive gestures, as if in a kind of reciprocating dance with the on-screen subject. As a slight tangent, a revealing analogy might be made with the choreographic choices in the dance scenes of the *Small Axe* episode, *Lovers Rock*. McQueen has expressed his passion for a more sensual, invitational dance form, the ethos of which would seem to apply here – the camera invites, waits, then follows, with each retaining a level of autonomy throughout the course of the movement (Gilroy and McQueen 2021). We see this arrangement early on in *Girls, Tricky* too. Tricky begins to bob his head to the rising beat and the camera follows quickly behind, subtly rising and falling. McQueen cannot keep up with Tricky though, as evidenced when his movement becomes too much for the video camera to contain. This *dance* – that is, Tricky's movement and McQueen's attempts to capture it – creates a blurred image. When Tricky begins to frantically jump, screaming 'I don't care', the camera stays still, as if McQueen has learned to not try to contain his subject. The performance ends with Tricky standing calmly at the microphone, whispering the lines, 'I'm not a Firestarter, because I'm a little smarter', as if slyly teasing us of his superiority in escaping subjection to restrictive identarian frames – not to mention the rigid frame of the video image.

The relationship between stillness and movement here, embodied at different times by McQueen's camera and Tricky's performance, works to undermine the film technology's ability to fully capture the Black male performer. Others have highlighted the importance of the dynamic between movement and stillness in McQueen's narrative films. Focusing on the endlessly tormented Patsey in *12 Years a Slave*, Rizvana Bradley locates 'an experimental mode of figuration and movement' as an alternative 'set of kinetic imperatives', which provide a level of cinematic agency (Bradley 2015: 173). Kimberly Juanita Brown has also discussed the way the film's 'clash of stillness and movement visualizes slavery's profound extensions', historicising the slave trade as 'the long stretch of modernity, horrifically ordered and repeatedly enforced' (Brown 2017: 121). It is notable that McQueen would utilise a gestural economy developed in his film installations for his epic historical reconstruction of a slave narrative. Eliding disparate times and spaces, the Black body's movement, and resistance to movement, carries what Grant Farred refers to as a 'disjunctive synthesis' which compels a momentary congregation of other resistant Black bodies in history (Farred 2014: 44). Between the ethical regard for proximity and a politicised aesthetic of (in)visibility, the filmic body of *Girls, Tricky* negotiates a space of agency for the Black performing body, which exists in a historical relationship of disjunctive synthesis with those other Black performing bodies in the history of the film technology.

The filmic body of *Girls, Tricky* ultimately exhibits the gaps between the real and the filmic, offsetting stillness and movement to interrogate surplus liveness, utilising the machinery of the recording studio to problematise the essentialised image of Black performing bodies. In so doing, it demonstrates McQueen's (intended or not) persistent concern for a racialised politics of the image. Rather than challenging McQueen's previous rejections of social commentary, or his recent avowed commitment to 'the burden of representation' (Olusoga 2020), I instead follow Jean Fisher in her claim that McQueen's work 'raises more general questions of where . . . political and ethical efficacy is actually located' (Fisher 2013: 73). In its testing of the limits of representation with regard to Black performance on-screen, *Girls, Tricky* 'accomplishes an understated political resonance through the poetics of the image itself' (Fisher 2013: 80).

CHAPTER 3

Eye Witness: Memorialising Humanity in Steve McQueen's *Hunger*

Eugene McNamee

INTRODUCTION

The 2008 film *Hunger*, directed by Steve McQueen, and co-written by McQueen and Enda Walsh, deals with the 1981 hunger strike and death in the Maze Prison/Long Kesh of IRA prisoner Bobby Sands.[1] McQueen's first feature film, it achieved enormous critical success, winning the Camera d'Or award at Cannes and numerous other international prizes.[2] Given the subject matter, it is of no surprise that it also generated a certain amount of controversy, some critics regarding it as a blatant 'hagiography' of a terrorist, and the dominant positive critical reception as a symptom of the unreflective romantic attachment to the underdog of naive liberal commentators.[3] This majority critical reception, however, seemed less characterised by support for the political position identified with Sands, but rather support for the artistic achievement of McQueen, tied to his own frequently stated position that he was neutral on Northern Irish political issues and interested in the idea of 'humanity' defined as the limits of what humans 'will inflict and . . . will endure'.[4] McQueen himself on at least one occasion made the point that such issues were particularly relevant given the ongoing debates on issues such as the use of torture on terrorist suspects, the abuses at Abu Ghraib, the detentions at Guantanamo Bay, and that the film was more than just an artistic intervention into the historical record, but spoke very clearly to 'now'.[5]

Accepting this version of the relevance of the film, on the abstract level as a filmic argument on the nature of humanity related to the more practical level of how certain issues of justice should be approached with an attention to the nature of humanity, gives rise to very obvious opportunities to consider the film as a text which raises specific legal issues and themes relevant to socio-legal studies. The field of 'law and film' as an area of socio-legal scholarship, however, has developed to the point where it is recognised that film as a 'multimodal' text is particularly rich in terms of what messages it communicates to an audience.[6] The analysis of films has moved beyond simply looking for legal themes or social themes with legal relevance, to looking for the (usually) hidden coherences in filmic texts which amount to imagined normative worlds with attendant 'alternative jurisprudences'.[7] This is a form of critical attention which comes closer to respecting the internal coherences of filmic creation and the way in which meaning is expressed through specifically filmic technique, and in short is a development which allows for a more transdisciplinary approach which moves beyond viewing films as a passive object for legal analysis and attempts to see the law of filmic language as much as the law in film, and therefore the ways in which film subtly encourages particular normative views of the world.[8]

The pathway of influence of film has also been theorised, rather than simply assumed, in terms of the mass exposure which film has, its persuasive and seductive qualities, and the likely or plausible effects of film read as argument, whether hegemonic or opening up alternative views and positions.[9] The particular quality of this mass-market appeal and seductive quality as an influence on the specific nexus between law and politics has also been examined, both in terms of influence on particular issues but also more broadly on the promotion of various subject positions which accord with visions of constitutional propriety.[10] The development of this point is that within various particular flexible constitutional systems the influence of film can be theorised as quite immediate in the constitutional legal realm, as is the case in moments of great constitutional flux where the line between law and politics becomes blurred.[11]

It is in this area of study that this essay seeks to examine more fully Steve McQueen's *Hunger*, as a particularly timely intervention into a legal constitutional field that is concerned with 'dealing with the past', and in particular with the idea of 'memorialisation', that is with achieving some kind of public marking of past events or the past generally.[12] This has a particularly local relevance to Northern Ireland, as it goes through various processes that span this divide of law and politics to try to achieve a sense of new beginning, but is also of relevance much more broadly to post-conflict societies as they attempt to grapple with issues of personal and social memory and the often fraught relationship of a past that must be dealt with to a future that is yet to be achieved.[13]

The film constitutes an intervention that is not only measurable, or even primarily so, in terms of a discursively coherent set of ideas. Rather, as befits the form, the filmic intervention is multimodal and by its nature invites a high degree of audience 'reading' which will differ from person to person, a form of engagement that is certainly reflected in the balance of this essay which, in 'transdisciplinary' fashion, is mixed film review and academic comment. The film is not an explanation, and the influence can never be expected to equate to producing a complete rational understanding, if such a thing were possible. The influence is based not only around grasping an idea or narrative, but also around sensory experience, in particular vision, and the production of emotional response, or affect.[14] Insofar as the human faculty of memory is concerned with affect and the recollection of images in 'the mind's eye', the suggestion here is that film, as it were, encounters memory where it lives. As a process, literally, of imagination (the creation of images) the film is able to span the territory between the recollection of images as memory and the creation of images of 'imagined worlds'. It allows for witnessing past events of which there were no witnesses. To develop this suggestion into an argument which partly grounds this essay, it is that the nature of film provides a formal quality which relates closely to memory and imagination. In films which aim at dealing with past subjects in a deliberately aesthetic way, in a way which pays close attention to form as resonant with subject matter, then the territory is close to that of public memorialisation.

In the particular scheme of ideas (as opposed to the form) that McQueen tries to convey through his particular approach in this film, the idea of humanity as nobility and resilience in the face of extreme physical situations to the point of death is offered to the public as a form of memorialisation that, I will argue, even if it cannot avoid political interpretation, manages to avoid political partisanship and cliché. In this it may have something to offer the wider social consideration on how to memorialise past conflicts, but importantly it must also be seen as a work of memorialisation in its own right.

The reception of the work, of course, is not something which McQueen or any other artist can control, and the reception is the element which most closely regards any idea of 'social effect' of the film. This essay will suggest that the reception of the film thus far gives hope that McQueen has managed to create a work of great beauty and power which has chimed with social consciousness in such a way that it may also have contributed to the developing social, political and constitutional landscape as regards 'the past' in Northern Ireland, and beyond.

MCQUEEN'S ART AND THE POLITICS OF MEMORIALISATION

Steve McQueen first came to public prominence in 1999 when he won the Turner Prize for contemporary art.[15] At the centre of his exhibited work on that occasion was *Deadpan*, a four-and a-half-minute 16mm black-and-white silent, recreating a famous Buster Keaton stunt. In *Deadpan* McQueen takes the part of Keaton and stares straight out into the camera while the tall facade of a building collapses around him in a shower of dust and debris, leaving him completely untouched as he stands precisely where an empty window frame falls to surround him. In its brevity and black-and-white starkness it has the quality of a pure image of courage in the face of eventual and inevitable collapse, a courage that is all the more striking in that it is played out as a comedy moment. Another early McQueen silent film, *Bear*, has the artist wrestling with another large man, both men naked. *Drumroll* has the artist rolling a large tin drum through the streets of Manhattan, filming the reactions of passersby. McQueen, in short, is primarily known as an experimental filmmaker who relies particularly on focusing the attention of the viewer on out-of-the-ordinary situations in which he himself is involved as a participant or actor and which are worked to a kind of super-normal aesthetic pitch through attention to the detail of the scenes, through encouraging an intense almost meditative attention in the viewer by the slow pacing of the changing image, and through the use of silence to sharpen the visual intensity of the sequences. His own presence in the scene serves to localise the action and to implicate the knowing viewer, yet the seeming unnaturalness of each occasion serves to create a kind of critical distance, thereby setting up a dissonance for the viewer between being in on the action and being radically outside it. The effect seems designed to unsettle and intrigue the viewer, but not to alarm or frighten, and there is in each case the sense that what is being explored is the strangeness of human behaviour and the variety of the range of human response.

In 2003, McQueen was approached by Channel 4 with the suggestion that he might make a feature film. For McQueen, perhaps bizarrely given his lack of obvious connection to Northern Ireland, the suggestion somehow recalled his childhood fascination with a TV image of Bobby Sands: 'it was to do with 1981, and Tottenham winning the FA Cup, the Brixton Riots and Bobby Sands popping up on my TV screen with a number beneath his image. It stayed with me. The seed was planted' (quoted in Mottram 2008).[16] The quote is typical McQueen; an invocation of the importance of memory that is at once personal and social, connected to a very defined image or very limited sequence of images, and married to a confidence that a form can be found to express this in a way that is both personally true and artistically engaging, in this case eventually leading to the film *Hunger*. Bobby Sands and his death forms part of a wider social tableau for a young Black boy in Brixton that has little to do with defined political positions, but has something to do perhaps with the idea of the underdog confronting authority (rioting against the police, the hunger strikers versus the government, and Tottenham weren't the kind of team who were supposed to win the FA Cup).

As if in ironic counterpoint to his decision to make a feature film on Sands's death, in 2003 McQueen also accepted an appointment as 'Official War Artist to Iraq', where he (briefly) accompanied British troops on a tour of duty.[17] His eventual artistic project issuing from this experience was the exhibition 'Queen and Country', comprising of a set of commemorative stamp sheets bearing the portraits of British service personnel killed in Iraq.[18] Discussing this work, McQueen commented:

> Strangely, it seems that for those who are against the war, my project is regarded as a good thing. For people who support the war, it is regarded as a good thing too. It is not pro- or anti-war. This work is like a sphere – roll it this way, roll it that way. In the end, it is an art work. When we hear about all the men, women and children killed in Iraq, we are numbed to it. I'm pointing out that these people are all victims, too. What happened to them all was a consequence of their participation. The MoD try to say that such and such many soldiers died in action – they don't include or count all the people who died in friendly fire, in traffic accidents and so on. Some were suicides. They chopped them all out. They deleted them. They're all part of this war. Nor do I think that soldiers have to have been manning a gun emplacement with one arm tied behind their back and doing a double somersault in order to be remembered or to get a medal. An 18-year-old kid gets killed by a landmine or catches a bullet. He has contributed his life. (Quoted in Searle 2007)

In this quote McQueen gives an indication of the artistic sensibility which he brought to what might seem politically incommensurable projects; the commemoration of the British soldiers killed in Iraq and the commemoration through film of the life of someone dedicated to the military overthrow of the British presence in Ireland. McQueen's declared concern is not with the politics in either case, but with memory and memorialisation of the dead, whatever his or her status, and the importance of the individual life lived as opposed to the political calculation of the value of a life in pursuit of an end. Frequently in interview he has stressed his concern with the 'humanity' in the story of Bobby Sands, rather than the politics, and on one occasion elaborated on this idea as follows:

> I am Davey and Gerry [prisoners in the film] and I am Raymond, the prison officer. It's not about right or wrong, good or bad, or the devil and Heaven. If you can answer it then you must be God – I'm not. (Quoted in Mottram 2008)

In this attitude McQueen is expressing a familiar non-judgemental 'artistic' idea of humanity that 'nothing which is human is alien to me'.[19] However, whatever McQueen's intention, the idea that a film could be made that would somehow avoid being regarded as political and embroiling McQueen in political controversy whether he wished it or not, is, on the face of it, extremely implausible. It is an accepted fact of political history in Northern Ireland that the hunger strikes represented a turning point in the conflict and one to which a direct line of heritage may be traced from the current political arrangements, the functioning Executive Government of Northern Ireland.[20] The hunger strikes, in other words, are grandly over-determined as not only political events, but events of such massive political significance that they may be fairly regarded as events of constitutional foundation, in both the general and the legal sense.[21] Not only this, but on the level of local experience the hunger strike period may be taken as a kind of distilled version of the entire 'Troubles'; the violence, the grand issues of constitutional politics mixed in arguable degree with issues of human rights, the local effects in terms of the polarisation of communities and political opinion, the public displays of certain political positions revealed by later events and histories as postures hiding very different strategies and calculations, a seemingly irresolvable argument between implacable foes.[22] It was, in short, a time of political ferment which inflamed and polarised Northern Ireland. It was one of those periods of the extended 'Troubles' where it was impossible to maintain the everyday fiction of a generally normal society with some trouble around the edges.[23] The hunger strike period is not only a site of the genesis of institutional and constitutional reformation, but is also a site of vivid and raw personal memory for the general population who lived through it.[24]

Not only this, but the film was released in 2008 at a time when the issue of remembrance of the past was a hot political topic in Northern Ireland. The 'Consultative Group on the Past'[25] (also known as the 'Eames–Bradley Commission' after the two co-chairs) had begun sitting in 2007 to review and suggest proposals to overhaul the hitherto piecemeal approach to 'dealing with the past' in Northern Ireland, and already certain leaks as to their proceedings had created political furore.[26] This is an indication of the extent to which Northern Ireland is still dealing with the past as an active element of the continuing present. Sectarian attacks are still fairly frequent, and are the tip of an iceberg of continuing sectarian segregation and tensions.[27] 'Dissident' Republican groups still oppose the constitutional settlement through 'armed struggle'.[28] Education is still, in the main, conducted in schools segregated along sectarian lines, and people, in the main, still live in segregated areas.

An extended treatment of the Eames–Bradley detailed report is beyond this essay, but I would like to pick up on a core point of fundamental approach that grounds many (arguably all) of the detailed recommendations within it. The point relates to the following statement, contained in the section on 'Developing a road map for the future':

> Buried memories fester in the unconscious minds of communities in conflict, only to emerge later in even more distorted and virulent forms to poison minds and relationships ... Most importantly for present purposes, one should emphasise that, although the past is past, it continues to exist in people's minds. That past affects how people live their lives and how they experience the world. Divided communities carry different experiences and understandings of the past in their minds, and indeed it is this that divides them ... If these conflicting moral assessments of the past are to change, then all sides need to be encouraged and facilitated to listen and hear each other's stories. This listening must then lead to honest assessment of what the other is saying and to recognition of truth within their story. In such a process it might be possible to construct a remembrance of our past which is more humane, comprehensive and rounded. (Consultative Group on the Past 2009: 52)

Unpicking the thematic threads of this statement, there are several issues to note. The first is the striking philosophically nominalist view of the past as relative and conditional on the 'stories' of those who refer to it. The second is the focus on what might be unkindly termed a 'pop psychological' version of the relationship between past trauma and present life, in the reference to memories 'fester[ing] in the unconscious minds of communities in conflict'. This is connected to the theme of the relativity of truth positions and to the consequent need for storytelling from all sides and for each side to recognise the truth within each other's stories. In other words, there is a presumption of 'sides' to truth, and of truth within all stories. The technique for managing the past is that this truth, or these truths, should be let out into the open air, not for judgement as to its (their) value as truth, but for recognition of the value of the very exercise of 'truth' telling. Truth gives way to a process of truth-telling, a kind of psychosomatic tool, a species of 'talking cure'.

Whatever the merits of this position (and in particular the extension of a recognisably therapeutic individualistic idea to the level of community conflict resolution), there is an implicit core presumption behind even these presumptions as to the relativity of truth, and it deserves serious attention. It is that the past should be bent to the service of the social health of the present, and in particular the future, or, as the 'key principle' laid out in the document states:

> The past should be dealt with in a manner which enables society to become more defined by its desire for true and lasting reconciliation, rather than by division and mistrust, seeking to promote a shared and reconciled future for all. (Consultative Group on the Past 2009: 23)

While on the face of things it would seem churlish to argue with the sentiment behind such a position, there is perhaps too much of an easy move from sentiment to an idea that 'telling stories' is the way forward without any working through of a coherent moral framework within which such stories might stand or fall in relation to each other. To translate this moral idea to a formal equivalent in the artistic realm, there is a kind of blind faith in the democratic nature and value of storytelling, without consideration of the idea that some people, for whatever reason, are better story-tellers than others, not to mention that some will certainly reject the idea of experience as 'story'.

Furthermore, the understanding of memory implicit in such an Eames–Bradley approach has certain ineluctable features. Implicit is that the past somehow owes a debt to the present, the debt of offering up some route to reconciliation.[29] The past, in other words, is not so much about what happened, but about what we presently need to have happened in order to construct our future. The past becomes an area to be mined to produce some good-quality hardcore on which to build. Memory as truth is malleable in the service of a good story of reconciliation. To put it another way, it seems that everyone is being given the responsibility to tell their own story, but a prior condition to do so must be the acceptance of a responsibility that their story and their telling is something that works for the common good. This seems not only philosophically incoherent, but also something likely to be practically unachievable, and therefore opens up as many questions as it resolves. It tries to marry the ethical (ought) questions of responsibility to the ontological (is) questions of people's memory of their lived experience.

The intention here is not to embark on an extended critique of the Eames–Bradley document, but to highlight the continued significance of 'dealing with the past', and to further highlight the complexity and difficulty of finding a form through which this might be achieved, and the likely controversies which will dog any attempt. McQueen's approach, as already foreshadowed earlier in the discussion of his work in relation to the British war dead in Iraq, is very different from that of Eames–Bradley.

HUNGER AND LINGERING WITH THE IMAGE OF HUMANITY

The film is split into three distinct sections. In the first and final sections there is practically no dialogue, while the second section consists entirely of an extended duologue which is almost all shot in a single 18-minute-long 'two-shot' take, the actors facing each other while the camera remains static. This scene was scripted by Enda Walsh[30] and consists of an extended theologico-political debate between Sands and a priest. This scene, as a 'landmark' in cinema form (the extended single take), gathered a huge amount of critical attention, but the fact that it was scripted by Walsh while McQueen as director seems to have decided to almost withdraw from the scene, makes it less interesting for this analysis, and so I don't propose to dwell on it further.[31] The third section catalogues Sands's progression towards eventual death, principally through a series of slow-paced scenes and images that recall the discussion of McQueen's art above, yet draw heavily on Christian and in particular Catholic iconography of the Passion of Jesus Christ. Likewise, this section is less interesting for this analysis. Insofar as it relates to the form of image-making, this will be discussed in relation to the images in the first section. On the level of ideas the story is simple; Sands completes his hunger strike to the death. The idea of the impact of how this story was told on the reception of the film will be discussed in the conclusion.

The first section of the film deals in parallel with the contrasting experience of two characters. One is a new prisoner arriving in the prison, and the other is a prison officer going about his daily routine of travelling to the prison and starting his work shift. The prisoner adopts the 'dirty protest' techniques in refusal of the status of a normal prisoner.[32] He strips naked before prison guards, is led to his cell, meets his cellmate and is gradually over time introduced to the routine realities of prison claustrophobia and brutality. In parallel to the viewer's introduction to the realities of the prison through the experience of this character, we are also introduced to the realities of prison life from the 'other side of the fence', as we see the daily routine of a prison officer, having breakfast, checking under his car for bombs, driving to work in civilian clothes, changing into uniform, entering into the gang of warders having tea and sharing jokes before they clock on for their shift.

While this opening portion of the film develops a context for what follows, the idea of context here is only obliquely a notion of political context, as this relates to the political situation outside the prison. At one point, for example, one prisoner manages to use a tiny smuggled radio to gain access to news from the outside world about how the political and military struggle is progressing. But the real force of the scenes regarding the radio within the film is that we are shown it being smuggled into the prison by a female visitor who, at visiting time, takes a cellophane-wrapped, sausage-shaped package out from beneath her skirt and passes it to a prisoner who puts it down his trousers before smuggling it back to his cell, where he is shown retrieving it from his anus. The radio is one of many items which are used to illustrate the theme of the rebellious bodies of the prisoners, and their ability to find ways to subvert the rules of the prison.[33]

The viewer is introduced to these scenes with the new inmate, and the depiction of the physicality is accentuated by the camera periodically adopting the prisoner's perspective. The viewer is made to recoil with him as he is pushed into a cell and takes in his new surroundings, the shit smeared on the walls in patterns to create a kind of cave art, and out of the darkness looming his cellmate resembling a caveman, naked, filthy, long hair and beard matted and unkempt.[34] There are horrific scenes of the naked men being beaten by a riot squad of prison officers that recalls scenes of cattle being beaten and prodded towards their death in an abattoir. The zenith of this thematic illustration of the conditions in which these men find themselves (or have created for themselves as a refusal of the condition of normalised humanity as it exists for the prison regime) is a scene in which this prisoner stands at the metal grille which covers the broken window from his cell to the outside and toys with a fly that has come through the window and into the cell (or perhaps hatched as a bluebottle from the maggots infesting the rotting food and shit on the floor). The scene seems to suggest that the prisoner is so abject that even a fly is good company, and the prisoner seems to play with it not in cruelty but in empathy. In a trademark gesture of McQueen's art, the camera lingers in silence for a long time on this odd and moving interaction.

In a parallel scene, the prison officer through whose eyes the film was introduced is shown standing alone in the prison exercise yard, smoking a cigarette as snow gently falls. The camera lingers as the flakes settle down on his grazed knuckles, knuckles that have been picked out previously in several scenes of the film. They were grazed in a horrific scene where he beat the prisoners as he tried to force them to wash, and the impression is given that this is a frequent practice and that the wounds on his hands are practically permanent. The snowflakes settle like a balm on the open wounds of his hands as he stands starkly alone and seemingly alienated even from himself. Only nature comforts him. In the film's opening scene of his home life his wife is so anonymised that her face is never shown; the crumbs that fall from the table are paid more attention. In scenes with his fellow officers he is raucous and sociable, but to the point where it seems like an act that he is putting on, a mask that he wears. In his final scene in the film he is visiting his mother in a rest home. As he sits trying to communicate with her it becomes obvious that she is in the late stages of dementia, and does not recognise him. A killer walks in and shoots him from behind, his blood splattering the unreacting face of his mother. The overall characterisation (in keeping with McQueen's declaration, cited above, that 'I am Raymond . . .') seems one of immense sympathy for the plight of this officer who is so dehumanised in his loss of capacity for authentic human interaction, and where this loss of capacity seems brought on by the abnormal and inhumane conditions of prison life.

The context, in other words, is a remarkable context of human ingenuity in the face of extremities of human experience. Men who are imprisoned for terrorist crimes refuse to conform to the definition imposed on them that they are criminals, and in order to assert a different status they embrace a condition of a kind of animality. They refuse to wear prison uniform and so are naked, wrapped only in a single blanket. They refuse to do prison work and so are confined to their cells without rights of exercise or association with other prisoners. They refuse to 'slop out' and so smear their cells with their own excrement to diffuse the accumulated shit. They build channels of rotted and rotting food to direct their urine out underneath the doorways and into the prison corridor. Their only concession to the normality of a prison regime is to don clothes so that they can avail themselves of visiting rights, and therefore to a degree of contact to the outside. Such attitudes necessarily create conflict with the guards inside the prison, who react with physical violence against the kind of systemic violence that the prisoners have, paradoxically, managed to inflict on the guards through wresting control over the physical environment; the guards must also live and work in shit and stench. The first section of the film then, opens up a context which is not only a kind of super-humanisation in terms of human ingenuity, but also a context of a kind of cyclical dehumanisation. In each case the concern is with what McQueen expressed as his idea of humanity, 'what we, as humans, are capable of . . . What we will inflict and what we will endure.'[35]

However, even as this broadly narrative element of the film is gradually unfolded, it is important to bear in mind two things, one itself a condition of the narrative and the second a condition of the filmmaking process. The first is that practically none of this opening narrative development concerns Bobby Sands. It is the parallel story of two men, one a prisoner and one a warder, and the physical and human context in which they live. The connected filmmaking point is that of how this story is unfolded, in particular as it focuses in on the two men as, on some occasions and to some degree, divorced from the context. Each of these men is offered several striking scenes where we, as an audience, are made to stay with them as they go through the most mundane of actions that are elevated and heightened into something extraordinary by the attention of the camera, by the details of lighting and sound. The prison officer washing his knuckles beneath running water, slowly smoking a cigarette beneath the falling snow, eating a piece of toast. The prisoner stripping naked before the guards, toying with the fly by the window in his cell, trying to masturbate to a tiny smuggled picture as his cellmate stirs on a filthy mattress a couple of feet away. The lighting and camera effects emphasise the darkness and claustrophobia of the environment. There is no dialogue and a focus on periods of silence punctuated by resonantly loud episodes; a clanging prison door, prisoners' screams, warders' raucous laughter. The effect is, through contrast, to heighten those periods of silence and to draw the attention to the significance of those mundane tasks; the unbuttoning of a shirt, the smoking of a cigarette. The audience is asked to linger in silence with a heightened sense of the significance of the mundane details of the lives of men trapped in extraordinary conditions. This lingering echoes McQueen's earlier silent films, and has the quality of creating a kind of secular, humanistic, devotional imagery. What we will inflict and what we will endure are the poles at either end of a much more normal gamut of sensation and endeavour that joins us all just as the former often divides us; the unbuttoning of a shirt, the smoking of a cigarette. In the midst of conditions of absolute horror, McQueen takes time to linger with such images of the banality of ordinary human experience and to remember that it can be beautiful and moving. The form and the idea are merged in the simple act which is requested of the audience: to watch and to wait, to witness and to feel.

AESTHETICS AND TRANSFORMATION

In his review of the film, that is on one level extremely perceptive, the Irish cultural commentator Fintan O'Toole (2008) regrets what he sees as McQueen's surrender to the 'narrative of the hunger strikers'. He writes:

> There is an obvious reason why artists return again and again to the 1981 hunger strikes, and it is not primarily political. It has to do with the sense in which the hunger strikes themselves were a kind of art. They functioned, as art does, on the plane of metaphorical transformation. They were all about definition and language. They began with the prisoners' determination to define themselves as political actors rather than as criminals. And as they developed they acquired the potential to transform the prisoners from victimisers to victims, from those who had inflicted suffering to those who had suffered. With that transformation they achieved what most artists dream of: a reordering of perceptions.

Further in the same review he reiterates and elaborates his point, as a pointed critic of what he sees as McQueen's political naivety:

> The whole point of the hunger strikes, after all, was that aesthetics trumps politics. The fusion of a visual imagery that deliberately tapped into images of Christ and the potent drama of slow death worked to simplify and transform a complex political reality. It obliterated the reality that the prisoners were killers. It even obscured the stark fact that far fewer prisoners than prison officers died in the H-Blocks conflict – 10 dead hunger strikers against 29 prison officers murdered by the IRA. Whatever its intentions, any film that plugs into that aesthetic power will always repeat that act of obliteration . . . it is utterly naive to think that you can both plug into the hunger strikes as an aesthetic event and give them a neutral political treatment.

There is a very good point here as to the hunger strikes as aesthetic events, even if in making it O'Toole himself is doing some simplifying and transforming of complex political realities. This is true on a simple factual level (not all the prisoners were killers, for example).[36] On a more complex political level, many Republican 'terrorists' would accept that they were victimisers in the sense of creating victims, but it is striking how many ascribe their political commitment to a response to personal victimisation – Gerry Adams, for example, in his autobiography ascribes his political commitment to his family having been forced out of its home (Adams 1996). In other words, the boundary between victim and victimiser is not quite as neat as O'Toole suggests.[37]

There are other simplifications at play here, which lie on the borders of the political and the aesthetic that are traced out by O'Toole himself. He does not want to concede that the hunger strikers, in performing a 'work of art', did something that was positive on a political plane. He can accept the status of their gesture as art, but can only see it as transformative through its 'obliterative' power over the political reality of the death of the prison officers. For a cultural commentator and an art critic this seems an odd surrender of the notion of nuance, which is particularly strange in that the move to cast the hunger strikes as performance art is so bold. If the hunger strikes were transformative in an artistic sense, in that they reordered perceptions, were they not also transformative in a political sense that was not merely a negative obliteration, or in a personal sense? The answer to the first of these questions is certainly 'yes', in a way that is both totally banal and yet utterly significant. The promotion of Sands as a candidate in a parliamentary by-election, as a deliberate tactic to draw attention to the support his protest had in the wider community, had the ancillary (and well-acknowledged) effect of shifting the balance of power within the Republican movement away from the military and towards the political.[38] In a personal sense, there are few who would argue that the movement from murder to self-immolation as a means of protest has at least the virtue of demonstrating the same level of life or death commitment to an ideal without involving unwilling participants in the gesture. O'Toole can't bring himself to concede that the hunger strikers could have done terrible things and yet that there was something extraordinary in what they were doing through their protest, or the even more simple point that even as victimisers (or victims) they were human beings putting themselves at the limit of human capability. He is performing his own act of obliteration of a complex relation between aesthetics and politics, a relationship which he himself has exploited in his comments.

In effect, what he is doing is trying (ironically for a cultural commentator) to promote politics beyond aesthetics because of his disapproval of the power of the aesthetic gesture of the hunger strikers, and his sense that any approach to this aesthetic power (such as McQueen's) has to take the nature of a surrender.

What McQueen has managed, however, together with his co-writer, actors and crew, is to plug into the humanity of the hunger strikes, in his own fascination with human capabilities and limits, and to match this humanity with an aesthetic of his own which performs an alternative work of transformation, the transformation of dehumanised figures hidden behind prison walls – and this is not just Sands but all of the characters, whether prisoner or warder – into figures of humanity who are worth remembering, and worth remembering with a steady and slow eye to the detail of their existence. This is an aesthetic based on captivating images and on dwelling with these images in silence.

Unlike the Eames–Bradley Commission then, which strays towards an idea that the dead somehow owe the living a chance to heal, the idea here seems that the living gain a measure of their own humanity by dwelling with the past for a while, by, in the gracious words of another recent commentator, simply bearing in mind these dead (McKay 2008). Perhaps film as a form which allowed McQueen, and allows generally for, a structure of imagining a past (or a future) but without the need for text 'shot through with explanation'[39] and which therefore allows for and indeed calls for and relies upon a range of response, is particularly suited to this kind of work of memorialisation, of marking the fact of memory yet leaving room for that public act to respect the individual community acts that it should somehow constitute and unify.

While the film garnered, in the main, positive critical comment (and many prizes), this is not something that would necessarily indicate that it would have a positive social effect in Northern Ireland. Of note here are two points. The first is that the film was warmly received by Republicans, even ex-hunger strikers. While for some (such as O'Toole, discussed above) this is simply evidence that the film 'surrendered' to the Republican narrative, a more convincing point is that the Republican movement itself has now moved to a point where the humanist portrayal of Sands, all but shorn of constitutional political elements, is one that they feel comfortable remembering. The second is that the film opened and ran in Belfast without any protests or demonstrations of any kind. An illustration, perhaps, that the form of memory was, if not something that could be shared equally by all, at least one that was tolerable.

Central to the exploration undertaken in this essay is the idea, not only that everyone has their story, which is of course true, but that the right story be told in the right way, notwithstanding that the person telling the story has no particular right (in that they did not live it) to tell it. Sands's story was the right story for McQueen, as discussed above, because of the personal imprint of the TV news image that, coming as an element of a time, place and emotional landscape, over twenty years before, planted the seed. The eventual telling is marked, as so much of McQueen's work, by the dominance of image over narrative, and by a fascination with humanity, with human capacity and human response. The reception of the film would suggest that the film succeeded in striking a positive chord, both in Northern Ireland and beyond, and that the marriage of form and idea somehow managed to express and consolidate an inchoate social idea of just memorialisation.

NOTES

Thanks are due to various people for conversations regarding this essay, in particular Stephen Douds, Gráinne McKeever and Catherine O'Rourke. The contribution of the students in my 'Law and Film' class, in particular Roisin Devlin and Mary Baxter, has been central to the completion of this piece in its current form. Thanks also to Dermot Feenan and Melanie Williams, the editors of this special collection, for their detailed suggestions. And special thanks to Sara Ramshaw for invaluable help and forbearance.

1. Sands, within the command structure of the Irish Republican Army, was the prison 'Officer Commanding' or 'OC'. The IRA (and its political component Sinn Féin) was dedicated (politically) to the establishment of a socialist republic throughout the whole island of Ireland, and militarily to the overthrow through 'armed struggle' of the British presence in Ireland. The IRA, formed early in the twentieth century to expel the British from Ireland as a whole, had waned in significance following the 1922 partition of the island, after which the newly constituted entity of 'Northern Ireland' remained a part of the United Kingdom. The organisation was rejuvenated by the outbreak of the modern Northern Ireland 'Troubles' period of political violence in 1969. In 1972, coincident with the introduction of a policy of internment without trial of those suspected of involvement in political violence, the internees and prisoners were awarded 'special category' status, modelled on the status of prisoners of war under the Geneva Conventions. The policy of 'criminalisation' of political violence in Northern Ireland – initiated under Home Secretary Merlyn Rees in 1975 – was marked by the cessation of the award of 'special category' status (in 1976) and the replacement of Nissen hut 'cages' at Long Kesh with newly constructed H-Block structures, renamed as the 'Maze Prison'. Those prisoners (and their supporters) who wished to maintain the claim to political status, generally refused to adopt the new name and continued (and continue) to refer to 'Long Kesh'. In search of the restoration of 'political status' some prisoners instituted a 'blanket' (refusal to wear prison uniform) and eventually 'no-wash' or 'dirty' protest (the refusal to remove body and food waste from cells). When this was unsuccessful, the decision was taken to go on hunger strike in pursuit of 'political status' and Sands was the first of ten men to die before the tactic was abandoned.
2. Aside from Cannes, the film also won prizes at the Sydney, Venice, Toronto and Chicago film festivals.
3. An extreme example of a frequent criticism that the film constituted a 'hagiography' of Sands appears as a feature comment by David Cox on *The Guardian* filmblog website (Cox 2008). See also comments on 'worshipping at the shrine of terrorism' (Tookey 2008).
4. The film, for example, was awarded the inaugural Sydney Film Festival Prize, for 'its controlled clarity of vision, its extraordinary detail and bravery, the dedication of its cast and the power and resonance of its humanity'.
5. See McDonald (2008).
6. Multimodal texts are those that combine different expressive modes, typically sound, image and discourse; see Schulenberg (2003).
7. See, in particular, on alternative jurisprudence, MacNeil (2003; 2005).

8. For specific discussion of 'transdisciplinarity' in this context, see Manderson and Mohr (2002). For examples of such transdisciplinarity in action, see Moran et al. (2004) and Manderson (2004).
9. For relevant discussions of legal pluralism in this context, see Kleinhans and Macdonald (1997).
10. See Chen and Churchill (2007). While not specifically a legal text, this book deals with the idea of 'citizenship' and thus precisely with the nexus of constitutional law and politics.
11. See, in particular, Duncanson (2008) and the provocative reading through each other of *Four Weddings and a Funeral* and the BBC coverage of Princess Diana's funeral; see also McNamee (2004); see more generally on this point, Kahn (1999).
12. Two other films, *H3* and *Some Mother's Son*, which deal directly with the hunger strikes of that period, have been made but, unlike *Hunger*, in those films the director and author had personal connection to the hunger strikes and/or the Republican movement.
13. For an introduction to this area of study generally, see Campbell and Ní Aoláin (2003) and particularly Bell (2003).
14. For the sketching of the beginnings of exploration in this area, see Buchanan and Johnson (2009).
15. The Turner Prize is awarded annually by a committee of jurors organised by the Tate Gallery London, in memory of radical landscape painter J. M. W. Turner. Instituted in 1984, it is the mostly highly publicised of UK art awards and has become associated with conceptual art which 'provokes comment on art'.
16. The number beneath the image referred to the number of days Sands had been on hunger strike.
17. The appointment is made by invitation of the Imperial War Museum. An account of the limited access afforded to McQueen in this process of 'embeddedness' (which he described as almost literally being forced by the army to remain in bed for his own safety in Iraq) is given in an interview with Searle (2007).
18. McQueen also promoted the idea that such a special edition of UK stamps should be issued into general circulation, 'all first class'.
19. The quote is originally from one of Terence's comedies, but has been reproduced almost to the point of cliché.
20. There are by now many histories of this period which look behind the scenes at the multiple interactions in play. For the most readable journalistic accounts, see McKittrick (1994) and Mallie and McKittrick (1996). For academic history, see Bew and Gillespie (1999) and Bew (2007). For a privileged internal account, see the book by the American 'Special Envoy to Northern Ireland' who was heavily instrumental in the talks process; Mitchell (1999).
21. The question of origin is a persistent one in constitutional terms, in particular within the Constitution of the UK. Aside from an elaborated argument on this point, I confine myself to noting that the political arrangements under the Belfast Agreement (and which were a precondition for its acceptance), under which 'terrorist' prisoners were released under licence after having served as little as two years of life sentences for murder, represent such a definitive victory for politics over the rule of law that the idea of revolution is not entirely misplaced.
22. For a highly controversial recent account from an ex-prisoner close to the hunger strikers, see O'Rawe (2005).
23. In the midst of his hunger strike, Sands stood for election as Member of Parliament for the constituency of Fermanagh and South Tyrone, and was elected with over 30,000 votes. When he died, the crowd at his funeral in Belfast was estimated at 100,000 (the overall population of Northern Ireland being approximately 1,500,000).

24. It is also an extremely 'commemorated' event in that there are multiple murals throughout Northern Ireland which picture the ten men who died, as well as an annual commemorative parade. As one example among many of international reaction to the hunger strike and the perceived injustice of the British position, 'Winston Churchill Avenue' in Teheran, the street on which stood the British Embassy, was renamed 'Bobby Sands Avenue'. This is not to suggest that international opinion was uniformly anti-British on the issues, rather to point to the raising of the international profile of the Republican cause.
25. The Consultative Group on the Past was an independent body set up under recommendation of the Secretary of State for Northern Ireland to report jointly to the British Government and the Northern Irish Assembly on dealing with the legacy of the past. It held public meetings, private meetings with individuals, and received written submissions for a period of about eighteenth months up until January 2009, when the report was submitted (Consultative Group on the Past 2009).
26. Press leaks, for example, that the Group were considering using the term 'war' to refer to the conflict, and that 'compensation' payments were being considered for the relatives of those killed.
27. On 24 May 2009, Kevin McDaid, a community worker, was murdered by a sectarian mob in Coleraine when he intervened to try to calm a violent altercation after a Rangers vs Celtic football match.
28. On 7 March 2009, Sapper Mark Quinsey and Sapper Patrick Azimka were killed outside Massereene Barracks, Antrim, in an attack by the 'Real IRA'. Two days later, Constable Stephen Carroll was murdered in an attack in Craigavon by members of the 'Continuity IRA'.
29. The idea of 'reconciliation' is not one that should escape critical interrogation. For an introduction, see Bell (2003; 2008).
30. Enda Walsh is an award-winning Irish playwright known for the complexity and vivacity of his writing in plays such as *Disco Pigs*, *Bedbound*, *The Walworth Farce* and latterly *The New Electric Ballroom* (all published by Nick Hern Books, London). He is only secondarily known as a screenwriter – *Hunger* is his second credit in this role.
31. In relation to this scene, McQueen's concern seems to have been far from the contest of political ideas expressed: 'I was interested in the whole notion of intimacy, the intimacy of the conversation . . . so it's just a two-shot of those two having a conversation . . . you have a situation where the audience thinks it shouldn't be involved, so your attention is heightened, your focus is sharpened . . . you become the camera' (McQueen, quoted in Mottram 2008).
32. For an explanation of 'dirty protest', see note 1.
33. One visiting room scene is almost comic in the mass and variety of material that is removed from enclosed body parts, mouths, ears, noses and anuses and passed across to be transported out of the prison, with a similar volume of material moving in the other direction. There is an extensive anthropological literature on the 'body as a site of resistance' developed through studies in Northern Ireland, in particular in the prison system, and more particularly in relation to the blanket protest, dirty protest and hunger strikes. For an explanatory introduction to this literature, as well as an extensive bibliography of material, see Wilson and Donnan (2006).
34. The adoption of the perspective of any individual character, with the attendant promotion of identification with the literal 'point of view' of this character, is done rarely throughout the film, which in general maintains an 'objective' viewpoint. An interesting exception which relates to this scene mentioned above is a scene in which a (sympathetically portrayed) prison orderly enters (clad head to foot in protective clothing) and pauses to

remove his helmet and stare at the 'art' on the walls; the viewer being offered this point of view.
35. McQueen, quoted in O'Hagan (2008).
36. Sands was serving a fourteen-year sentence for 'possession of firearms'.
37. The recent and ongoing response to the Eames–Bradley Commission Report throws up this whole issue once again; who is a victim, is there a parity of victimhood? The likelihood is that the extensive work and multiple recommendations of the group will be lost in the blaze of controversy over their proposal that the 'nearest relative' of those who died (whether civilian, security force personnel or paramilitary) in the Northern Irish conflict should be awarded an ex gratia 'recognition payment' of £12,000. The proposal was flatly rejected by the Secretary of State for Northern Ireland and the First Minister of the Northern Ireland Executive.
38. This movement was marked by IRA publicity officer Danny Morrison's 1981 address to the Sinn Féin (the political wing of the IRA) Ard fheis (Annual Conference), where he stated: 'Who here really believes we can win the war through the ballot box? But will anyone here object if, with a ballot paper in this hand and an Armalite in the other, we take power in Ireland?'
39. For discussion of this idea in relation to cultural forms, see Benjamin (1968: 84 and Foreword).

CHAPTER 4

Shame and the City: Subverting Neoliberal, New York Singleton Culture in *Shame*

Niall Richardson

In one of the most memorable scenes in Steve McQueen's *Shame*, Sissy (Carey Mulligan) performs a unique version of the song 'New York, New York'.[1] Sissy's rendition is so ritardando, and employs such an extreme rubato, that the song assumes a completely different timbre from the theme song of the Scorsese musical *New York, New York* (1977) (Blum 2015). Instead of being a celebration of the hope and opportunity offered by New York city – a place where career and romantic dreams come true – Sissy's version is a 'hymn to loneliness, loss and despair' (Featherstone 2016: 34).

This musical scene can be read as a metonym for one of the key themes of *Shame*: a critique of the type of neoliberal, sexual utopia narratives of New York which found popularity in many 1990s romantic comedies – not least the HBO series *Sex and the City*. *Shame* represents a dystopian version of the fantastic sexual freedom of earlier representations of New York: a 'ghoulish response to the early 1990s sexual utopia of New York singles, *Sex and the City* (1998–2004)' (Featherstone 2016: 34). Recent critical writing about *Shame* has focused on how it interrogates the dynamics of male (rather than female) shame (Stepien 2104; Schiller 2011); how it represents the concept of sex 'addiction' (Iwen 2014); how the film subverts sexual utopia (Featherstone 2016); and how Michael Fassbender's performance of Brandon challenges hegemonic masculinity (Akyildiz 2021; Braid 2014). This chapter, however, will extend these debates by analysing how *Shame* can also be read as a critique of contemporary neoliberal culture in which the obsession with individuality and career success means that relationships are now focused on personal fulfilment and organised around work schedules. While the film does allow the possibility of reading Brandon's sex 'addiction' as the direct result of some unresolved childhood trauma (see below), *Shame* also suggests that Brandon is merely someone who has retreated into a succession of physical encounters to insulate himself against a neoliberal context where relationships are so difficult to forge and maintain. In this respect, the shame of the film's title is not Brandon's realisation of his supposed sex 'addiction' but the shameful society which facilitates this type of behaviour and the spectator's recognition of the self in this contemporary sexualised culture.

Through textual analysis, this chapter will examine how McQueen's distinctive visual style (his characteristic long takes, expressive use of colour, visual symbols, sound/music) and his negotiation of the genres of the rom-com and musical are mobilised to subvert the signification of the glamorous Manhattan setting – the backdrop for countless rom-coms and musicals – to render the sexual utopia of neoliberal New York as nightmarish.

SEX ADDICTION FILMS

Shame tells the story of Brandon (Fassbender), a thirty-something executive who lives in Manhattan. Brandon is a classically handsome, heterosexually-identified, white, cisgender man who appears to lead a life of middle-class success in New York. However, behind the economic prosperity, he is revealed to be a sex 'addict' who fills his leisure (and sometimes even his worktime breaks) watching pornography and engaging in casual pick-ups – either with random women or sex workers. Brandon's routine of endless porn consumption and sex hook-ups is disturbed when his sister Sissy – who works as a nightclub singer – needs to crash at his apartment for a while. The film progresses through a series of casual sex encounters for Brandon, and relationship disappointments for Sissy, and culminates in Sissy's attempted suicide and Brandon's emotional breakdown.

Shame can be seen as an example of the cycle of films identified by the journalist Tom Shone as 'sex addiction films' (Shone 2014). Other films include *Diary of a Sex Addict* (Joseph Brutsman, 2001), *I Am a Sex Addict* (Caveh Zahedi, 2005), *Choke* (Clark Gregg, 2008), *Thanks for Sharing* (Stuart Blumberg, 2012), *Don Jon* (Joseph Gordon-Leavitt, 2013), *Nymph(o)maniac* (Lars von Trier, 2013) and *Welcome to New York* (Abel Ferrara, 2014). Alistair Fox argues that there is a difference in tone between the sex addiction films produced in the USA and those in Europe. While the American texts are often comedic or, at the very least, have funny moments, the European films (of which *Shame* is an example) are 'unrelievedly grim and harrowing' (Fox 2016: 15). Yet despite tonal differences, both brands of sex addiction film represent sex 'addiction' as involuntary and something which the practitioner finds very difficult to give up (Fox 15). Most importantly, all the films assert that sex 'addiction' is 'harmful to the individual who suffers from it' (Fox 15).

The concept of sex 'addiction' has been debated by many critics, with several psychologists arguing that it is merely a media discourse which has no basis in psychiatric-medical science (Ley 2012; Reay et al. 2015). Many of the films in this cycle can be read as reinforcing the myth of sex 'addiction' by reducing the practice to a simplistic concept of unresolved trauma within the individual. What distinguishes *Shame* from the other films is that it offers a more nuanced representation of sex 'addiction'. Although it is possible to speculate that Brandon's sex 'addiction' may be the result of unresolved childhood trauma, which might have involved incest with Sissy, this is never confirmed within the film narrative. Indeed, the only scene which suggests the possibility of this incestuous relationship is the sequence where Sissy sneaks into Brandon's bed one evening. While this can be read as suggesting incestuous desire, it can also be interpreted as a deliberate challenge to prejudices which see sex 'addiction' as the result of childhood sexual trauma. The spectator is forced to realise that it is only the context of the film (in which debauched sexual acts have been so plentiful) that can lead them to read this sequence as anything more than Sissy seeking some emotional support from her older brother. Similarly, Sissy is first introduced in the film through her repeated voicemail messages to Brandon which, given his succession of one-night stands, the spectator initially reads as the pleadings of one of his previous tricks rather than his sister. In this respect, the film is forcing the spectator to realise that they are diagnosing sex 'addiction' in accordance with clichéd narratives of childhood trauma rather than acknowledging that the practice may simply be the result of contemporary, metropolitan culture and its celebration of neoliberal sexual expressions.

NEOLIBERALISM

The latter half of the twentieth century saw the development of post-Fordist economies in which industries of mass manufacturing have been succeeded by new production methods which often specialise in the sale of images, such as the media and tourism. As a result of this economic shift, post-Fordism requires continuous innovation necessitated by the instability of capitalism. It is this economic uncertainty which has inspired a type of governance in the West which advocates protecting individual autonomy, personal choice and the free market (Tauss 2012). Neoliberalism, in this respect, is underpinned by the philosophy that nations are not responsible for an individual's social welfare and that instead citizens should take charge of their own social and personal well-being (Rose 1992: 12). On the level of everyday culture, this discourse of neoliberalism can be seen in how society has rejected the intervention of state control (Harvey 2005) to create instead a culture of choice. Indeed, it is this celebration of choice that underpins the current practice of self-help and self-development, ranging from lifestyle and career planning through to diet, fashion and beauty advice (Tudor 2011).

Alistair Fox points out that this discourse of neoliberalism – especially its focus on freedom of choice – can also be seen to underpin the politics of sexual expression in the USA (Fox 2016: 10). Recent forms of feminist and queer rights activism from the past sixty years, which have promoted socio-cultural acceptance for gays and lesbians, sex beyond marriage and queer/alternative forms of sexual and gender practice, can be read as 'consonant with the country's neo-liberal commitment to "freedom" in other areas of life' (Fox 2016: 10) (see also Allyn 2001). Hilary Radner notes that there is an obvious similarity between the personal satisfaction identified as the goal of consumer culture with the fulfilment that is supposed to be afforded to the sexual subject through sexual expression (Radner 2010: 1–25). This freedom of sexual expression has led to what is often termed a pornographication of culture (McNair 2013), which denotes how mainstream entertainment has become increasingly sexualised, often adopting the codes and conventions previously associated with pornographic representation. One possible benefit of pornographication is how it can facilitate a 'democracy of desire' (McNair 2002) in that this new sexualised culture challenges heteronormative and patriarchal expectations of gender and sexuality.

However, as Fox argues, the inevitable outcome of the neoliberalisation of sexual expression is not only unregimented access to sexualised material but a loosening of the framework of dating rituals and therefore the rise of contemporary 'hook-up culture' (Fox 2016: 10). Indeed, in a recent interview, both Steve McQueen and Michael Fassbender explained that they felt *Shame* was not suggesting there was a problem with the individual (Brandon) but that the issue was simply that there is now a culture in which there is too much choice and easy availability (Studio Q). When this ready availability of anonymous sex is combined with the pressures of work, it is only to be expected that individuals will avail themselves of easy options rather than pursuing the romantic labour involved with dating practices. Featherstone argues that *Shame*'s Brandon represents the horror of what has happened in neoliberal sexualised society, in which all the citizens of the city are autonomous individuals whose relationships are structured around work (2016: 33). Most importantly, these sexual relationships lack stability due to the excess of choice (ibid.). The terror of *Shame* is that it represents how, in contemporary metropolitan culture, there is often 'nothing beyond the fuck itself' (ibid.).

From the opening sequence, *Shame* suggests that Brandon's sex addiction is a result of cultural regimes, rather than an inherent psychological problem. The introductory shot represents Brandon, filmed from overhead, lying in his bed waiting for his alarm clock to ring. The fact that Brandon is already awake, yet waiting for his alarm clock to sound, demonstrates that he does not need the alarm clock but has one merely because it is a societal requirement. This rather small visual element can be read as symbolic of the theme throughout the rest of the film: the difficulties of Brandon's sex 'addiction' are as much a structural issue as any form of internalised problem. The cool blue sheets of the bed anticipate the colour motif which will feature throughout the film (Brandon's clothes are all blue-grey toned and blue lighting often illuminates the scenes) to suggest the isolation of New York city – despite the heated pick-ups that Brandon experiences. The off-centre framing of Brandon suggests that everything is not 'centred' in this character's world, while the aerial shot suggests that the film will be critiquing, or even satirising, a particular culture. Most importantly, when Brandon gets up and leaves the frame, the camera stays on the bed. By representing the protagonist leaving the shot, and then focusing only on an image of his environment, *Shame* is suggesting that Brandon's 'addiction' may be more a structural issue than a personal or psychological problem.

This theme of how Brandon is merely a component within the wider regime of neoliberal sexual expression is emphasised in other visual motifs throughout the film. One recurrent image throughout the film represents Brandon gazing out of windows over the vista of New York, sometimes while having anonymous sex. This is a reversal of the motif often found in melodramas (and made especially popular by Douglas Sirk) of the character filmed while framed by the window – thus suggesting their domestic captivity. By contrast, Brandon is shown while gazing through the windows, over the New York landscape, thus suggesting that it is now the very city of New York itself which is the captor.

However, what makes *Shame* such a discomforting experience is that its critique of the structural problems of contemporary neoliberal society is further emphasised by the way the narrative reworks, and on occasions even subverts, the structural constraints of the filmic genre itself. As Matthias Grotkopp argues in this volume, McQueen often appropriates and transforms popular genres to make a political point, and *Shame* negotiates the generic expectations of both the rom-com and the musical, two genres that have been synonymous with a New York setting.

FROM ROM-COM TO HOMME-COM TO SHAME-COM

As critics have noted, New York has often been the setting of romantic comedies (Jermyn 2008; McDonald 2015; Morrison 2010). As Deborah Jermyn explains, New York (rather than LA or Chicago) became the setting for romance narratives not simply because the city emerged as the 'urban capital of US modernity' (2008: 15) but because New York also served as the 'gateway to expansive American immigration' (2008: 16). For the millions of people who emigrated to the USA in the pursuit of happiness, the attainment of romantic love was one of their key goals alongside freedom, liberty and economic success. Although heterosexuality has always been, and continues to remain, 'Hollywood's great subject' (Hayward 2006: 177), in that most plot resolutions require 'the heterosexual couple formation' (Hayward ibid.), the packaging of heterosexuality into romantic love has been a format that has needed to evolve throughout the genre of the rom-com. The screwball comedies of the 1930s were a response to the Hays Code constrictions on explicit representations of sexuality and circumvented this censorship by sublimating sexual tension into the metaphor of the couple fighting and bickering (Glitre 2006). The rom-coms of the 1970s, responding to the rise of Western feminism (Alberti 2013: 160; Mortimer 2010), assumed a much more nervous quality (Krutnik 1990) in which the male lead was hesitant in his advances. This changed again in the conservative decade of the Reagan-led 1980s, where there was a rise of neo-traditional rom-coms (McDonald 2005) in which the traditional narrative dynamics of a male hero actively pursuing his female love interest returned to the screen.

Most recently, critics have argued that the genre has developed to include films targeted more to a male spectator (Hansen-Miller and Gill 2010; McDonald 2009). Tamar Jeffers McDonald labels these 'homme-coms' (2009). She argues that these are romantic comedies distinguished by how they rework the rom-com conventions in accordance with a male perspective. As opposed to female-centred rom-coms, the 'meet-cute' in the homme-com represents the male lead as the point of focalisation and the spectator is invited to share his point of view when the romantic female lead enters his life. While 'chick-flick' rom-coms usually focus on the heroine's life (her place of work and her social life provide the setting for most of the sequences), the homme-com features the male protagonist's home and work life as the backdrop to the romantic action. Some critics have argued that a sub-genre of the homme-com is the 'lad flick' (Hansen-Miller and Gill 2010), in which much of the comedy, and interpersonal tension between the characters, is inspired by the hero struggling with contemporary expectations of masculinity. These films often represent masculinity as 'a troubled category' (Hansen-Miller and Gill 2011: 36) and represent men who are struggling to live up to society's expectations of hegemonic masculinity.

Shame initially appears to accord with the tenets of the homme-com/lad flick in that it focuses on an Irish-American male lead (the New York immigrant seeking not only career but romantic success) who is navigating the contemporary dating scene and most obviously struggling with competing discourses of masculinity. Most importantly, the early pick-up scenes can, at first glance, appear to represent 'the male fantasy of a sexual utopia, where women are free and easy and sex always comes with no strings' (Featherstone 2016: 33). Throughout the early scenes of the film, it becomes apparent that casual pick-up culture secures an easy and efficient fuck while traditional dating is a lot of hassle and often leads only to disappointment. In one early scene, Brandon accompanies his boss David (James Badge Dale) to a bar where David is determined to impress a group of young women and pick up one of them (it seems that anyone will do) for casual sex. David performs many of the 'adorkable' pick-up antics which have been popularised by romantic comedy heroes of the past: he not only buys the women drinks but tells self-deprecating jokes, praises his wing man Brandon (to show that he is a nice guy who supports his friends) and, of course, performs goofy disco dance moves on the dance floor. This, however, is all coded as a considerable amount of hard work which, in the end, fails to attain the desired result. The women are still not interested in David. By contrast, Brandon merely needs to stand at the bar, making eye contact with the woman he fancies, to secure a casual pick-up fuck with her in the street outside. The scene makes a clear point: in contemporary New York, if someone is as handsome as Brandon then why bother with gestures of traditional rom-com chivalry when casual sex is only a mere eye-meet away?

Brandon's easy bar pick-up is then contrasted with the later scene where he goes on a traditional dinner date with a work colleague – Marianne (Nicole Beharie). Far from being a romantic experience, the date is represented as one of the most awkward and tense scenes in the film. The waiter, lacking any sensitivity whatsoever, interrupts at the most inappropriate moments and, characteristic of McQueen, the scene is one long take to convey the sense of discomfort between the characters. A fixed camera extends this sense of unease to the spectator, who is made to feel like a viewer of a wildlife documentary watching animals engaging in a mating ritual. This is also one of the few scenes which does not feature any music, while other 'sleazy' pick-ups have often been anchored by a romantic, non-diegetic soundtrack. In short, *Shame* asserts that pick-up culture works while traditional dating practices do not.

Yet what makes *Shame* such a disconcerting experience is the way it pushes the genre of the homme-com into a world of anguish rather than comedy. Instead of coding Brandon's pick-ups as fun, the film represents these as unsettling or even horrific. One of the earliest sequences in *Shame* depicts a 'meet-cute' on the New York subway. While pick-ups on the subway have more usually been associated with gay culture, the sequence may initially be read as the natural development of sexual liberalisation in which heterosexual culture (as predicted by critics such as Michael Warner (1999)) is adopting many practices that had once been the preserve of queer culture – not least online dating and hook-up culture. However, the scene does not code the sequence as sexually liberating but as oppressive and even terrifying. Filmed in the blue-hued lighting that is characteristic of the film, the subway sequence shows Brandon cruising an attractive woman sitting opposite him on the train. What makes the sequence so uncomfortable for the viewer is its deliberate confusion of consent.

At first, it appears that the woman welcomes the advances and, in accordance with one of the key sensibilities of postfeminism (Gill 2007: 151–2), embraces the masculine gaze as a form of flattery – even sexual empowerment – rather than objectification. However, there is then a shot of Brandon's face which is represented as a blurred image. In this distorted shot, Brandon's pallid face resembles the ghoulish, nondescript mask of Michael Myers – Hollywood's most famous stalker and women-slasher – and so codes the subway flirtation as something considerably more sinister. (See Figure 4:1.)

This image also emphasises *Shame*'s critique of the neoliberal colour-blindness associated with rom-coms. Although the film initially appears to be invested in a colour-blind culture in which racial difference is coded as irrelevant in contemporary Manhattan culture (Brandon's sexual tricks and dates include both white women and women of colour), the film critiques this by challenging the aesthetic of whiteness associated with rom-coms. The use of the blue-hued lighting and the out-of-focus shot make Brandon's pale skin assume a ghoulish, almost deathly, pallor. This is the very opposite of the romantic 'glow' usually associated with white-skinned glamorous female stars but which, in recent years has also been used to romanticise male leads (see Dyer 1997: 122–42). Instead of a radiance, connoting concepts of enlightenment and sophistication, Brandon's pale skin suggests exhaustion, fatigue and, on occasions, even resembles the iconography of vampirism or other living-death creatures.

Following the shot of Brandon's terrifying white face, the film cuts to the woman, who is now looking uncomfortable with Brandon's gaze – as signified by her head gestures and the way she crosses her legs tightly to give him the message that she is not interested. Yet, despite the woman's indications of

Figure 4.1. Brandon's deathly white face represented in an out-of-focus shot so that it resembles the ghoulish mask of Michael Myers. (Fox Searchlight, Film4, UK Film Council.)

discomfort, Brandon persists in cruising her. This attempted subway pick-up is intercut with flashbacks of Brandon's sexual experiences from the previous days. We see a shot of him with a sex worker and then a scene of him jerking off in the shower. These flashbacks subvert the ideology of the homme-com, in which the male protagonist may well articulate a desire merely to have sex but is always coded as secretly wanting a long-term, meaningful relationship. In contrast, Brandon is driven only by sex.

By this point, the woman cannot bear any more of this predatory gaze and stands up to leave the train. However, Brandon stands behind her in an action that now resembles a subway stalk rather than a cruise. The woman flees the carriage, but Brandon pursues her, only then to lose her in the crowd of commuters. Throughout the sequence, non-diegetic romantic music plays in the soundtrack, thus making the predatory actions even more disconcerting. What started as a contemporary, queer-inflected 'meet-cute' has become an attempted assault. As Brandon stands on the subway platform, desperately looking around to locate the woman, high-key lighting illuminates Brandon's perturbed and confused facial expression. The camera revolves around him, not only suggesting his disorientation (Where has she gone? Did she not want to have casual sex with me when I thought she did?) but also suggesting that he now feels like a public spectacle, on display in front of the crowds, and shamed because of a failed sexual pick-up. Yet, it has been the very culture of hook-ups that has facilitated this type of meet-cute in the first place (it would not have been out of place on *Sex and the City*) and led the spectator to infer that the sequence would develop into an erotic encounter. In this respect, the sequence subverts the ideology of neoliberal romantic comedies, such as the *Sex and the City* franchise, where 'New York is shown to be a place of freedom and safety' for women whose casual pick-ups have 'lost the danger of a sadistic or reproving masculine gaze' (Arthurs 2003: 93).

DYSTOPIA AND THE MUSICAL

If New York has been the setting for innumerable rom-coms, it has also served as the backdrop for the genre's sibling: the film musical (Bukatman 2003; Foulkes 2015; Shearer 2016). Like rom-coms, the musical's great obsession is heterosexuality (Dyer 2012). Most musicals represent a heterosexual couple who initially appear to be incompatible, due to oppositions of socioeconomic class and personality type, but by the end of the film this couple are united and all their differences are overcome (Altman 1989: 24–5). The joy of musicals is that this union of the seemingly unsuited couple then demonstrates how this is possible for the wider community (the pairing of the couple is always a model for partnerships occurring throughout the rest of the characters) and so the musical offers the fantasy that everyone can form a happy community (Wolf 2006: 352).

Richard Dyer labels the pleasure of musicals 'utopia' (2005). This utopia in musical sequences is not so much a visual representation but instead, through the mechanism of music, song and dance, is a sense of how utopia might feel. The musical sequences offer a temporary escape from the drudgery of everyday life by suggesting the very opposite sensations that are usually experienced from the daily slog. Instead of the lethargy of chores, the song and dance sequences offer exuberance and vitality; instead of dreariness and lack of emotion, there is intensity of feeling, and, most pleasurable of all, instead of alienation and loneliness, the musical numbers offer harmony and community as everyone is united in the music.

This chapter commenced with a description of one of the most memorable sequences in *Shame*, where Sissy sings an extreme rubato version of 'New York, New York', the theme song from Scorsese's 1977 musical of the same name. *New York, New York* was noteworthy for its distinct departure from the gritty and bleak New York that Scorsese had previously represented in *Taxi Driver* (1976) and instead was an homage to the earlier musicals of the Golden Days of Hollywood. The song 'New York, New York', performed by Liza Minnelli in the musical (and most famously recorded by Frank Sinatra a few years later), is one of the most famous love letters to New York city, proclaiming the singer's optimism of how they will 'make it there' by attaining both career success and romantic fulfilment. It is hard to find another song that is as full of life and confidence as 'New York, New York', and indeed there are few other tunes that are as instantaneously recognisable after only hearing the first new notes of the introduction.

Sissy's version, by contrast, completely subverts the original meaning of this most famous billet-doux to New York city. As Adam Blum explains, Sissy's rendition is performed so ritardando that it reaches 'the point of absurdity' as its sense of harmonic trajectory is 'fragmented into taps of diminished triads' which often fade into an uncomfortable silence (Blum 2015: 126). This is also one of the rare moments in the film where Brandon shows any genuine emotion and, in an acting technique that has become characteristic of Fassbender's performances (and much beloved by his fans or 'Fassinators' (Braid 2014b)), he borders on the verge of crying.

Therefore, instead of extending a sense of the utopia usually evoked in a musical performance (both to the diegetic characters and the spectators who feel the joy of the musical performance), this rendition of 'New York, New York' conveys only loneliness, disappointment and heartache. This dystopia is further emphasised by the setting and cinematography. Filmed in the bar at the top of the Standard Hotel, the setting is altered by the addition of overhead spotlights shining down directly on the tables. Although this lighting

SUBVERTING NEOLIBERAL, NEW YORK SINGLETON CULTURE

creates a warm glow, it also has the effect of isolating each table, suggesting each group is like an island separated from the rest of the community in the bar. Most dramatically, this overhead lighting bounces off the tables' surfaces so that the characters are lit from below and therefore, in yet another nod to Michael Myers, this below-chin illumination (often referred to by gaffers as Halloween lighting) blanches the white faces and creates a ghoulish effect. This sets the background for the boss's pick-up of Sissy – an action that Brandon finds distressing not least because he recognises his boss's behaviour in his own previous actions. What should have been a song sequence conveying the utopia of a musical becomes instead a scene of despair, isolation and dystopia. (See Figure 4.2.)

CONCLUSION

According to fan review websites, *Shame* remains the least popular of McQueen's films (rottentomatoes.com). While it is impossible to guess why viewers like or dislike a film, it is fair to speculate that many spectators were troubled by how *Shame* refuses to represent sex 'addiction' as a pathology, or the result of trauma, but instead codes it as the *inevitable* consequence of neoliberal, pornographied society. As has been argued in this chapter, this message is conveyed not only by the unique aesthetic of McQueen's cinema but through his deliberate subversion of the genres of the rom-com and musical, demonstrating that sex 'addiction' is facilitated by structural issues rather than personal problems. Therefore, at its core, *Shame* is a critique of contemporary, metropolitan neoliberalism.

Figure 4.2. Halloween lighting emphasises the sense of dystopia and makes David's pick-up of Sissy seem very sinister. (Fox Searchlight, Film4, UK Film Council.)

The problem this may pose for spectators (especially those based in the USA) is that a critique of neoliberal ideologies – especially their relation to sexual expression – is a sensitive issue in the highly divided USA. This is because differing permutations of neoliberalism underpin the ideologies of *both* the Democrat and Republican parties. While critics are correct to note that 'the Republican Party and its incumbent governments in recent US history are prime examples of the social mandate of neoliberalism' (Gwynne 2021), it should not be forgotten that *both* sides of the aisle are united by neoliberalist economic policy (Gerstle 2022). However, while both parties share a broad agreement on political economy, which underpins neoliberal ideology, they are very divided in how this should be demonstrated in social policy. The Republican Party embraces what Gary Gerstle labels a Neo-Victorianist form of neoliberalism: an ideology which celebrates traditional family units and, most importantly, disciplined and conservative attitudes towards consumption and sexuality. The belief is that this moral code prevents overconsumption and debt. Given that neoliberalist ideology objects to government involvement in disciplining people's choices, another narrative is needed to regiment activities and, for the Republicans, this is usually an adherence to conservative interpretations of Christianity.

The Democratic Party, on the other hand, advocates the neoliberalist sensibility which Gerstle titles 'cosmopolitanism': a political stance which embraces pluralism, diversity and, most importantly, free expression of gender and sexuality beyond the confines of the traditional family unit. As can only be imagined, cosmopolitans attack Neo-Victorians for their discrimination against gays, people of colour and their restriction of women's rights. In reverse, the Neo-Victorians attack cosmopolitan ideology for embracing sexual immorality in its efforts to tolerate difference. In recent years, this differing view of appropriate social policy has condensed into heated congressional debates in relation to gay rights (such as extending marriage rights to same-sex couples and protection against homophobic discrimination in public services) or women's reproductive health (a woman's constitutional right to an abortion continues to divide North American culture and, in a controversial ruling, was removed by the Supreme Court in 2022 when it overturned the landmark case known as Roe versus Wade).

Shame, therefore, as one of the first films to actively critique neoliberal cosmopolitanism – especially its acceptance and facilitation of casualised sexual expression – may be interpreted as a film that is conservative – or Neo-Victorianist – at its ideological core. Given the strength of the current socio-political division in the USA, this makes the film a highly emotive text within the culture wars of gender and sexual expression. For example, many USA-based commentators found the gay sex-club sequence – in which Brandon, desperate for a sexual fix, seeks relief in a casual blow-job from a man – to be a homophobic representation (see Jagernauth 2013). Although the scene demonstrates how, despite the labels that Western culture attributes to sexual acts, there is only carnal desire animating bodies, it unfortunately also echoes earlier cinematic cliches of representing gay sex as depraved, dirty and trapped in a hell-like dungeon (Shadow and Act 2011; Jagernauth 2013) and suggests that a casual gay sex encounter is the ultimate downfall in Brandon's sex 'addiction'. The scene implies that a sex 'addict' has fallen to an all-time low if he must succumb to same-sex fellatio. Given that gay rights remain such a heated issue across the Congressional aisle, it can be understood why liberal-leaning commentators had difficulties with such a depiction.

It could be speculated that, as a European director, McQueen may not have been fully aware of the implications of setting a story which demonstrates that sex 'addiction' is the inevitable outcome of cosmopolitan ideology, in the largest city in the USA. Alternatively, it could also be argued that, similar to McQueen's other work, which draws attention to structural racism and gender inequality, *Shame* demonstrates that systems of oppression survive *beyond* a simple two-party political divide. Sex 'addiction' is something facilitated by contemporary metropolitan culture and not something forged by one political group.

Perhaps this point is best made in one of the most visually striking sequences of *Shame* (and the one always praised by the journalists who reviewed the film), in which Brandon jogs through the avenues of New York while listening to music on his iPhone. This scene occurs just after Sissy has picked up David, following her performance of 'New York, New York' in the Standard Hotel, and brings him back to Brandon's flat for a quick fuck. Brandon, distressed by seeing his own lifestyle now reflected in his sister and, most importantly, brought into his own neatly ordered apartment, needs to flee his home and vent his frustration into the physical release of a run. This extended tracking sequence not only offers Brandon a way of dealing with his anger but also a temporary escape from the oppression of his living environment. The tracking shot represents the beauty of the New York backdrop while also conveying Brandon's temporary isolation from this culture. Insulated in his sound bubble of Bach's music, Brandon jogs through the avenues.

The baroque music – Bach's Prelude No. 10 in E Minor (BWV 855) – further emphasises Brandon's distance from contemporary New York culture because it is not the genre usually associated with the city or the action of jogging. If Sissy's performance of 'New York, New York' inverted the anticipated pleasures of a musical, by creating a sense of dystopia, this jogging sequence is one of the few where the music offers a temporary relief from the oppressions of the film's story. As in a musical, this sequence pauses the narrative to offer a spectacle of physical experience, suggesting energy, life and, most importantly, endorphin-fuelled pleasure. Indeed, the jogging sequence is probably the *single* feel-good moment in this overwhelmingly bleak film.

However, while the sequence may offer the pleasures of the musical it also subverts its ideology. As Dyer has argued, a key element of musical moments – especially those involving dance or physical expression – is a white expansionist ideology in which the white performers claim the space through their movements (Dyer 2002: 39–41). By contrast, Brandon's jogging sequence may offer a moment of respite from the film's despondency, but this is only because Brandon is now distanced from New York society. Instead of colonising the space, he is now retreating from it, insulated in his sound bubble. It is only within this Bach bubble that Brandon (and the spectator) experience the sense of pleasure afforded by a musical moment in cinema. Through attaining some distance from the culture of contemporary New York – the iconic setting of rom-coms, musicals and their contemporary ideology of free sexual expression – Brandon can gain (and the spectator also enjoys) a moment of fleeting utopia in such a depressing film. For this utopian moment, Brandon may well be in the very heart of New York but, in this brief jogging sequence filled with energy, life and pleasure, he is happily not – to quote from the famous song – 'a part of it'.[2]

NOTES

1. 'New York, New York', by John Kander and Fred Ebb.
2. 'New York, New York', by John Kander and Fred Ebb.

CHAPTER 5

If it is to be done, how?: Considering a Robeson Biopic

Shana L. Redmond

In 2014 the popular press on both sides of the Atlantic lit up with reports that the famed Oscar-winning director Steve McQueen had joined forces with the self-described Paul Robeson 'disciple' and singer-actor-humanitarian Harry Belafonte in production of a Robeson film. The announcement followed closely on the heels of McQueen's 2012 gallery installation, *End Credits*, which toured a number of major cities in the US and UK and was composed of audio readings of Robeson's redacted surveillance reports from the US Federal Bureau of Investigation (FBI) that scrolled end to end on a screen in the style of film end credits. A stunning reveal in and of itself, the display is a curious prelude to McQueen's plans for the cinematic story of a Black giant. Robeson's dense critiques of the film industry and the ample record of his political beliefs provide guidance in consideration of what, if anything, should become of his life on film. With those resources in mind, I offer this brief meditation as a critical premise for an impossible film.

The ongoing spectral nature of this Robeson film is appropriate as it is a long-standing dream project for McQueen. It is the film that he hoped to make after his debut *Hunger* (2008) but, according to him, he didn't have the 'juice' to make it. It's not the genre but the subject that would require substantial amounts of influence and power. Despite being a highly lucrative and award-winning genre, biopics are not for people like Paul Robeson. He's simply too large for the form as we know it. He devastates straightforward, linear storytelling that relies on purely beloved or purely scandalous characters. At one point in his career, an entire world chose sides over him. How to understand someone who was not an elected official nor an inheritor of influence, but was, instead, an innovator in most all things he tried, turning the cultures and struggles of his father's enslavement into political and emotional fortitude. He does not fit the tropes of the mainstream imagination, evades the dichotomies that defined his time, and confounds the logics of our own.

Perhaps knowing this himself, Robeson had no desire to see his life on-screen, let alone be its star. He believed that he was unexceptional; he'd seen and read about the flowering of Black talent all over the country and world, and understood that what divided his success from the widespread impoverishment and marginalisation of his people was opportunity and luck. His stardom was not a measure of his talents but those of the communities from which he came – he was an ambassador sent by the people, rather than a king who rose above them. 'I've managed to get some success,' he said, 'but there are thousands who haven't had the chance. It's not enough for one to be able to do it. I want everyone to have the chance' (Robeson 1978: 120). The genre of the biopic, with its investment in singularity and triumph or notoriety, could only support Robeson's heft if framed as and by a collective. To conceive of a film in which 'everyone [has] the chance' to tell (t)his story – to make it theirs – is a fitting reflection of and dedication to Robeson's lifetime of labour.

Robeson struggled mightily with the film industry over his career. Even after fantastic success in Oscar Micheaux's *Body and Soul* (1925) and the film version of Eugene O'Neill's play *The Emperor Jones* (1933), he increasingly took public issue with his films in the middle and late 1930s, including *Sanders of the River* (1935) and *Song of Freedom* (1936), while also harbouring quiet reservations about returning to his career-altering role as Joe in the 1936 film version of the musical *Show Boat*. In one spectacular read of an interview from 1937, he broke the industry down to its parts and all of them were junk. Fatigued by lies and misrepresentation, he publicly threatened to retire: 'I shan't do any more films after the two that are being finished now. Not unless I can get a cast-iron story – the kind that can't be twisted in the making. There's room for short independent films. I might try to do those. But for the rest, I'll just wait until the right story comes along, either here or abroad.' His dreams for the form could never match its reality nor the needs of his people: 'I thought I could do something for the Negro race on the films: show the truth about them – and about other people too. I used to do my part and go away feeling satisfied. Thought everything was OK. Well, it wasn't. Things were twisted and changed – distorted. They didn't mean the same.' He ultimately understood his defeat as part of an intentional system of limited gains and prevailing losses: 'One man can't face the film companies. They represent about the biggest aggregate of finance capital in the world: that's why they make their films that way. So no more films for me' (Robeson 1978: 120). 'No more,' he sang. 'No more.'

McQueen appears deeply enamoured of Robeson, which may explain his ambition in creation of the film, even with all that will stand in the way of its success. He learned of Robeson far earlier than others of his generation. As he tells it, his Grenadian neighbour Milton was fond of leaving mail for him that extolled Black history and heroism. It was in one of those mailers that McQueen discovered a pamphlet about Paul's intimate relationship with the Welsh miners. A heroic, sometimes mythological camaraderie, Paul's many decades of performing with and supporting the miners was enough to bestow him with honorary citizenship in that country. To be introduced to Robeson through the stories of affinity and righteous struggle in his own backyard undoubtedly contributed to the enduring nature of Paul's influence on McQueen. His 2016 discussion of and through Robeson with Cornel West at the Whitney Museum in New York was genuinely inquisitive, with passion abounding for this man. I know it when I see it because I too feel the same way. I'm eager for the mention of his name, captivated by his unending talents, titillated by his enduring influence. After years of study, I remain stunned by the very fact that he ever existed. How one displays or, even better, earns that sense of awe in viewers is a tall task. Yet anything short of that – short of the viewer leaving the cinema or walking away from the couch having begged with incredulity the question of 'How?', short of having been transformed – has not met the challenge of his too-large life.

What then shall be made if not an industry-backed, blockbuster biopic? Inspired by his five-part television film series *Small Axe* (2020), in which the details of Black life and living are tenderly carried in open palms, I want from McQueen a fidelity to the mundane elements of Paul's life that, for others, were spectacular because who else can do that? Who else can draw crowds from spontaneous, improvised singing based in the laments and triumphs of his ancestors? Who else, in refusing to answer a single question, upends a federal tribunal? Who else has a title so hyphenated (scholar-singer-athlete-humanitarian-actor-linguist-organizer . . .) that we tire in saying it as the letters become irrelevant for the length of the dash? 'The tallest tree in our forest' (see Noble's 1977 film). I want his singing on the tarmac in Berlin, his singing in his sister's living room in Philadelphia, his singing from the bed of a pick-up truck from Washington state USA over the Canadian border into British Columbia, his singing as answer to the theremin, his singing in the shower. While on the topic of singing, I want ALL of the music: the Negro spirituals – especially 'Didn't My Lord Deliver Daniel?' – 'O Isis und Osiris' delivered from an Egyptian pyramid, Welsh hymns, Yiddish and Spanish folk songs as the cannons cease, Nigerian lullabies, 'Ode to Joy', his one and only recorded blues, and *his* 'Ol' Man River'. McQueen understands that, by singing in other people's languages, Robeson was 'breaking their heart with [his] voice' (McQueen and West 2016). Show the heartbreak that happened all over the world and continues to happen. Make every viewer's heart break too.

Extend the beauty of his commitments and study. Portions of the film should take place in one of the two dozen-plus languages in which he sung and spoke; he can switch in and out at will with or without caption, depending on the scene. What he will never say, in any language, is whether or not he is now or ever has been a member of the Communist Party, singing instead the Russian national anthem as response. I want him to playfully run around and over people in Harlem, winking and waving all along, only to freeze as a Heisman trophy in anticipation of all that he would deserve but never receive. I want to see him laughing with Basque children in 1938 and those of Camp Kinderland in 1949. I want to see him, in that same year, in the back of the car as it approaches the Peekskill campground. Show in prolonged detail how his look of fright transitions to anger and finally sadness. Then, without a scene break, reveal him again, a week later, in the same back seat looking out of the window and beaming with pride and a sigh of relief as the union workers who volunteered to be his front line on stage come into view. I want to see him eating the tomatoes and climbing the trees and mountains named in his honour, and follow his admirers as they seek the stars underfoot and above head dedicated to him after his lifetime (Redmond 2020). We must see him on stage for encore after encore juxtaposed with those same stages as they were forbidden to him only a few years later. Show him with his son in the studio in which he sang into telephones and recorded greetings and songs for an eager, co-ordinated global majority.

We can't envision anything bigger than what he actually was, so show the world for what he knew it to be. What if the film, inspired by *End Credits*, didn't focus on Paul at all? What if it, true to form, was unambiguously populated by conspiracy and half-truths created in service of US empire? What if Paul was the agent of that reveal rather than the exceptional star of the state's dreadful fantasy? McQueen argued that 'those documents were sheets of music' (McQueen and West 2016). Let the terrible song they compose cause our ears to ache in exposure of its terror. Protect us from nothing that he was not spared. The extensive, structuring gaps, ▆▆▆▆▆▆, and silences in their story should overflow with those things with which they were never concerned: flowers, laughter, love, passion, ▆▆▆▆▆▆, solidarity, and peace of mind (Redmond 2020; Sharpe 2016). Paul's film should respect and reflect the form and integrity of storytelling that he chose for his own career. As he told Cuban writer and activist Nicolás Guillén in 1938, 'What I won't do any more is work for the big companies, which are headed by individuals who would make me a slave, like my father, if they could. I need to work with small independent producers, in short films with songs, until the moment comes to make something with greater breadth and a more positive meaning than has been possible so far' (Robeson 1978: 126). Create a filmic world around him as if he were cast as its star because he is, after all. 'Robeson never got a chance to play anybody close to what he was,' argued film historian Clyde Taylor (Bourne 1999). What would it take for him to be cast in this role? What would he need to see and hear and feel to accept? To produce anything less is a further violation, another loss, another ▆▆▆▆▆▆▆▆.

In his discussion of musician and psychologist Don Shirley's life and film representation, Hanif Abdurraqib wishes something more for him than what *Green Book* (2018) offered – something grand.

> I want a movie in which Don Shirley sleeps for a while. I want a movie in which Don Shirley goes to the store and holds a magazine in his hands, thumbing through the pages before sighing and putting it down. I want a movie in which Don Shirley goes to the movies and watches a movie in which no one Black suffers for the imagined greater good. I want a movie in which Don Shirley visits the grave of someone he loved dearly and lays a haphazardly arranged handful of flowers on it before going home and speaking to no one. I want a Don Shirley movie that isn't tasked with solving any problems it didn't create. (Abdurraqib 2021: 189–90)

This mundane list of daily non-events and routines ends with a most terrific bit of rest. I too want this for Paul. What I'm requesting is what he displayed in life and deserves in death: the dignity of living in his fullness. It's messy and complicated and vast, exceeding the big screen. In that case, I'm also requesting that McQueen embrace the possibility of failure, for in it we may get closest to understanding what's truly at stake.

CHAPTER 6

The Slave Narrative and Filmic Aesthetics: Steve McQueen, Solomon Northup and Colonial Violence

Philip Kaisary

In recent years, the cultural and political memory of slavery has occupied an unusual prominence in public comment and debate. Various explanations for this can be found in the re-emergence of calls for reparations, renewed scholarly attention to the relationship between slavery and capitalism, and several anniversaries commemorating the abolition of slavery in the Atlantic world.[1] Concomitant with this heightened awareness, there has been a dramatic upsurge in popular cinematic works of widely varying quality and ideological intent focused on Black history and the legacies of slavery. In some cases, slavery has merely served as a backdrop to Hollywood action-drama – for example, Quentin Tarantino's *Django Unchained* (2012), a stylised revenge thriller that revives the archetype of the 'Black cowboy' – while in others, Black experience is subordinate to the further mythologisation of a small number of 'white anti-slavery heroes', such as Abraham Lincoln and William Wilberforce; Steven Spielberg's *Lincoln* (2012) and Michael Apted's *Amazing Grace* (2006) exemplify this approach.[2]

Popular and critical discussion peaked in the winter of 2013–14 with the release of Steve McQueen's *12 Years a Slave* (2013), an adaptation of Solomon Northup's 1853 account of his kidnapping, enslavement and eventual return to liberty. This film, the first cinematic adaptation of a slave narrative, immediately garnered overwhelmingly positive reviews. Consider David Denby's assessment in *The New Yorker* that *12 Years a Slave* is 'easily the greatest feature film ever made about American slavery' and Peter Bradshaw's view that the film constitutes a triumphant 'essay in outrage and injustice'. *12 Years a Slave* has rapidly become regarded as the definitive feature film about slavery.[3] However, I argue that McQueen's *12 Years a Slave* elides the formative role slavery has played in the creation of the modern self and modern world.

Notwithstanding McQueen's undoubted gifts as a filmmaker and artist, his adaptation fails to register the larger meaning of slavery and implicitly presents racism as anachronistic rather than as continuing systematised oppression. This is especially ironic given that McQueen's wider oeuvre – especially his art films and video installation work – has criticised contemporary racialised labour exploitation, its roots in colonialism and chattel slavery's intricate relationship to capitalism.

To substantiate these claims, I proceed along two lines of inquiry. First, I compare McQueen's adaptation to Solomon Northup's text to identify systemic patterns of omission and addition in the McQueen version and consider their impact. As Stephanie Li has noted, 'film adaptations of historical texts inevitably raise questions about how true they are to their original sources' (2014: 336). My objective, however, is not to find fault with McQueen's version for any lack of fidelity to the original source material. Northup's narrative is, after all, itself a mediated text: it was transcribed and edited by David Wilson, a New York lawyer, writer and politician, to whom Northup told his story. The text is thus not without its own inconsistencies and tensions, and it cannot be uncritically treated as authentic testimony to Northup's lived experience of slavery. For example, while some critics have noted the veracity of many elements of Northup's narrative, others have drawn attention to its striking similarities with Harriet Beecher Stowe's 1852 anti-slavery sensation, *Uncle Tom's Cabin*, which was published one year before Northup's text (Eakin and Lodgson 1968: xvi).[4] Hence, faithfulness to Northup's original should not automatically be considered a positive, nor is any lack of it necessarily detrimental. Instead, I seek to answer Li's question, 'what has been lost or gained in the translation to the big screen?' (2014: 336), and address the implications of this translation.

I will also address the impact of McQueen's signature filmic language, which frequently blurs the boundary between narrative and non-narrative form, in the context of debates over the representability of slavery. Questions centred on the ethics and aesthetics of configuring slavery take on a new pertinence given McQueen's gift for sumptuous cinematography, an art perfected over many years' collaboration with cinematographer Sean Bobbitt, and his penchant for giving primacy to the suffering body in his work. Critics have noted that the writings of Édouard Glissant and Toni Morrison, among others, demonstrate that it is possible to construct an ethical aesthetic out of the horrors of slavery.[5] However, McQueen was unable to negotiate this minefield of ethics and representation while working within Hollywood – an intricate machine created for and by capitalism. Furthermore, ironically, the film's extremely moving visual and aural poetics deepen its problematic occlusion of slavery's 'systematicity'.

COMPARING SOLOMON NORTHUP AND STEVE MCQUEEN

In comparing McQueen's 2013 adaptation to Northup's 1853 narrative, it is necessary to recognise the challenges inherent in adapting a work for a very different socio-political milieu. In 1853, Northup was writing for a US audience preoccupied with debates surrounding slavery. Northup's narrative was published amid a maelstrom of heated discussion surrounding *Uncle Tom's Cabin* and three years after the notorious Fugitive Slave Act of 1850, a piece of draconian pro-slavery legislation that deprived runaway slaves of habeas corpus, the right to a jury trial and the right to testify on their own behalf. As Daniel Sharfstein contends, this Act placed 'the federal government in the service of slaveowners pursuing their runaways' (2012: 57) and 'allowed slaveowners and their authorized agents to "pursue and reclaim" escapees on free soil', hence encouraging the kidnapping of free Blacks (2012: 87).[6] Moreover, the passage of the Kansas-Nebraska Act in 1854, 'which allowed settlers to vote to determine whether Kansas [would join the Union as] a slave or free state', was just months away (2012: 58). Although the secession of the slave states and the outbreak of the Civil War were still more than seven years away, Northup's narrative constituted an intervention into what Sharftstein describes as an 'escalating national crisis over slavery' and a political and public discourse dominated by fiercely contested and polarised debates over bondage and freedom (2012: 58).

In contrast, McQueen was operating within a contemporary context in which, as Paul Gilroy (2013) has noted, 'slavery has been written off as part of the pre-history of our world' and racism itself is commonly 'presented as anachronistic'. This changed context of reception informs Thomas Doherty's contention that in the twenty-first century, 'the didactic purpose of the slave narrative – to rebuke the institution of slavery and the racist ideology that sustained it – is a dead letter' (2013: 4). However, Doherty's assessment overlooks the potential role of the slave narrative in promoting a robust conception of the significance of slavery to global capitalism. This point was certainly not lost on McQueen. In many publicity events pertaining to the release of his adaptation, McQueen took pains to make the case that he viewed his *12 Years a Slave* project as serving myriad progressive political purposes, from highlighting the widespread existence of new forms of slavery to the persistence of socially entrenched, pernicious racial iniquities.[7] Such a perspective has long been a prominent theme in McQueen's video installation work. Consider, for example, *Caribs' Leap* (2002), *Western Deep* (2002) and *Gravesend* (2007), each of which uses techniques of historical and geographic juxtaposition to communicate a concern with the racialised and systemic character of capitalist exploitation and the connections between slavery, imperialism and intensified extraction capitalism. *Caribs' Leap* links colonial genocide in the seventeenth century to poverty and underdevelopment in present-day Grenada, while *Western Deep* addresses labour exploitation under neoliberal capitalism in the gold-mining industry of post-apartheid South Africa. Similarly, if more obliquely, *Gravesend* evokes an understanding of a radically uneven world system that emphasises the way in which the 'high tech' depends on the 'low tech' by depicting coltan mining in the Congo and its final processing in Britain for use in electronic devices. Unlike these films, and despite McQueen's assertions of its contemporary political relevance, *12 Years a Slave* does not succeed as a vehicle for a radical politics.

The limitations of Hollywood should not be underestimated in seeking to understand this discrepancy in McQueen's work, but a partial explanation for it can be found in the attempt of *12 Years a Slave* to capture the universality of Northup's narrative without sufficient attention to its particularity. Of course, revisionist depictions of slavery in popular culture from D. W. Griffith's *The Birth of a Nation* (1915) to the present have tended to dramatically overemphasise slavery's particularity while also sustaining the potent fantasy that slavery was essentially benign and paternalistic. In this discourse, the so-called 'peculiar institution' has long been mistakenly considered a relic of an outmoded society that bears little relation to our own. This perspective – which denies the centrality of slavery to capitalist modernity – has also proven an effective means of disavowing the slave experience as a potential source for an emancipatory politics. Translating Northup's narrative to the big screen and emphasising its universal dimensions might have implicitly contested this pernicious mythology, but McQueen's adaptation instead manufactures a platitudinous universality based on sentiment rather than historical specificity. For example, the film's musical score – a repeated four-note theme written for cello and violin – has been described by Hans Zimmer, the composer, as a deliberately conceived strategy for communicating the 'timelessness' of Northup's story. The unfortunate effect of this gesture to timelessness is the reduction of slavery in antebellum America to a simplified story of human greed, cruelty and pathos.[8]

The prolific character of the slave narrative genre elaborates a further point of contrast between Northup's text and McQueen's adaptation. Solomon Northup's *Twelve Years a Slave* is one of 204 published North American slave narratives (Andrews). This genre, considered to have limited literary value until the institutionalisation of Black studies in American universities in the 1960s and 1970s, had been a key propaganda weapon in the hands of anti-slavery activists and abolitionists in the United States before the Civil War. The most well-known examples of the genre include Frederick Douglass's autobiographies (the first of which, *Narrative of the Life of Frederick Douglass* [1845], was a bestseller and is widely regarded as being the best-written example of the genre), Harriet Jacobs's *Incidents in the Life of a Slave Girl* (1861), and *The Interesting Narrative of the Life of Olaudah Equiano* (1789). However, Solomon Northup's *Twelve Years a Slave*, also a bestseller, was an unusual example of the genre for several reasons. First, the arc of Northup's narrative is unique within the tradition of the antebellum slave narrative since the movement is initially from liberty to bondage. Second, as Sue Eakin and Joseph Lodgson note in the introduction to the 1968 edition, 'no other slave has left such a detailed picture of life in the Gulf South' (xi). In fact, Northup's narrative is our only first-hand account of slavery in the Deep South from the perspective of a former slave. Third, no other slave narrative contained such dramatic material, which was heralded by the full nineteenth-century title: *Twelve Years a Slave, Narrative of Solomon Northup, A Citizen of New York, Kidnapped in Washington City in 1841, and Rescued in 1853, From a Cotton Plantation Near the Red River in Louisiana*.[9] This was particularly important to McQueen, since he considers Northup's narrative of freedom in the North before his illegal enslavement more accessible to a twenty-first-century audience (McQueen 2013b).

The narrative begins with Northup's variation on the slave narrative's opening convention, 'I was born,' instead announcing, 'Having been born a freeman'. He then provides the reader with a brief outline of his family history, in which he explains his status as a free Black in the North. Northup's ancestors on his paternal side, as far back as he could ascertain, 'were slaves in Rhode Island' and belonged 'to a family by the name of Northup' (1853, 2014: 5). Northup's father, Mintus Northup, was 'emancipated by a direction in his [master's] will', and Solomon goes on to note that he received an education 'surpassing that ordinarily bestowed on' children of his status (6). Significantly, Northup comments that even in the North, slavery was far from a benign institution, and that although his father held 'the warmest emotions of kindness, and even of affection towards the family in whose house he had been a bondsman', he nevertheless 'comprehended the system of Slavery, and dwelt with sorrow on the degradation of his race' (6–7). This perspective on the condition of enslaved Blacks north of the Mason–Dixon Line, as well as the view that slavery could not be ameliorated by the kindness of individuals, is not communicated in the film. Indeed, it is the first in a series of omissions that obscure slavery's systematicity, elevate Northup's status to high bourgeois and undermine his accounts of resistance.

McQueen's version transforms Northup's linear memoir into a narrative structured by flashbacks, memories and emotions – a change apparent from the outset. The film begins in media res as a white overseer issues instructions to a sugar cane cutting gang that includes the already enslaved Northup. The camera is immersed in the foliage of green cane leaves before entering a clearing in which the cutting gang is at work. The toil of cane cutting and the sound of machetes at work merge with the singing of a work song. The camera then leads us back through the cane leaves before darkening and fading to a view from above a bedroom in which we can make out perhaps ten slaves turning in for the night. Next, in a brief scene of communal eating in silence, we see Northup come upon the idea of using blackberry juice, running on his supper plate, as pen ink, followed by him fashioning a rudimentary pen by candlelight and attempting to write. Although he is unsuccessful – the blackberry ink is too watery – the sequence pays an oblique tribute to Northup as an author and to the literary genre of the slave narrative. It conveys the determination of slaves and former slaves to record their experiences and affirms their dignity and humanity.

This elegant opening sequence that powerfully bestows a sombre decorum and dignity to slave life is then broken with an invented scene. Once again, the screen fades into darkness before the camera intrudes on perhaps a dozen slaves sleeping communally on the floor, followed by a brief sexual encounter between Northup and an unnamed female slave, whose name we never learn and who never reappears in the film. Although the encounter evokes feelings of betrayal and indignity – the slave woman turns away from Northup in tears while Northup recalls lying in his marital bed with his wife before his enslavement – McQueen has spoken of this scene as intended to demonstrate how slaves were owned yet could, in certain moments, take control of their own bodies.

In the 1853 text, Northup discusses meaningful romantic liaisons between slaves very differently. Following a description of how slaves in the Bayou Boeuf region celebrated Christmas, 'the only respite from constant labor the slave has through the whole year' (140), Northup writes: 'Cupid disdains not to hurl his arrows into the simple hearts of slaves.' He notes that Christmas presented an opportunity for slave couples to make a public show of 'an exchange of tenderness' by sitting opposite each other during the 'fun and merriment' of a rare social gathering that involved food, music and dance long into the night (142). Thus, while Northup discussed relationships among slaves with reticence and with an emphasis on their nourishing qualities, McQueen depicts slaves' sexual desires and presents shame and guilt as integral to slave life. While neither of these dichotomous representations may in fact reflect the actual and more complicated sexual lives of slaves, the distinct ideological thrust of each representation remains telling.

Another significant departure in McQueen's version is the representation of Northup and his family before his kidnapping. They are shown to be living a comfortable bourgeois life, complete with fine clothing and a finely furnished house in a glamourised Saratoga Springs. Perhaps alluding to a flashback in which the Northups are out shopping and encounter impeccable manners and conduct, Doherty notes that McQueen's Saratoga in 1841 'might just as well be Cambridge, Massachusetts in 2013' (2013: 5). The danger of this resemblance is that McQueen's representation augments a familiar and insufficiently nuanced narrative of the antebellum United States in which the genteel North's mirror image is the barbarous and slaveholding South. Although Walter Johnson has noted that elements of Northup's narrative 'may reflect [his] pride in his Northern origins and legal freedom' (1999: 67), it certainly registers both a less sanguine picture of the North and the family's humbler social status.

Through descriptions of his occupations in the 1853 text, we learn that Northup scraped together a living by various means. These included labouring as a hired hand on canal construction, woodcutting, small-scale farming, and playing his violin at local dances. In 1834, Northup moved with his family to Saratoga Springs, New York, in pursuit of better prospects. These, however, failed to materialise, and he found himself labouring on the railroad before securing employment in the tourist season driving a hack; in the winter season he once more relied on his violin. By 1841, the year of his kidnapping, Northup writes of his disappointment: 'The flattering anticipations which, seven years before, had seduced us from the quiet farm-house, on the east side of the Hudson, had not been realized. Though always in comfortable circumstances, we had not prospered' (11). It is striking that the visual representation in McQueen's adaptation does not accord with Northup's description of his family's social situation. As a freeman in Saratoga Springs, McQueen's Northup looks like a well-to-do country gent in a fine three-piece suit, and when Northup is seduced by his kidnappers' promise of a good salary for playing his fiddle in their circus troupe, his eager acceptance appears guileless. The temptation of a decent wage – 'one dollar for each day's services,' plus three dollars for each evening's performance (13) – is much more convincing in the original. Moreover, McQueen's decision to portray the Northups in Saratoga Springs as possessing impeccable bourgeois tastes, and the inclusion of scenes in which the Northups are greeted with great deference and cordiality by white shopkeepers and strangers, dramatically embellishes the lives of free Blacks in the North, where freedom was legally and socially restricted and racism remained rife.[10] Thus, McQueen's representation of the North is one of the means by which the film obscures Northup's descriptions of slavery's systemic character – a character that Northup recalls his father also understanding when he observes the inadequacy of seeking to explain the evil of slavery by levelling blame at individuals. Indeed, midway through his narrative, Northup writes that '[i]t is not the fault of the slaveholder that he is cruel, so much as it is the fault of the system under which he lives' (1853, 2014: 135).

In addition, Northup's narrative is notable for its detailed descriptions of the processes of cotton (107–13) and sugar (37–40) cultivation and production as they were practised under the system of slavery. Critics have noted that these descriptions 'are recognized classics' within the literature of slavery (Eakin and Logsdon 1968: xvi). Although his perspective as an enslaved field hand did not enable him to perceive slavery's global dimensions, Northup's descriptions indicate an understanding of the role of slave labour in the production of valued market commodities and the stringency of consumers' requirements for such commodities. Hence, Northup describes the importance of precision when cutting cane – the need 'to sever all the green from the ripe part' – to avoid souring the molasses that would render the product 'unsalable' (138). Furthermore, he describes processed 'white or loaf sugar' as 'clear, clean, and white as snow' when packed in hogsheads, 'ready for market' (140). This emphasis on the production of a commodity for the market as a mode of explanation for plantation slavery is absent in the McQueen version, which instead conceives of slavery as either paternalistic or barbarous based merely on the contrasting personalities of individual slave owners. For example, in McQueen's version, Northup's first master, the aristocratically mannered William Ford, is recognisably the man that Northup described as being 'kind, noble, candid, [and] Christian' (57). However, Northup described not just the individual but also the impact of his circumstances on his perspective: 'The influences and associations that had always surrounded him, blinded him to the inherent wrong at the bottom of the system of Slavery' (57). Thus, Northup makes explicit that the institution of slavery could not be comprehended at the level of the individual.

Later in the narrative, reflecting on his period of enslavement under Epps – a violent, psychotic and lusty slave owner who anticipates William Faulkner's Sutpen in *Absalom, Absalom!* (1936) – Northup expands on his analysis of the relationship between the individual and society as a mode of historical explanation: 'There may be humane masters, as there certainly are inhumane ones – there may be slaves well-clothed, well-fed, and happy, as there surely are those half-clad, half-starved and miserable; nevertheless, the institution that tolerates such wrong and inhumanity as I have witnessed, is a cruel, unjust, and barbarous one' (135). C. L. R. James's evaluation some eighty years later, in his history of the Haitian Revolution, *The Black Jacobins: Toussaint L'Ouverture and the San Domingo Revolution* (1938), offers a compelling comparison: 'There were good and bad Governors, good and bad Intendants, as there were good and bad slave-owners. But this was a matter of pure chance. It was the system that was bad' (1938/1963: 35). Such analysis is lost in McQueen's adaptation. The impact of the excellent performances of Benedict Cumberbatch and, especially, Michael Fassbender, who play the contrasting slave owners – the saintly Ford and the monstrous Epps – compounds this problem. While McQueen has insisted that 'Epps is a human being' and that 'as much as we want to think of him as a monster [or] as a devil, he's not', it is hard to witness Fassbender's virtuoso performance of Epps as psychotic and borderline deranged, ravaged with drink and lust, and not be persuaded otherwise (Lee 2013).[11] The dichotomous presentation of saintly or monstrous individual slave owners was of course present in Northup's original, but it was tempered by an emphasis that in slave society, where everything was infected and debased, analysis of individuals had limited explanatory power.

More extraordinary still than the omission of Northup's perspective on slavery as a system, however, is that his accounts of slave resistance are either eliminated or distorted in the McQueen version. In his narrative, Northup asserted that the temptation of flight and rebellion among enslaved populations was ever-present. For example, Northup described the plans he claimed to have made with two of his fellow captives, Arthur (also a kidnapped freeman) and Robert, to attempt a mutiny on the *Orleans*, a paddle steamer that was transporting them to the New Orleans slave market. Northup describes how their planned attempt to take possession of the brig and sail the vessel to New York was meticulously thought through over a period of days and how various components of the plan were carefully tested for feasibility (such as how they might reach the deck from the hold in the dead of night). Ultimately, we learn that Northup and his fellow conspirators never had an opportunity to put their plans into action – the designs were derailed by Robert's death from smallpox four days before they were to arrive in New Orleans (40–3). Although Northup's account of these plans also reveals his disdain for what he perceives as the limited revolutionary capacity of many of his fellow enslaved men and women, the way in which the episode has been transposed into the McQueen version supplants resistance with abject hopelessness.

All of the careful planning is absent, and Northup's unwillingness to trust his fellow slaves, whom he considers servile (41), is distorted in the speech of Arthur, who in the film is renamed 'Clemens Ray': 'Three can't stand against the whole crew. The rest here are niggers, born and bred slaves. Niggers ain't got no stomach for a fight, not a damn one.' As Marc Norton observes, these lines signal the end of the planned insurgency in the McQueen version. Furthermore, Robert does not die from smallpox. Instead, he is slain by a white sailor in the dead of night for attempting to prevent the rape of Eliza, a former slave mistress who has been sold downriver to William Ford by her former master's heirs. The insertion of Robert's murder is troubling for a number of reasons.

First, as Stephanie Li notes, 'the scene is historically suspect. The sailor does not own the slave [whom he murders] and [he] would certainly be punished for the loss of such a valuable commodity.' Moreover, Li explains, 'McQueen's version of Robert's death' serves 'to contextualize the passivity that defines much of Northup's response to the horrors he witnesses throughout the film' (2014: 328). While in his narrative Northup was never naïvely optimistic about the prospect of successful resistance, in McQueen's version, Northup's powerlessness is profoundly exacerbated.

McQueen's exposition of passivity, impotence and relentless suffering endured by enslaved Blacks thus fails to capture the nuances of Northup's original narrative. For example, entirely absent from the film are the ideas Northup narrates in a section titled 'The Idea of Insurrection' in chapter seventeen. Here, Northup tells the history of an attempted slave uprising in the Bayou Boeuf region led by the slave Lew Cheney, with whom Northup had become personally acquainted. Northup explains that Cheney travelled from plantation to plantation preaching the idea of 'fighting a crusade' all the way to the free land of Mexico, but that, at the last moment, the would-be slave-rebels were discovered, and Cheney, 'in order to curry favor with his master . . . determined to sacrifice all his companions' (163–4). However, notwithstanding Cheney's treachery and the ultimate failure of the rebels' plan (as well as the brutal response from the plantocracy), Northup writes eloquently of the ever-present and empowering allure of contemplating violent resistance to enslavement:

> Such an idea as insurrection, however, is not new among the enslaved population of Bayou Boeuf. . . . They are deceived who flatter themselves that the ignorant and debased slave has no conception of the magnitude of his wrongs. They are deceived who imagine that he arises from his knees, with his back lacerated and bleeding, cherishing only a spirit of meekness and forgiveness. A day may come – it will come, if his prayer is heard – a terrible day of vengeance, when the master in his turn will cry in vain for mercy. (164–5)

It is instructive to note that a version of Northup's narrative, stripped of its accounts of Black agency and rebellion, has become a successful and critically applauded feature film while Danny Glover's planned biopic of Toussaint L'Ouverture, the great architect of the Haitian Revolution, remains in limbo, unable to secure sufficient funding due to its 'lack of white heroes' ('Danny' 2008). It thus seems that the most radical event of the Atlantic world's age of revolutions still presents a narrative deemed too dangerous for the mainstream, while even projects focused on 'lesser' Black slave rebellions have remained almost entirely beyond the pale for Hollywood.

ETHICS AND AESTHETICS

Having considered McQueen's adaptation alongside Northup's original narrative, I now turn to the impact of McQueen's filmic language on the ideological thrust of *12 Years a Slave*. Melissa Anderson (2013) poses the following question to highlight what she sees as the central dilemma of McQueen's adaptation: is it 'even conceivable to graphically represent the unimaginable without further cheapening the lives one sets out to honor or diminishing the horrors of a monstrous epoch?' Anderson's question suggests that the ethical-aesthetic tightrope that must be walked in any artistic recuperation of historic trauma is especially treacherous when it comes to visual representations, which lend themselves to voyeurism more readily than other cultural forms.

The danger of visual aestheticism diminishing historical trauma is especially real for a director such as McQueen, whose work, his critics have suggested, tends to give 'primacy to the fastidiously composed image over human emotion' (Gonzalez 2013). While the mere act of filmic aesthetic construction inevitably prettifies reality, McQueen's eye for stunning visual harmonies and his cinematographic skill ensures that *12 Years a Slave* is, despite its horrors, a visually striking film. This prompts a question that dovetails with Nick Nesbitt's work on the Haitian writer Edwidge Danticat: how does one 'turn the partial guilt of artistic representation' back on the total guilt of slavery (207)? In an attempt to address this problem, I consider the effect of McQueen's technique – manifest most prominently in exquisite representations of the natural world and his penchant for nonnarrative filmic grammar – on the treatment of violence and torture.

The tension in McQueen's *12 Years a Slave* between representing the horrors of slavery and displaying the splendour of the natural world of the South has drawn considerable comment.[12] McQueen's long-time cinematographer and collaborator, Sean Bobbitt, has stated that it was an intended goal to 'embrace and use for a number of different effects' the 'inherent natural beauty' of Louisiana (Moakley). In several interviews, McQueen has attempted to defend this approach as a mode of artistic truthfulness. For McQueen, the coexistence of beauty and horror is to be explained as part of 'the perversity of the world', and he suggests that his filmic representation of this depravity belongs to an artistic tradition stretching back to Goya:

> In terms of art, it goes back to Goya, the Spanish painter who was creating some of the most horrific images of torture and devastation and war – and yet they're beautiful paintings. . . . [R]eality is perverse. . . . That's the haunting thing – and the difficult thing. It's like when a child asks you, 'Why is the world so unfair?' The only answer is that it just is. The world is unfair. That's reality. So rather than fighting against the reality, you embrace it – which in turn makes it even more horrific. (McQueen 2013a)

Whether or not McQueen's embrace of Louisiana's magnificent scenery succeeds in exacerbating the horror of Northup's narrative is arguable, but beyond dispute is the visual beauty of McQueen's *12 Years a Slave*. McQueen's resplendent and sumptuous cinematic chiaroscuro depicts the natural world of Louisiana in all its splendour. The beauty of its flora and its numerous waterways – lagoons, bayous, inlets – is exquisitely enhanced by a kaleidoscopic array of subtle variations of light and shade; dappled sunlight plays on majestic live oaks and cypress trees adorned with creepers and Spanish moss; and even the cane and cotton fields, sites of intense suffering, are evoked as intensely beautiful. Such stunning filmic artwork confirms McQueen's standing as a visual artist of extraordinary talents. Yet these sensual visuals of the Gulf South undercut the representation of daily miseries endured under slavery, existing uneasily with Northup's descriptions in the 1853 text of the natural world around him as a source of terror and a barrier to escape: '[T]he nature of the country is such as renders it impossible to pass through it with any safety' (159). While Northup narrates in considerable detail the dangers posed by a wilderness teeming with wild animals, snakes and alligators (90–1), McQueen's version evokes an intensely hospitable natural environment. It thus becomes necessary to ask whether McQueen and Bobbitt's gorgeous cinematography reproduces the colonial gaze of the tropics as paradisiacal. This question assumes even greater analytic and probative value when we recall that this colonial gaze was also paradoxically charged with apprehensions of unseen evil and forbidden sensuality. It appears that McQueen's critical judgement erred: what the camera perceives as beautiful was a source of terror and despair for Northup and the enslaved populations of the Deep South.

An additional effect of the film's aesthetic is that, far from intensifying perception of slavery's extremities, the ordinary brutality of slavery is lost. In fact, still shots that afford pleasure are deployed immediately following scenes of distressing suffering, as if to comfort the audience. While McQueen does depict harrowing scenes of brutal violence and torture, the daily miseries and hardships of slavery – evoked very clearly in the 1853 text – are diminished. While McQueen's version shows some scenes of slave work, they fail to register the impact of hard labour on the slave body. This is especially ironic given his emphasis on the body as a site of suffering elsewhere in the film and throughout his other works. For example, in *Western Deep*, which journeys into the physical interior of the deepest gold mine in the world, the Tau Tona mines in South Africa, McQueen takes us into the darkness and claustrophobia of the lift and mine shafts, showing us the hot, dusty and dangerous conditions of labour and the faces and bodies of the miners. Thomas McEvilley notes that the message of *Western Deep* is unequivocally that 'labor in a capitalist society is a hell of exploitation and humiliation'. This is especially apparent in an extended sequence in which we observe Black miners carrying out mandatory, supervised physical exercises in unison, stepping up and down as red buzzers sound and light up above their heads, before having their body temperatures monitored. This sequence evokes chain gang and plantation labour, as well as the institutional repression of prison regimes, but it also emphasises the strength and stoicism of the miners by depicting their capacity to survive in an extreme environment. There are no comparable sequences in *12 Years a Slave*. Instead, attention to the conditions of slave labour is supplanted by prolonged and graphic torture scenes: Patsey's whipping (the most horrific episode of torture) and Northup's near death by lynching are drawn out for over four minutes each. The film thus gives primacy to the traditional focus on slavery as punishment, physical torture and sexual exploitation. 'Slow', or structural, violence is usurped by spectacular, or super-structural, violence.[13] The problems with this approach are manifold and are encapsulated in the words of Joanne Laurier: '[S]lavery was not simply the sum total of beatings and whippings – as real as they were and as much as they were an integral part of the institution' (2013). McQueen's representation thus misconceives slavery as an aberration rather than identifying it as a system of capitalist labour fundamental to the making of the modern world and the modern self.

Moreover, slave labour is usurped by McQueen's fondness for what Dana Stevens (2013) has described as 'contemplative insert shots', which often focus on a detail from nature, such as 'cypress trees reflected in peach-colored bayous at sunset, [or] caterpillars crawling over cotton bolls'. Such visually commanding shots stand at the threshold of narrative and non-narrative cinema; yet, while McQueen shows us close-ups of cotton plants, he refrains from focusing on what cotton picking does to the pickers' hands. McQueen misses an opportunity here to inform his audience of one aspect of the mundane suffering of cotton pickers. Instead, when representing slave suffering, McQueen stages highly theatrical and harrowing incidents of torture.

NORTHUP'S LYNCHING AND PATSEY'S WHIPPING

The scene in which Northup is lynched by Tibeats and two of his companions is one of the film's most harrowing. The representation of the lynched or hanged slave, suspended either from ropes, hooks or chains, is, as the work of Marcus Wood reminds us, one of the most iconic and notorious cultural symbols of the atrocity of slavery (2000: 38–40, 230–2). The lynching scene in *12 Years a Slave* seeks to evoke this cultural history by using a long take – an uninterrupted shot that disrupts the film's narrative rhythm – during which the camera remains unwaveringly focused on Northup's torture. In interviews subsequent to the making of the film, McQueen stated that there was a twofold purpose in lingering on Northup's lynching. First, McQueen explained that he wanted to force the audience to watch long after they wanted to turn away. Second, McQueen spoke of his wish to commemorate not only the untold numbers of slaves murdered by lynching but also the many thousands of post-slavery Jim Crow lynchings (McQueen 2013b). Thus, the visual medium of film breaks the temporal bounds of Northup's original memoir. Yet the scene fails in its intention as a memorial to the victims of Jim Crow lynchings by omitting other well-documented tortures – mutilations, castrations, and the burning out of eyes with hot irons.

Although McQueen's representation of Northup's lynching is sufficiently disturbing to its twenty-first-century audience, it does not apprise them of Northup's prolonged torment under the white legal property codes of antebellum Louisiana. It is the chattel mortgage that Ford has taken out on Northup that ensures his agony must last until his owner returns to cut him down. In the absence of historical analysis, this enactment of depravity becomes merely a horror show that, as Laurier observes, inflicts suffering on the audience while failing 'to arrive at its truth'. Thus, McQueen's strategy cannot accurately be dubbed 'didactic'.[14]

Moreover, his strategy of dramatically emphasising the horror of slave torture might be considered especially fraught in the twenty-first century, since audiences have become so accustomed to cinematic, televisual and internet images of grotesque violence that shock tactics are no longer effective. While it was essential in 1853, to further the abolitionist cause, for Northup to narrate the facts of the sexual abuse he had witnessed and the viciousness to which he was victim in visceral detail, transposing these elements to the big screen in the twenty-first century runs the risk of unwittingly pornographising historic sexual atrocity and violence. Consider, for example, the film's emotional crescendo, 'an interminable, lurid sequence' (Laurier 2013), in which Patsey endures a sadistic whipping. While this critique illuminates the problematic question of how one depicts the true nature of plantation violence without driving one's audience away, it also constitutes another example of how McQueen attributes suffering under slavery to the evil of individual 'mad masters' rather than systemic issues. In this schema, Epps becomes an exemplar of utter evil as shown by his savage torture of Patsey. Patsey's torment is compounded further by the fact that Epps's infatuation with her disgusts his wife, who is driven by extreme sexual jealousy to further abuse Patsey. Yet this representation is also problematic, as Jasmine Nichole Cobb has argued, since it encourages the audience to 'observe Mistress Epps . . . as sadistic and jealous' without appreciation for her entrapment within a domestic sphere dictated by nineteenth-century gender politics. Similarly, Cobb notes, McQueen's representation of Tibeats, '"the poor white trash" overseer', emphasises his status as an ignorant, racist scoundrel but does not offer the audience 'a broad enough view of slavery as a system to understand labor competition as a counterpart to the racism we see in his character' (2014: 343). We cannot overlook that Tibeats forms a sharp contrast with Northup's first master, William Ford, who is the epitome of the 'gentlemanly master' in McQueen's version. With this portrayal, McQueen appears to have inadvertently given new credence to the archetype of the honourable, aristocratic Southern gentleman. It should also be noted that Ford's demeanour contrasts starkly with that of Tibeats and Epps, whose viciousness correlates to their class positions, one a poor white, the other an upstart member of the planter elite. *12 Years a Slave* thus fails to contextualise the agency and suffering of its dramatis personae and reduces the institution of slavery to little more than the backdrop to a sensational costume melodrama.

CONCLUSION

While McQueen's adaptation of Northup's narrative is polished and cinematographically accomplished, it fails to capture the fundamental fact that, as Greg Grandin has recently put it, 'slavery created the modern world, and the modern world's divisions (both abstract and concrete) are the product of slavery' (2015). Instead, McQueen's *12 Years a Slave* elects to explain away the horrors of slavery by focusing on individual 'evil-doers'. However, Northup's original memoir conspicuously denies the accuracy of this explanatory mode.

Furthermore, the aestheticised filmic language of *12 Years a Slave* diminishes the attempted representation of the human devastation wrought by slavery. Additionally, whereas three of McQueen's art films and video installation works, namely *Caribs' Leap*, *Western Deep* and *Gravesend*, use filmic language to conjure race as a vector of oppression under capitalism across space and time, *12 Years a Slave* forecloses any such analysis. However, it could be argued that McQueen's art-house techniques could not have been adapted to the Hollywood feature film. In this context, it is worth considering two other recent and popular examples focused on the subject of the Black diaspora that demonstrate that a focus on individuals need not result in the occlusion of systemic explanation.

David Simon and Eric Overmyer's HBO series *Tremé* (2010–13) and Lars von Trier's *Manderlay* (2005) are examples of successful televisual and cinematic forms that have succeeded at the level of systemic explanation. The production and circulation histories of these two examples differ from McQueen's *12 Years a Slave*, and this reminds us to be attentive to the question of what may or may not be possible in a Hollywood form. Nevertheless, a cross-genre comparison effectively reveals some of the limitations of McQueen's adaptation. In *Tremé*, which tracks the lives of several individuals living through the aftermath of Hurricane Katrina in New Orleans, the creative use of 'lens language' locates individual narratives within a larger, systemic tragedy. For example, Stephen Shapiro reads the moment in which one of the central characters, the downtrodden La Donna, finally tracks down her brother's body in a makeshift mobile morgue comprised of refrigerated white trucks. The camera rotates around La Donna clockwise before spinning counterclockwise, as the viewer and La Donna both take in the dizzying number of trucks, which all contain other victims of Katrina's long durée. Shapiro notes that the uniformly white trucks recall New Orleans's levees but also the slave ship. Via such simple but effective lens language, the viewer is reminded not to lose sight of the systemic tragedy while focusing on the story of an individual.¹⁵

A sensitivity to transhistorical, underlying systemic connections can also be found in Lars von Trier's *Manderlay*. Trier emphasises that the abolition of slavery in the United States did not usher in a new age of racial equality and happiness by setting the story in an Alabama community that was ignorant of the fact that slavery had been abolished. Although repugnant in many ways – the film is both misogynistic and deeply problematic in its portrayal of Blacks as complicit in their own enslavement – *Manderlay* refuses to overlook the horrors of continuing and systemic Black immiseration. As the end credits roll, we see a montage of American racial atrocities and ironies from the nineteenth century to the twenty-first century, including iconic images of the Ku Klux Klan, anti-desegregation protests, police brutality, African Americans serving in Vietnam and Iraq, and the Black Power movement. The radicalism of this approach – which juxtaposes disparate images of oppression, violence and resistance, thereby suggesting a deep causal explanation – is arguably more faithful to the spirit of Northup's narrative than is McQueen's adaptation.

Moreover, McQueen's own work includes powerful examples of the explanatory potential of the technique of juxtaposition. In *Gravesend*, McQueen uses the technique to vividly convey the dependence of advanced technological society on resource extraction in the deprived peripheral location of the Congo. The dynamic of this relation is also recalled by the title, the point of departure in Joseph Conrad's 1899 novella *Heart of Darkness*. Such techniques could also have been deployed in *12 Years a Slave*: McQueen could have interspersed among the many beautiful shots of Southern landscapes images of the cotton mills in Lancashire, of middlemen in the North profiting from slavery, or of the cotton-trading markets in London. Notably, Gillo Pontecorvo's 1969 film *Burn!*, which narrates a story of late-nineteenth-century anti-slavery revolution and Machiavellian colonial manipulation, adopts such a strategy. The existence of a colonial global network of capitalist exploitation is evoked throughout the film, most explicitly in a scene in which traders at the London Stock Exchange react with excitement to the rising share prices of the world's leading sugar companies. Pontecorvo's representational strategy ensures that slavery is not portrayed as an evil contained entirely in the US South and makes clear that its end did not herald a new chapter of civilised humanity. On the contrary, as recent scholarship has made clear, the end of cotton slavery in the southern United States was the catalyst for the massive expansion of cotton production in India, Egypt and Brazil and concomitant new forms of labour exploitation in those territories.¹⁶

Coming hot on the heels of a series of Hollywood feature films about Black diasporic experience – for example, *The Help* (2011), *Django Unchained* (2012), *Belle* (2013), *The Butler* (2013) and *Selma* (2014) – the success of *12 Years a Slave* prompts us to wonder whether having long overlooked slavery and its legacies, Hollywood is now cashing in on Black history and engaged in the manufacture of new fantasies and denials about slavery, Black lives and Black suffering. Although *12 Years a Slave* is powerful and assured filmmaking that retains the emotional and personal drama of Northup's memoir, it also lacks the dynamics of historical change and drains Northup's narrative of its politics and specificity. This is regrettable since the film looks set to become a cultural touchstone about slavery for many years to come.

NOTES

1. On the renewal of debate over reparations, see Coates 2014, and the work of the CARICOM Reparations Commission. For recent scholarship addressing the relationship of slavery and capitalism, see Edward E. Baptist, Sven Beckert, Ada Ferrer, Greg Grandin and Walter Johnson. Recent anniversaries of major events in the history of slavery and abolition that have been officially observed include the sesquicentennial of the American Civil War and the bicentenaries of the Haitian Revolution and the British 1807 Abolition of the Slave Trade Act.
2. The generic mixture of revenge thriller and Black cowboy film in Quentin Tarantino's *Django Unchained* (2012) does, however, contest slavery stereotypes with long histories, for example, via the revenge exacted on the Uncle Tom figure played by Samuel Jackson. It is also noteworthy that in other recent films addressing slavery there has been a sustained attempt to meditate more seriously on slavery and its inheritance. Lars von Trier's *Manderlay* (2005) is a notable example, notwithstanding its crude polemics.
3. Moreover, the film has already attracted considerable academic interest, including a special 2014 forum in *American Literary History*: '12 Years a Slave: An ALH Forum'.
4. It is also noteworthy that Solomon Northup dedicated his narrative to Harriet Beecher Stowe and that he offers his narrative as 'another key to Uncle Tom's Cabin'.
5. See, for example, Wood (2000: 266–7), Nesbitt (2003: 207) and Kaisary (2014: 59–61).
6. For further analysis of the Fugitive Slave Act of 1850, see Blackett (2013: 32–67).
7. See Nelson George for examples of how McQueen sought to connect his *12 Years a Slave* project to contemporary politics and realities inherited from slavery.
8. A relevant contrast can be observed in Richard Wright's *Uncle Tom's Children*, a collection of novellas first published in 1938, in which Wright's universalist depiction of Black experience in the Deep South in the post-slavery era is always inflected by historical specificity. This dimension of the work drew the praise of Ralph Ellison (1941: 22).
9. As Sue Eakin and John Lodgson also note, 'the abduction of a free Negro adult from the North and his enslavement in the South . . . provides a sensational element which cannot be matched in any of the dozens of narratives written by former slaves' (1968: ix).
10. Leon F. Litwack's *North of Slavery* (1965) remains the classic account of racism and oppression in the antebellum 'free states'.
11. Michael Wood assesses the impact of Fassbender's performance: 'Fassbender is terrific [as Epps], but the result is similar to Hannibal Lecter's running away with *The Silence of the Lambs*. . . . So that was the problem: a few crazy sadists like Epps. Remove the bad apples, and the crop will be as good as it ever was. This is not where the film has any intention of going, but it is where it gets' (2014: 23).
12. See, for example, McQueen 2013.

13. On 'slow' violence, see Nixon 2013.
14. The film has attracted much praise for its alleged didacticism. See, for example, Brody 2013.
15. Stephen Shapiro's analysis will appear in his article 'Cultural Realignment and Televisual Intellect: The Telepraxis of Class Alliances in Contemporary Subscription Television Drama', forthcoming in *Precarious Television*, edited by Sieglinde Lemke and Wibke Schniedermann.
16. For analysis of forms of labour control and exploitation that developed in the wake of abolition (in the context of cotton cultivation, sharecropping was the dominant form), see Beckert (2004: 1405–38, especially 1424).

CHAPTER 7

Working for/working with/ working against – *Widows* and the Politics and Poetics of Genre

Matthias Grotkopp

Following his previous work as a video artist and after the feature films *Hunger* (2008), *Shame* (2011) and *12 Years a Slave* (2013), Steve McQueen's next film seemed not to be an obvious choice. Instead of complex stories about freedom and different kinds of oppression and imprisonment, both internal and external, now we have *Widows* (2018), a heist film that follows the modes of action and sentimentality of popular genre cinema? That must either be a lowering of artistic standards or an elaborate con that substitutes what the audiences expect with a complex study of real power relations.

At least this was the tenor of a large part of the film's critical reception. There was an insistence that *Widows* must be about #BlackLivesMatter and about #Metoo in a meaningful way that disrupts the levels of mere entertainment (Simmons 2019). There were some reactions that took this attention to questions of class, race and gender and found the film lacking, precisely because of its relation to genre templates. One critic wrote that *Widows* does not provide 'any real discussion about the realities of American women' and that '*Widows* was fun to watch, but I wonder how many women will actually see themselves reflected on screen' (Mercer 2018).

Another very strong critique was levelled at the portrayal of the Blackness of the film's protagonist Veronica, played by Viola Davis. What struck me, when I was reading it, was the very particularity and authority from which it was voiced, in contrast to the encompassing claim to speak for 'American women' in the review above. Referring to the early scene in which Veronica mourns her dead husband, looking out of the window in a melancholic way, putting on a vinyl record of Nina Simone, Kristen Warner writes: 'I do not believe Veronica has always been who she is. I do not believe Veronica was always affluent [. . .]. I do not believe that Veronica has always listened to Nina Simone' (Warner 2019: 187).

What Warner wishes for is a choice of music that is more nuanced, more culturally specific. In the sense that: even a white male from practically anywhere could have come up with Nina Simone. What Warner brings to the film is a sort of tacit knowledge that is more akin to a home movie than a fiction film.[1] And that is something which is totally beyond me to judge, as an almost-white, cis-male person from Berlin, Germany. Therefore it opens up the debate towards differentiated notions of spectatorship and marks my vision of *Widows* as audio-visual discourse as equally partial (and by acknowledging partiality and the plurality of different media memories and audio-visual enculturations marking it as equally objective) in this sense.

Even those voices that reviewed the film positively – and they are by and large the majority – often sounded quite apologetic. They admit that being 'a heist movie is no shame' and that 'genre escapism needn't be shorn of real-world context or curiosity' (Lodge 2018). But somehow reviewers felt obliged to excuse the film's genericity and emphasise in how many ways the film 'transcends the tropes of the genre' (Sinha-Roy 2018).

At one point in the build-up to the heist sequence, the film seems to ask this question itself, when Veronica drops off her dog at a Deluxe Sit & Stay. Framed by the black outlines of a car window, the slender front of the triangular building is in the centre of the image and on both sides the symmetrical vanishing points are lit by warm yellow lights. Veronica is standing at the centre in a wide shot, holding her dog before she enters the building. The visual composition of this shot, which lasts for about 25 seconds, urges us to feel this moment of diverging paths: will they or won't they? Veronica is literally at one of the generic crossroads described by Rick Altman:

Figure 7.1. Veronica at the crossroads. (New Regency Productions, See-Saw Films, Film4, Lammas Park)

> To the extent that they are indebted to specific genres, Hollywood films incorporate a series of paradigmatically designed and often repeated 'crossroads'. Each one of these moments depends on a crucial opposition between two paths open to the text, each representing a different type of pleasure for the spectator. Strategically simplifying, we may say that one fork offers a culturally sanctioned activity or value, while the other path diverges from cultural norms in favour of generic pleasure. (Altman 1999: 145)[2]

The moment of truth comes for the characters but also for the film itself: Do I take the road towards art, critique and deconstruction? Do I work against the genre? Or do I aim at popular culture, commerce, pleasure? Do I work for the genre? And in the conclusion of the heist sequence, we find the answer that the film gives, when the van with the money driven by Jatemme Manning (Daniel Kaluuya) crashes into an intersection where the street forks into two tunnels, hitting the barrier between them, at the centre of the image. As it crashes, the windshield crumbles, the structure of the car deforms and becomes a mass of dark, crumbled shadows, turning this shot into a kind of disorderly mirror image of the balanced shot of Veronica at the dog-sit. What I take this to mean is that *Widows* is going right through the middle of the opposition of working for or against. It is working with the genre.

This kind of answer also underlies the constitutive conflict of the heist film genre. If one follows Daryl Lee's argument, its function is

> to reflect on the raison d'être and condition of the film artist in a commercial medium from within a commercial genre. The heist film serves as a vehicle for exploring aesthetic value and artistic creation as a problematic in which capitalist economics, labour and pure aesthetic value face off against each other. (Lee 2014: 10)

In an early scene, Mulligan Sr (Robert Duvall) mocks Mulligan Jr (Colin Farrell) and his acquisition of a painting by an upcoming artist, calling it first a masterpiece and then a '50,000 dollar piece of wallpaper'. It seems obvious that this price tag also refers us to the budget of a film like the one we are seeing and to the necessity to regain this money at the box office, which is thought to always threaten the ambitions of creating art. I would argue, however, that this predicament of the artist working in a commercial medium is itself only the particular version of a very general conflict: namely our historically and culturally entrenched antinomic relationship to the question of work: What the heist film dramatises is the difference between work as labour, as the never-ending task of sustaining life, of fighting entropy, on the one hand, and work as creation, as the making of a shared world, as a means of self-realisation, on the other hand – and how both never stop interfering with each other. The heist-film genre can be used as an aesthetic experience of both suspending and accentuating these antinomies of working, making and acting, of individual self-sufficiency and independence on the one hand and of the ubiquitous dependence on others in a society based on the division of labour. The utopian aspect of the genre, when it is turning the act of stealing into an emphatically collective working together, is expressed in a short exchange: When Veronica states: 'Your husbands have been working a long time for my husband' and stands immediately corrected by Linda (Michelle Rodriguez): 'With your husband.'

This question of work and community, of making a shared world, is inherently bound to short- and long-term historical figurations. I will not go into depth here, but I just want to hint at the fact that anthropological studies emphasise even those hunter-gatherer societies that live in adverse environments have shorter working hours than people in affluent societies.[3] So why do we live in a society that demands about 40 hours or more – and even that is not enough for some low-income jobs? The answer is that we have surrounded ourselves with a world of needs and desires that go beyond feeding, clothing and housing ourselves; we have surrounded ourselves with power structures and fictions – fictions like money or race.

HOW GENRES WORK

And then there is another reason why the discussion is misleading when it recognises the social relevance of a film like *Widows* only when the film transcends its genre condition. Because this attitude follows a logic of genre that only looks at genres as sets of conventions and iconographies, as a taxonomy for sorting films into categories, for easy communication between industry and audiences. In opposition to that, I would follow Christine Gledhill's intervention into genre theory. She argues that genres do not follow the neat order of taxonomies, but create historical dynamics of differentiating and interacting expressive modalities. Genre poetics is the dynamic process of the permanent refiguration of different ways to perceive, feel and think in embodied processes. Genres thus shape the way we understand the most basic conflicts of being in a world that is gendered, ordinary, historical, full of racial, social and political struggles. They do this not by depicting these conflicts but by creating expressive modalities which in the case of film means audio-visual patterns of time, space and bodies:

> the notion of modality, like register in socio-linguistics, defines a specific mode of aesthetic articulation adaptable across a range of genres, across decades, and across national cultures. It provides the genre system with

a mechanism of 'double articulation', capable of generating specific and distinctively different generic formulae in particular historical conjunctures, while also providing a medium of interchange and overlap between genres. (Gledhill 2000: 229)

Based on this notion, it becomes possible to regard genre not as a sorting tool but as the dynamic principle of a history of creating spaces of diverse and intersecting sensibilities and experiences. It helps us analyse films not just as representations of sets of circumstances in our reality but as interventions into the affective modalities of experience that form the basis of different cultural communities: 'Genres are always only to be observed historically as a specific figuration, transformation, ramification, and fusion of a variety of modes of poetic making' (Kappelhoff 2018: 96).

You can see this in *Widows* in the sense that this film, like all genre films, includes already more than one register, one affective modality (Grotkopp and Kappelhoff 2012). We have the modality of the action film but also a lot of melodrama as well as moments of comic relief. We have the dramatisation of the urban from the gangster film, which oscillates into political drama and the menacing thriller performance of Daniel Kaluuya. And then we have the moments of bodily labour, which one can argue belong to a modality that cuts across a lot of customary genre categories. One could call this 'the process genre' (Skvirsky 2020).

Widows follows the heist film's standard scenes of process: the assembling, planning, rehearsing and executing as well as its usual constellation of multiple lines of betrayal and parasitic relationships. Based on the theoretical background I have just hinted at, it is clear that I do not regard these actions under the category of representation of criminal acts: we do not see these criminals *as* criminals, but rather as an exaggerated version of ourselves, of workers, artists, making and consuming, being made and being consumed. Hustlers in the struggle of everyday life in a post-industrial economy, but viewed from an oblique, shifted perspective: 'the delinquent exists only by displacing itself, [. . .] its specific mark is to live not on the margins but in the interstices of the codes' (De Certeau 1984: 130). In this way, they lay open the ways of poetic world-making and make it possible to imagine change.

At the origin of the genre, one finds the question of class as the central code or category of differences. I think it is no accident that the heist film as a genre emerged after the Second World War, when the outlines of the post-industrial era became foreseeable. From the working-class melancholia in John Huston's *The Asphalt Jungle* (1950) to the image of the heist as industrial labour and an almost Marxist theory of expropriation in Michael Mann's *Thief* (1980), the American Dream of achieving affluence through hard work is revisited as a tragic condition of self-deception. In addition to that, the history of the genre also becomes the history of appropriating this constitutive conflict of the genre for the contested areas of race and gender: two prominent heist films by white filmmakers – *Odds against Tomorrow* (Robert Wise, 1959) and *Blue Collar* (Paul Schrader, 1978) – focus on the fact that racism divides the working poor and 'undermines the possibility of class solidarity' (Munby 2017: 122). Then there are films that interweave the heist film with a very frontal affirmation of Black politics and resistance, like *The Spook Who Sat by the Door* (Ivan Dixon, 1972), based on the book by Sam Greenlee.

As far as a problematisation of gender is concerned, the genre system offered a different kind of response: female caper movies of the 1960s like *How to Steal a Million* (William Wyler, 1966) or *Penelope* (Arthur Hiller, 1966) rather playfully equate capitalism and theft, making it all about the maintenance of a consumer lifestyle (Dassanowsky 2007), and in this sense are not part of the heist-film genre but rather a complementary genre in Cavellian terms.[4] But with *Set It Off* (F. Gary Gray, 1995) we have an important milestone of intersectionality, a female and partially queer sisterhood, which is largely motivated by inter-racial injustice but also intra-racial socio-economic divides (Munby 2017).

And finally there is the British TV series *Widows* (Lynda La Plante, 1983–5), which gave its title and the central premise to McQueen's film, but has a slightly different focus and a different dramaturgy of affect. Here it is mostly the relationship of a surrogate all-female family which emerges through a soap-operatic rhythm of escalation, reconciliation and repetition of conflicts within the group as they learn to perform the actions of the male criminal – something we can attribute to the affordances of the serial format (and one can find an echo of this dynamic in the relationship between Veronica and Alice in the film). The comparison of the female gang and their husbands is more direct in the series through the use of compositional repetition and montages, both in the preparation and in the execution. But one thing both series and film have in common is the question of 'womanliness as a masquerade' (Doane 1982)[5] and the possibility to hide in plain sight – even though the film does not emphasise this in the aftermath of the heist whereas the series gives this a lot of space, and also because its second season is entirely about keeping the loot and staying alive.[6]

CINEMATIC WORKSPACES OF LIFE AND DEATH

It is in relation to this genealogy, the different echoes and reverberations, repetitions and differences on the one hand and the concrete socio-political materiality and cartography of Chicago on the other hand, that *Widows* creates its cinematic world projection. Before I go into detail with the actual heist sequence, I want to share some general observations about important aspects of the film's composition.

After the already famous shots of the boisterous kiss between a Black woman, Veronica, and a white man, Harry (Liam Neeson), the opening scene alternates the aftermath of the men's heist, at first shot entirely from the inside of the escape van, with flashbacks to everyday interactions with their wives. This scene correlates violent action with gender relations, relations which in themselves lay out the continuum of bodily passion, economic exploitation, abusive violence and cruel indifference. The central coordinates of this film's world are thus clearly marked: gender, money and race. And the vanishing point of these three is: death and mourning.

This prologue in itself works like the end of a conventional heist film: the perfect plan went wrong, the law is on their heels, someone got hurt ... And the framing of the ensuing shooting and explosion through the gate of the warehouse can be thought to play with the genre's equation of crime, work and film art if one compares it with *La Sortie de l'usine Lumière à Lyon* (1895) – only that McQueen's workers will not leave this factory.

One important feature of the heist film that is much too seldom put into the foreground in the academic discourse is its relation to the everyday arrangements and rhythms of social life. For the heist to be successful it must insert itself into the recurrent events and the gaps between them. For us, the films provide a map of the otherwise unseen ordinary: from the routines and routes of cops and security personnel to the opening times of shops or the time a florist's gets its deliveries in the morning in *Du Rififi chez les hommes* (Jules Dassin, 1955). In *Widows* this is tracked down to the regular interval of a cop's urinary urgencies, which provides the possibility to catch the security at the house off guard. Not only do the films create spatial outlines of the criminal's targets but dynamic mappings of spatio-temporal relations and interactions, movements and durations, and most importantly they create a perception of the gaps and shadows, the blind spots and layers of possibilities.

Widows extends these surveys to the spatial arrangement of social differences and questions of power, with the contrasted private spaces of the Mulligans, the glossy hotel rooms or spas and Veronica's aseptic, crystalline apartment on the one hand and the stuffed, chaotic but warmly lit places of Linda and Belle (Cynthia Erivo) on the other hand. At the beginning there is a conspicuous abundance of large public and semi-public spaces, from the Preston Bradley Hall to a gym or Rev. Wheeler's (Jon Michael Mill) large church, which seem to spatially encode the masculine game of power, intimidation and oppression – which for instance Veronica is trying to pass on to the other women in their first meeting in the sauna. The contrast between public transport and individual transport is another re-occurring trope, as well as the socio-economic metaphorisations of high and low positions.

One remarkable moment is the scene where we move in one shot from a poor neighbourhood to a block of wealthy mansions. The ride itself that connects and separates the extremes only takes 1 minute 49 seconds.[7] The windshield screens us spectators from the passengers as much as the car screens them from any real interaction with the outside, while the dialogue between Mulligan Jr and his assistant/girlfriend Siobhan (Molly Kunz) negotiates a crude intermingling of gender roles, racist stereotypes and power dynamics. This scene foregrounds the successful execution of an artistic challenge, the terrible beauty of making art in a world of inequalities, oppression and a constant death threat. And this is true for quite a number of other sequences, like the execution of two underlings by Jatemme Manning, which is shot in one swirling continuous steady-cam shot.

If these questions of craftsmanship seem to work only on a surface level, then this is precisely the point. Surfaces and reflections can be found in abundance in this film and there is a constant struggle between a movement towards transparencies and layers and a nesting of boxes and receptacles – from coffins and cars to the locker box with Harry's notebook and of course the safe. In addition to that, a whole article could also be dedicated to the interplay of colours and textures, the whites and blacks of dresses, dogs or the redness of Veronica's dress in the scene where she realises that Harry is still alive. These surface features are important both for the allegorisation of the heist with the craft of filmmaking but also with reference to a world in which appearances of race and gender are matters of life and death.

And that is also the importance of the inclusion of the flashback to the murder of Veronica's and Harry's son Marcus, which is not just flashing police brutality in our face in order to check this box as well,[8] but if one looks at the surfaces it becomes clear that it is much more than that. The intense red of the car and the bright blue of the police uniform match the colours of the iconic Obama-Hope posters that suddenly are plastered over all the walls. This shows the painful ambivalence of hopeful messages.

Figure 7.2. Obama posters in the background of Marcus's murder. (New Regency Productions, See-Saw Films, Film4, Lammas Park)

But also on a dramaturgical level, this scene is important. From the flower that Veronica lays on his gravestone during Harry's funeral and the first flashback to Marcus's funeral that comes twenty minutes earlier than the flashback to the actual shooting, to the donation of the money from the heist to the school library that shall bear his name in the final scene, it becomes clear that the work of the heist and the work of mourning each become the vehicle of the other. The dramaturgical macro-structure of the film is not interested in a linear emplotment of suspense or surprise (the fact that Harry is still alive is not exploited for dramatic effect) but rather we have an alternation of the heist narrative with phases in which death and mourning are foregrounded, progress is halted and in which especially the shots of Veronica drift in time and space. In this sense, Marcus's death pervades the film because 'the reference point of a racist culture [. . .] is death' (Engell 2021: 12). Until this changes, hope kills. If hope is the message, the message is death.[9]

WORKING HARD: PROPULSION AND DISRUPTION

What then is the role of the actual heist in this film, the reference point of the genre, so to speak? One thing seems apparent. It is not a bravura piece of daring proportions: nothing like *Du Rififi chez les hommes*' half an hour without a spoken word, or the temporal cubism of Kubrick's *The Killing* (1956), or the media-savvy trickery of Soderbergh's *Ocean's Eleven* (2001). For some, this is a reason for disappointment: 'in the end the heist itself is almost an afterthought, an armed stumble through a darkened house rather than the kind of complex artistic feat we've come to expect from the "Ocean's" movies' (Ross 2018: 47).

But I would follow the argument that this inconspicuousness is exactly the point, because the scene provides a kind of utopian moment of not having to combat expectations and public discourse. 'It could be that the widows' heist is, paradoxically, exactly that respite, because it pleasurably (at least for the viewer) suspends the sociopolitical circumstances of the women for a moment' (Simmons 2019). The heist sequence is special because it is in a way ordinary, it denies the exceptional gesture, it is political because it does not just provide 'kinesthetic empathy' for 'perfectly timed and coordinated movements' (Hanich 2020: 310) but also for the stumbling, the interruption, the improvisation, the will to persevere, to bounce back.

And still there is a critical commentary built into the scene's structural composition because in a way the scene is in itself many different scenes at once. I have already hinted at this plurality with the shot at the dog-sit initiating the heist sequence, opening different possible pathways. The scene, if one takes it to end with Belle walking off in Veronica's rear-view mirror, runs for about 10 minutes. In these 10 minutes no action goes uninterrupted and everything happens at least twice. The money is not stolen once but three times. In the vault, they enter the wrong code, then they enter the right code. The money is on the right, even more money is on the left. Everybody is blindsided by everybody: first the police and the security at the house by the widows, then the widows by Jatemme Manning, then Manning by the widows.

Two times we hear the political candidates over the radio in a clear double entendre: first Jack Mulligan claims 'We work harder', then Jamal Manning (Brian Tyree Henry) demands, 'Let us live!', and both times we hear the screenplay speaking for the widows. This insertion of the widows' action in the interstices of a male power struggle is central here, because it makes clear that it is not about the heist per se, but about the heist as an action within a world ruled by masculinity and racism as means to wield power, a world in which everything is implicated in crime and therefore everything is politics (or vice versa: in one of the flashbacks Harry and Mulligan Jr are on a yacht and shown in two shots that present them as graphic inverting of each other) and where the likes of Jamal Manning are themselves violently pushing towards a different position within this political economy.

The music by Hans Zimmer does not follow a linear progression of swelling tension but rather sudden bursts of intense beating and pulsing, and equally sudden break-offs into almost silence. Also the camera shifts between agility and dynamic movement and moments of sudden stasis. The expressive microstructure of the scenes thus mirrors the dramaturgical macro-structure of the film by alternating impulse and momentum with retardation and sudden stops. For example, after Belle distracts the cops, the other three start to move towards the house, but the movement is at first slow, cautious and arduous with darkness dominating the image, the camera always sliding and panning with them. As soon as the security guard opens the door, the music gets louder and the editing accelerates, only to make way for a longer Steadicam shot pursuing them through the ground floor and towards the staircase, the heavy, distorted breathing interlocking with the ticking sound of the music. The following shot continues the dynamic movement of circular panning, only to come to a very sudden stop and sudden silence with the shoulder close up of Mulligan Sr's private nurse. The shot-reverse-shot sequence with a quivering handheld camera is closed by a static long shot of the three, frozen like statues in the staircase, as the nurse quietly retreats into her room. It is this expressive pattern of momentum and interruption that is repeated throughout the scene during the cutaways to Belle waiting outside while they are in the vault, during a second encounter in the staircase, now with Mulligan Sr himself, and when they are being outmanoeuvred by Jatemme.

Another important aspect of the scene's design is that when the three women in disguise enter the mansion, they make themselves unreadable as women, as women of colour in the darkness, behind masks, using voice changers (the use of the latter incidentally inspired by children's play in an earlier scene). In this performance of passing, there is more at stake than to just claim that women can do all the things formerly reserved for men because it is about the effect that this claim has in different constellations.

As I have described, they are interrupted on the staircase two times. First by the nurse, then by Mulligan Sr. In a kind of spatio-temporally dismantled shot / reverse-shot construction (Åkervall 2018), the two moments are both mirrored and complementary. Both feature a static long shot with similar graphical composition – the widows are on the right side, positioned in a staggered manner, facing left towards their counterpart – but the two shots are from opposite directions, so that the first one looks from the open window towards the staircase and the second from the stairs towards the window.

In the first case the moment of recognition between the two women is a question of mutuality, as if the nurse can see herself in the eyes behind the mask, if you will. In the second case the moment of recognition is also a moment of mis-recognition, of cognitive dissonance. The fact that the old white man cannot comprehend that he is being robbed by the Black woman from the teacher's union provides the moment of hesitation that catches him off guard. Just as the fact that Manning does not reckon with the women's tenacity provides the opportunity to literally thrust him from his blind.

And finally, the shot of Jatemme Manning at the wheel of the van with its fixed view towards the back of the van and the street out of focus in the background, flickering indirect lights changing from warm to cold colours, is in itself multiply connected. First it refers to the opening chase scene of the film (which is not as static but in a fixed position inside the van, often aimed at the scenery behind it) and second, it is then taken up again in Harry's entrance in the next scene, which is also shot from inside the station wagon, looking towards the rear and using the window frame of the tailgate as a frame of the image. And this one also connects to the shot earlier, when we see Belle through the iron grid as the others step into the van and then Jatemme slowly enters the image from the right. So every moment in the film is interwoven with others, creating similarities and oppositions like the distorted echo of the men's heist in the women's which finds as one of its central points the different way of dealing with the injury of a team member: the latter stop at a hospital, the former don't.

THE WORK OF SPECTATORSHIP

A kiss is a cut. Beginning with the prologue and culminating in the heist scene, no action, no shot, no character is identical to itself, they are all multiple beings.[10] Every view is a blind spot, cache and cadre. And this is perhaps the point of the allegorical dramatisation of filmmaking and artistic creation in *Widows*, because it argues for a non-identity of work, artist, reception, meaning and referentiality. Not by denying authorship and responsibility, not by fulfilling or refusing representation of lived experiences, but by multiplying it and by loading the burden of counter-hegemonic work not only onto the Black artist but by putting it into the hands of the spectators, who realise the audio-visual world of these ramifications in their viewing experiences. In this sense *Widows* can be regarded as an example of what Michael Boyce Gillespie names film Blackness as an aesthetics that resists the straightforward demand that Black film must adhere to a 'consensual truth of film's capacity to wholly account for the lived experience or social life of race' (Gillespie 2016: 4) and that it

> demands a certain work of spectator, critical or otherwise, to revalue black film with the active labor of reading through and across blackness by treating each enactment of black film as discrete, if not ambivalent. (2016: 7)

Or in the words of Fred Moten:

> If the self is an artwork, if they are identical in the separation of artist, work, and observer – then art is the refusal of them and their identity-in-relation, their spectatorial or compositional rapprochement. Art consents not to be a single being. (2018: 118)

Art and fiction are not the process in which we resolve the contradictions in our reality, precisely because these contradictions are in themselves already saturated with fictions and desires. One must therefore navigate between two equally unsustainable attitudes, between working for the genre and working against the genre. Working for the genre, to simply reproduce stereotypes and fantasies, comes with a price for people of colour. The 'dream of becoming white' (Baldwin 1998b: 835) is fatal – and the same might be said for any female dreams of becoming masculine. But working against the genre also risks reducing and neutralising race and gender to metaphors of crossing or blurring boundaries and to put the burden of deconstruction on women and Black artists and other minorities, and thus to perpetuate the dependence on the background of a white masculinity and its claim to universality.

Therefore, I think that McQueen's approach in *Widows* can be described as working with the genre: this means that the film realises genre poetics not as the reproduction of rules and conventions but rather as poiesis, as the possibility to create something new by appropriating what has come before, by using, consuming, transforming, by discarding and compensating. Appropriating the heist film can lead to a new idea of what the heist means in a culturally and historically specific context and can mean a becoming-minor of the genre precisely not in the sense that the position of a hegemonic standard of the white, male majority is usurped by others, but that this position itself is carried away by a becoming woman, becoming Black (Deleuze/Guattari 1987: 106). This might mean that *Widows* shifts the utopian paradigm of the heist film from a 'transgression of boundaries' (Hanich 2020: 311) towards a desire to transgress the need for transgression, to achieve an image of solidarity without violence or compassion.[11]

This new utopian paradigm that *Widows* articulates is not about escape anymore, not about a socio-economic vertical ascension or horizontal exit, but it is about the right to stay, to stand your ground. And even though the typical Robin Hood economic rhetoric of the heist-film genre, taking from the rich and giving to the poor (us), is here restated – money, to be money, is always already stolen money and it only belongs to you in the measure of you being able to avoid being stolen from again – it is about a different 'art of practice' (De Certeau 1984). Not the art of strategic planning, craftsmanship and accumulation but the art of tactically reacting to circumstances, improvising and sharing. But the film denies us the naïve sentimental realisation of these in a utopian community of the women's work: the amount of shared screen time over the course of the film is surprisingly low, and if they are shown together, the external pressures and the corresponding internal fissures are always present.

If there is a possibility of a community, the film withholds it, referring us to an always eluding after of suffering, of grief, of generational trauma. But it is there in the absences, both in the absence of a catastrophe, of fatal consequences and reckonings for the four women, and in the absence of a happy ending. Or is this image of solidarity achieved in the final shot of the film, the hesitant encounter between Veronica and Alice, breaking the agreement to refrain from any further contact, which is held in suspense without crystallising into any category of relationships?

Already at the end of the scene inside the diner we start to hear the sad chords and vocalising of the Sade song that will accompany the end credits. A cut to the outside, Alice passes the camera, approaches a car. Off-screen we hear Veronica call her and with Alice stopping and looking up, the camera swirls around and approaches Veronica. We hear Veronica ask, 'How you been?', with a hitherto suppressed fragility in her voice, but we do not hear Alice's answer, we just see Veronica nod and smile. The incompleteness of the encounter is of the essence: the task of achieving solidarity, of achieving the extraordinary in the ordinary, is a task that has to be addressed again and again, for which the work of mourning can be a suitable beginning (Cavell 2005: 119). This idea of mourning as a new morning emphasises the interminability, its impossibility to achieve a new object of love representing the lost one. Instead, the film splits up this relation into a public affair – the naming of the library as a tribute to the ongoing violence and segregation in the United States, paid for by Veronica and owed by society – and a private affair. The film restitutes a certain air of unintelligibility to Veronica, letting her rise above the socially and historically grounded condition of being a Black woman. And in mourning her husband, her son and her old sense of self she enters what the title of the Sade song names *The Big Unknown*. This unknown is nothing else than her own sense of a 'black privacy' (Baldwin 1998a: 564), her claim to self-reliance, responsibility and self-knowledge that transcends the norms of subjectivity and judgement of a (male, white) culture and that 'we' as an audience may recognise or reject (Fay 2022) both as a mode of critique and as a mode of pleasure. Something we can work with.

NOTES

1. I am following here Jean-Pierre Meunier's phenomenological study of *The Structures of the Film Experience* (2019) that differentiates the fictional, the documentary and the home movie experience according to the spectator's embodied experiences of (not) knowing and/or positing the existence of the film's intended objects.
2. Thanks to Thomas Austin for pointing out this reference.
3. See, for example, Harari (2011: 56) or Suzman (2020: 143): 'for most of human history, scarcity was not the organizing feature of human economic life'.
4. In Stanley Cavell's descriptions, neighbouring genres like the Hollywood Comedy of Remarriage and the Melodrama of the Unknown Woman supplement and compensate each other (Cavell 1996).
5. See also Riviere 1986 and Johnston 1975.
6. This shift between the two seasons can be read as a shift in generic and gendered address and its expressive modalities: whereas the first season works to become a 'men's genre for women' (Brunsdon 1997), the second traps the widows in a melodramatic mode of victimisation and passivity (1997: 197–9).
7. 'As they drove around the city, they began to envision one specific shot that could drive their sociopolitical point home. Says Bobbitt, "[We wanted to] literally move a character from a poor area to a rich area and try to do that in one continuous shot so it emphasized just how close those two extremes are physically in the world of Chicago." It wasn't difficult to find such a spot in the city, and the scene they ended up filming follows a car along an eight-block course that takes it from 47th Street to a stony Hyde Park mansion' (Kilkenny 2018).
8. Russell 2019 accuses the scene of 'signaling police brutality just a bit too literally' (2019: 50).
9. I of course allude to Arthur Jafa's famous piece of video appropriation art *Love is the Message, the Message is Death* (2017).
10. And as a side note, I have referred to the four women as widows when actually only two of them are widowed at the beginning. Veronica killing Harry after the heist makes her the third one, being un/widowed in a processual mode rather than in a static civil status and thus perhaps proving her independence from this male-centred designation.
11. Because, as Nietzsche taught us, compassion is also a kind of violent, asymmetrical power relation (Nietzsche 2002).

PART 2

CHAPTER 8

Is *Small Axe* Cinema or Television and does it Matter? Discourses of Authorship and Production in the Publicity for *Small Axe*

Christine Geraghty

Towards the end of 2020, I reacted with some anger when the leading British film journal *Sight and Sound* decided that those invited to participate in their polls of the year could not vote for *Small Axe* in the Best Television poll. This was despite the fact that the five episodes of this epic work were screened from 15 November 2020 over consecutive Sunday nights on BBC ONE (the mainstream, general television channel) and that they were also, unusually, released over five consecutive Fridays from 20 November on US Amazon Prime.[1] Instead, potential voters were advised that three of the episodes could be considered as separate items for the Best Films poll. As a television viewer and an academic who has written about popular television drama, I have experienced the hierarchy of values, inside and outside the screen industries, which, even now, consistently puts television below cinema or film, and this seemed to be another example. In 2020, with cinemas closed during two national lockdowns because of the Covid pandemic, *Sight and Sound* had begun to review some new television programmes in a separate reviews section.[2] Despite this, the decision was taken to make the separate episodes of *Small Axe* eligible for inclusion in its famous '50 Best Films Poll' rather than the (smaller, only '20 Best') television poll, which seemed to reinforce the hierarchy between film and television so far as *Sight and Sound* was concerned.

The question of whether *Small Axe* was film or television was posed in much of the publicity which helped launch the latest work of Steve McQueen, its director and co-writer. In this article, I try to map this struggle over definition and assess its consequences. My main source is initially material published in *Sight and Sound*. This is supplemented by some material from interviews McQueen gave to other publications and by statements made by McQueen and those involved in the production who participated in various panels used to promote *Small Axe* for up to a year after the initial screenings. The publicity for the various festival screenings and for the television premieres was extensive and generally featured McQueen, sometimes alongside his executive producer, Tracey Scoffield, cinematographer Shabier Kirchner and writers Alastair Siddons and Courttia Newland. McQueen clearly worked very hard at promotion and, in many ways, this publicity barrage helped shape how *Small Axe* was received. It is important to note, however, that the interviews and panels were public performances given to particular audiences. This chapter is thus analysing the discursive positions which can be traced across these interventions rather than making a judgement about what McQueen or anyone else involved in the production 'really' thinks.

This chapter begins by examining the coverage given to *Small Axe* in *Sight and Sound*, and particularly the vocabulary used by its writers to describe it, before moving on to consider some statements made by McQueen himself. Despite the claim that what one *Sight and Sound* writer called the 'the hoary old "Film Vs TV"' debate does not matter in an era of convergence (Bell 2020/21: 102), I then argue that the vocabulary used to describe *Small Axe* which emphasised distinctions between film/cinema and television has consequences in relation to British Black filmmaking and public service broadcasting. This leads into an exploration of how some elements of production are discussed rather differently by the executive producer Tracey Scoffield in the *Small Axe* publicity material, which suggests that there might be ways to avoid the binaries of the film/television polarisation which found its apogee in the *Sight and Sound* polls.

FILM OR TELEVISON?

Sight and Sound certainly gave *Small Axe* exceptional coverage at the time of its television transmission. Vol. 30: issue 10 (December 2020) celebrated *Small Axe* extensively. The cover featured a picture of McQueen himself, looking straight out at the reader. Inside, *Small Axe* featured in an editorial by Mike Williams and an interview with McQueen himself. This was conducted by historian David Olusoga, who had given the Edinburgh Festival MacTaggart lecture in August 2020, in which he had asked whether the British television industry had 'the will to genuinely share power with those who have, for so very long, been marginalised and silenced' (Olusoga 2020a). In the same issue of *Sight and Sound*, and very unusually, there were reviews of each of the five episodes by celebrity reviewers (academic Kehinde Andrews on *Mangrove*; journalist and academic Gary Younge on *Red, White and Blue*; novelist Candice Carty-Williams on *Lovers Rock*; writer Kit de Waal on *Education*; poet Jay Bernard on *Alex Wheatle*) as well as standard reviews in the film reviews section of *Lovers Rock* by Nadine Deller and *Mangrove* by Alex Ramon.

The next edition, Vol. 31: issue 1 (Winter 2020/21), was the issue which announced the results of the two polls for Best Films and Best Television of 2020. *Small Axe* featured in the introduction to 'The Best 50 Films of 2020' by Kieron Corless and also in the features on *Mangrove*, which came in at No. 13, and *Lovers Rock*, which won the film poll. *Small Axe* was also discussed by James Bell in his introduction to the 'Television of the Year' and by US writer Nicholas Russell in 'The Year in Black Cinema'. The issue also contained reviews of the last three episodes in the film reviews section: *Red, White and Blue* by Hannah McGill; *Alex Wheatle* by Greg de Cuir Jr; *Education* by Nikki Baughan.

Then, finally, going beyond the time when *Small Axe* was being heavily promoted, we get Vol. 31: issue 7 (September 2021). Nearly a year later, McQueen is one of four people put on the cover[3] and he is interviewed again, this time by Kaleem Aftab, for an issue that focuses on the future of film. It is also worth noting that in October 2021 the BFI South Bank screened the whole series in separate showings with a programme note explaining that 'we take this opportunity to present these remarkable films on the big screen' (Boyea, 40).

In exploring this extensive written material, a number of things are worth noting. One problem in talking about *Small Axe* is the question of what to call it, which inevitably involves a categorisation. Nearly all the writers in *Sight and Sound* over this period use the term 'film'. In the lead interview, Olusoga consistently refers to films and does not take up the fact that these were made for television. Baughan describes *Education* as 'one of five films in Steve McQueen's BBC series' (130) and Russell goes so far as to refer to 'five feature films' (76). Both McGill and de Cuir Jr try to do something different but struggle to find the right words: McGill describes *Red, White and Blue* as a 'chapter in Steve McQueen's "Small Axe" anthology' (137), while de Cuir Jr speaks of *Alex Wheatle* as a 'bio-pic', as 'televisual cinema' and as 'part of his [McQueen's] new anthology series *Small Axe*' (126). No one uses the US term 'mini-series' for *Small Axe*, which was the term later used by the Royal Television Society and BAFTA when *Small Axe* was nominated for their television awards.

The cover of the Winter 20/21 issue which announced the results of the polls is itself interesting. It highlights 'the 50 Best Films' and then separately 'Small Screen, Big Pictures'. It is not clear what this latter byline refers to: the separate poll on television or the fact that films have gone online during the pandemic. Corless, in his introduction to the 'Films of the Year', says that Covid-19 had led to an 'online migration' (50) and acknowledges the role of the BFI Player and MUBI in screening films online. The cover represents all this by using bright colours of purple, pink and yellow to show an old-fashioned television set as a piece of furniture with legs, an image which is intended to be amusing but in a patronising way offers a representation of television in which all the changes in the technologies of domestic viewing have been erased.

Inside the issue, the clear distinction between the two polls is maintained and they are reported on separately. *Lovers Rock* takes the number one spot in the film section and Michaela Coel's *I May Destroy You* (2020) the television honours. Different reasons are given for treating *Lovers Rock* as cinema. Corless points to the difficulties of categorisation and remarks on the significance of *Small Axe* being shown on a national TV channel, but in a more forceful comment he proposes of *Lovers Rock* that 'Such an immersive film cries out to be experienced on a big screen, not least for the rapturous soundtrack to be blasted out as it should be' (53). The aesthetic qualities of *Lovers Rock*, it would appear, demanded that it be treated as a film best experienced in the cinema. James Bell, introducing the television poll, is more pragmatic. Although he calls *Small Axe* 'one of the most significant TV events of the year', he explains that 'it is only not included in our [TV] poll as we judged that as some of its five films had played in film festivals, and were conceived as standalone parts of a whole, it was eligible for our film poll instead' (2000: 102). In other words, the rules permitted some *Small Axe* episodes to be treated as cinema and since they were eligible for the film poll that was naturally where they went.

It would be unfair to suggest that *Sight and Sound* writers entirely ignored television in relation to *Small Axe*. Corless discusses the debate about film and television in some detail and calls *Lovers Rock* 'the most radical thing I've seen on TV since Alan Clarke's . . . *Elephant* (1989)'. Rather than take this as the opportunity to consider what changes in television had made *Lovers Rock* possible, he is content to be amazed: 'It's hard to credit that something so stripped-back in terms of narrative . . . should be shown on BBC1 [sic] on a Sunday evening!' (53). Two writers on *Mangrove* referred to television, perhaps because it was the first episode to be screened on television and thus got considerable publicity. Kehinde Andrews reflected that it 'radiated a sense of Blackness in Britain that is rarely displayed on a mainstream platform like the BBC'. He noted that *Mangrove* did not compromise in its use of language ('the embrace of dialect') and of music. In particular, he commented that this 'is the first time I have seen a genuine attempt to represent British Black Power on mainstream television' but was concerned that the BBC would not take this further forward: 'My only fear is that the BBC will feel it has fulfilled its requirement to cover Black power' (27). In his review of *Mangrove*, Alex Ramon began by commenting with some surprise on McQueen's move to the 'small screen': '*Mangrove* suggests that the series as a whole represents a return to the kind of distilled, focused storytelling and socially relevant themes that distinguished BBC's Play for Today.' But the resonances of this comparison are not explored and Ramon concludes by claiming *Mangrove* as 'among the most important films of the year' (71).

Only Jay Barnard, writer, artist, film programmer and activist, shows imagination and sympathy in using television as a context for a review of *Alex Wheatle*.

IS *SMALL AXE* CINEMA OR TELEVISION AND DOES IT MATTER? 117

Commenting on the role of Dread (aka Simeon), who passes on to Alex 'the intense, radical history of Black people, a history that has been deliberately kept out of schools and off our television screens', Barnard brings into his account some old BBC Arena films he has been watching; they take on the 'social history of carnival, the working-class roots of the steel pans, Black radical poets', subjects long ago erased as the 'struggle for Black cultural production has been characterised by censorship, avoidance, delays and underfunding'. He refers to the work of Horace Ové and Menelik Shabazz, and ends by pointing out that 'films, histories and even TV programming from the 1980s still have the power to shock us. So what is happening today that is too taboo, too difficult, too confronting?' (34).

MCQUEEN ON THE FILM OR TELEVISION DEBATE

The clashing polls gave the debate in *Sight and Sound* about whether *Small Axe* was cinema or television a particular force which would be repeated in publicity for the Academy Awards and the Emmys in the following year. But it is clear from other publicity about *Small Axe* that this was an issue in which McQueen himself took a particular interest. The director took a major part in the interviews and events promoting the series and, while many of his main points inevitably re-occur, it is interesting to see how he shapes his comments in response to the particular circumstances.

The early film festival screenings seemed to have provided a vehicle for placing the emphasis on *Small Axe* as films screened in cinema. The screenings at the NYFF in October 2020 were discussed in a Zoom panel with McQueen and others involved in the production. Shabier Kirchner, the cinematographer, begins to relate how McQueen had told him, 'Forget about TV, these are films.' McQueen interrupts, laughing and saying, 'The BBC didn't know that though', while Kirchner continues to explain that Steve said, 'Don't tell anybody, we're making these into feature films.' McQueen concludes the panel by thanking the festival for putting them on the big screen, 'where they are supposed to be' (NYFF 58). McQueen used a similar formulation when he welcomed *Lovers Rock* being added to the 2020 London Film Festival: 'I'm so happy to be screening *Lovers Rock* at the London Film Festival, to show it here where it belongs is a privilege' (Ritman).

This emphasis on films being screened in a cinema informs the promotion of *Small Axe* through press interviews and events. In interviews with US-based magazines, *Little White Lies* and *Rolling Stone*, McQueen talks, as a filmmaker, about the use of 35 mm and 16 mm film stock and the important work of colour grader Tom Poole at Company3 in New York in the making of *Small Axe*.[4] In this context, the possibility of adopting a television narrative format which centred the stories around one family is described as a way of getting the project going: 'To get my foot in the door, it started off as a sort of episodic situation,' McQueen said in an interview with the *New York Times* in November 2020. 'But then I realized they had to be individual films because there's too much interesting material' (Clark). John Winfield for *Drama Quarterly* gave a similar account of McQueen's story of developing the project: 'McQueen initially planned to make a more standard drama series with a single narrative, but later "realised these stories had to stand alone as original films, yet at the same time be part of a collective . . . These are cinema; these are films that happen to be on TV."'

Nevertheless, McQueen at this stage is also careful to acknowledge television. He several times refers to the antecedents of *Education* in the BBC's Play for Today series of the 1970s (see Ide, for example) and he sometimes hints at what might seem to be advantages of broadcast television in, for instance, the possibility of planning the order of transmission for viewers: '*Mangrove* had to be first, then *Lovers Rock*. I wanted the optimism of *Education* [at the end] . . . But it was very important to curate them in this manner' (Sepinwall). This was repeated in an interview to promote the screenings of the *Small Axe* films at the New York Lincoln Center in June 2021. McQueen again discussed the order of screening, admitting that, while people could dip in and out, he had wanted audiences to earn *Lovers Rock* by understanding the political and historical context that *Mangrove* provides: 'you see the narrative, you see the progression'. *Red, White and Blue* showed the children of the Mangrove generation trying to get 'a foot in the institutions . . . getting rejected', while at the end, *Education* offered 'the infinite amount of possibility we all have as human beings' (Film at Lincoln Center). In addition, he discusses the different lengths of the episodes as being appropriate for the story told in each one. As will be discussed later, this did initially cause problems for the BBC but the three which came in at 1 hour 10 minutes or less (*Lovers Rock*, *Alex Wheatle* and *Education*) would certainly have had difficulties getting screened as feature films in commercial cinemas.

In the promotional interviews and events surrounding the premieres, McQueen stresses that getting *Small Axe* completed was 'a lot of effort' but is nevertheless careful to express gratitude to the BBC 'because they supported us through this process for 11 years' (Craig). He regularly relates his desire for the films to be shown on television to his feeling that they tell the story of a generation which will be more likely to watch on broadcast television. In particular, when the interview context relates to television awards, he says that television is where they belong:

> *Finally, you've been adamant that these are films, not television. Amazon is submitting these to the Emmys as a limited series. What kind of conversations did you have with them about it?*

> ... These films were made for television. They can be projected in cinema, but *Small Axe* was all about the generosity and accessibility to these films. From the beginning, I wanted these films to be accessible to my mother, I wanted them on the BBC. It was always going to be on TV, the five films. (Sepinwall)

McQueen, indeed, does his duty to the BBC and Amazon in interviews which are highlighting the television awards. In an interview given in May 2021 in connection with the upcoming Emmys, McQueen gives a very positive response to the reception of *Small Axe* on television: 'But to release this in that way and come into people's homes, I think it was that fact that I was invited into people's homes and the emotion and the response that occurred was just quite overwhelming, really' (Hammond). Wendy Ide, in an Emmy spotlight feature for *Screen Daily*, quoted similar remarks by McQueen about accessibility – '"This was always for television or streaming"' – and reported that 'McQueen conceived *Small Axe* as a television project rather than a cinema venture'. In some ways, in the interviews where it was important to acknowledge television, McQueen seemed to resolve the issue of film or television by saying it could be either or both: 'It was always going to be on TV, the five films. But at the same time, they premiered in the cinema. There's no absolutes anymore. There shouldn't be. Because it's about how people want to see things. That's about it' (Sepinwall).

But as time went on and the impact of the television screenings and awards receded, the emphasis began to shift back to film again. In an interview for *Sight and Sound* in September 2021, McQueen appears in a feature on 'The Future of Film' and expresses a strong preference for cinema as a space for enjoying a film:

> I love being in a cinema with an audience. I love the 'oohs' and the 'ahhs', the applause, the titters, the communal viewing. . . . I always prefer to consume and see something in the cinema . . . the experience of watching something in the cinema is far superior to watching something at home. (Aftab)

This response is then related to his own work when he is asked, '*Small Axe* was made for television and played in the cinema? How should people see them?' He replies, 'I always made them for the cinema' and states that 'the cinema mix informed the TV mix, which is a smaller and less sophisticated situation'. Later in the interview he discusses 'storytelling [as a] craft . . . you need to complete that story in that moment'. He argues that the viewing situation of cinema is thus an advantage: 'So cinema having that limit to around a couple of hours to tell a story and hold an audience's attention is valuable because it's about craft' (Aftab, 45).

With this comment, McQueen is reverting to views on television he had expressed when he was publicising *Widows* (2018). He explained to James Bell why he had remade the 1983 British television series as a feature film: 'Some of this new TV is so rubbish because they try to squeeze out every drop and keep it going.' He criticises 'even the best TV drama over several series' for being overlong and narratively slack: 'usually . . . you could stitch them together as one shorter thing' (2018: 26). And to Ben Travers he said, 'There was a moment in the '90s or early 2000s when it was amazing. And now it's just, "Get stuff done. We need stuff."' It seems possible that the preference for cinema that McQueen expresses here is linked to a desire for the storyteller to be in control: in the cinema, the carefully crafted and pared-down story is shown to an audience which is encouraged by the viewing set-up to give its sole attention to the film. In any case, by the autumn of 2021, McQueen apparently feels freer even in the UK to drop any ambiguity about *Small Axe*. In October 2021, at a panel event promoting the screening of all five films in the cinema at the National Film Theatre, McQueen seemed to exude a sense of relief when he told the audience, 'These were feature films. I can say it now.' It would seem that *Sight and Sound* had made the correct decision with regard to its polls.

Going into this detail about where *Small Axe* should be placed may seem to be nit-picking. Maybe I have fallen into the trap and fulfilled Bell's prediction that 'the hoary old "Film vs TV" debates will be rehashed past the point of tedium' (2020: 102). It would be easier, indeed, to settle for McQueen's commitment to openness in December 2020: 'There's no absolutes anymore. There shouldn't be. Because it's about how people want to see things' (Sepinwall). Maybe, as both Corless and Bell suggested in *Sight and Sound*, the convergence of film and television solves the problem of medium specificity and renders film/television debates redundant. This would have the benefit of fitting in with the reality that British cinema and television have been intertwined at least since the 1980s, that the BBC and Channel 4 in particular have effectively subsidised British cinema over the years and that films have been a recognised and valued format on British television through Film on 4 and BBC Films (see Hannah Andrews 2014 and chapter in this volume). In particular, as Kulraj Phullar suggested at the conference at which this paper was first sketched out, there is a long history of 'blurry boundaries when it comes to British diasporic film and television', citing *My Beautiful Laundrette* (1985) as another film made for television which found an enthusiastic audience when premiered at a film festival.

CONSEQUENCES

Nevertheless, to drop this discussion would be to disregard McQueen's very specific engagement with issues about cinema and television. As we have seen,

McQueen takes this seriously, and the *Sight and Sound* polls in 2020 are one illustration of distinctions still being made to television's disadvantage. The positioning of *Small Axe* in this film/television discourse does have consequences, particularly for those working or seeking to work in British film and television. Olusoga introduced his interview with McQueen with the suggestion that *Small Axe* should mark 'a moment of transition ... in the story of British film and television. After this there are no viable excuses for marginalising Black stories and Black voices' (2020b: 26). I want to look at Olusoga's suggestion that *Small Axe* should open up a path that can be followed and to suggest that, in the light of the issues raised in the debate, it needs to be tested out a bit further.

Firstly, the *Sight and Sound* insistence that *Small Axe* should be considered as cinema confirms McQueen as a film auteur. *Mangrove* and *Lovers Rock* are used as further evidence of how cinema has continued to give McQueen the kind of spectacular status he had achieved in the visual arts. This is reinforced by his executive producer: 'He has a creative genius that most directors don't have, in my experience', Tracey Scoffield said in her interviews (Ganatra, 11). And he did it on his own terms. 'People say I'm fast. But I don't know that I'm fast,' he said, when discussing comments on how quickly he worked when filming. 'I've never been on anyone else's set' (Hunt). 'I don't do "no",' he told the audience at the National Film Theatre in an account which emphasised the importance of not compromising (NFT panel 2021). McQueen has spoken strikingly of the struggles he has faced as a Black artist and identified himself with Leroy Logan and the difficulties he faced when joining the police force ('the Establishment say "yes" but "no"' (NYFF 58)). Nevertheless, as a Turner Prize winner, an Oscar winner and as a successful filmmaker, able to make two films in the US during the long process of making *Small Axe*, McQueen is acknowledged as exceptional and positioned outside the history of British Black filmmaking.[5] He provides his own explanation and the context for his work is himself, his art, his earlier films, his status as an artist and an auteur. The use of him as an example sets a very high bar for others to follow.

Secondly, McQueen's exceptional position is reinforced by the effacement of the work of Black filmmakers before him. Speaking of *Small Axe*, McQueen tells Olusoga, 'For me, these films should have been made 35 years ago, 25 years ago, but they weren't and I suppose in my mad head, I wanted to make as many films as I could to fix that' (2020b: 26). In his identification of this great lack, there is no reference here or in other interviews to the work of Horace Ové with his film *Pressure* in 1975 and his Play for Today, *A Hole in Babylon* (1979), or to Menelik Shabazz's *Burning an Illusion* (1981) or his much later documentary, *The Story of Lovers Rock* (2011). In the 1980s, Channel 4 funding in part supported workshops such as Black Audio Film Collective and Sankofa but the subsequent careers of John Akomfrah and Isaac Julien in visual arts or the more mainstream work of Maureen Blackwood and Nadine Marsh-Edwards are not referenced. When actually asked about some of this history at the New York Film Festival, McQueen responds with uncharacteristic awkwardness; replying to a question from the audience about how *Small Axe* might be situated in relation to, for example, *Handsworth Songs* (1986) and Franco Rossi's *Babylon* (1980), McQueen mumbles that 'we looked at them', there are 'so few', 'we're happy for them to exist' (NYFF 58). I am not suggesting that any of this previous work influenced the development of *Small Axe* in any way. Nevertheless, given his emphasis on telling stories that had been suppressed or could not be told, it seems odd that, in all the publicity around *Small Axe*, McQueen did not take the opportunity to say something about the difficult history of Black work in film and on television which might have been informative for those seeking to follow on.[6]

Thirdly, the other omission from the promotion interviews in *Sight and Sound* and elsewhere is detailed discussion about the input of the BBC. McQueen does not bring this up in his interview with Olusoga, who himself does not ask questions about the BBC's support despite the fact that he argues that *Small Axe* 'stands as an indictment of the UK film and television industry and its failure to value Black stories and harness Black talent' (26). Nor is the question of how *Small Axe* came to be on the BBC's mainstream channel explored in the rest of *Sight and Sound*'s coverage; Corless resorts to exceptionalism again, saying that this 'is surely testament to the clout wielded by Steve McQueen' (53). But that doesn't tell us anything about what agreements were made or why the BBC thought it was worthwhile to make such a huge commitment over so many years to such a project. Certainly, *Small Axe* can be understood as a commitment arising from the BBC's status as a public service broadcaster. It was indeed referenced as such in September 2021 when the BBC Director General Tim Davie commented on the Conservative government's proposals that the BBC should promote 'distinctly British' content. He used *Small Axe* as an example of how the BBC was already working on this basis and commented that this kind of policy need not be associated with 'flag-waving or editorial control' (Waterson). But McQueen makes no comment about the merits or otherwise of PSB funding except indirectly when he appreciated the lack of commercials on *Small Axe* (Lincoln Film Center). Since he lives in Amsterdam and has made his career largely outside the UK, PSB may not be part of his filmmaking culture but he has now been a recipient of the BBC's funding and distribution systems. At a time when the BBC is under threat, McQueen's reticence about this crucial aspect of British screen production is striking, and if *Sight and Sound* is going to take on reviewing television seriously then an analysis of the BBC's contribution to *Small Axe* would have been informative for its readers and, in particular, would have helped other filmmakers learn from McQueen's experience (good or bad) of getting BBC support.

CURATING *SMALL AXE*

Nevertheless, there is something in the publicity around *Small Axe* which might be valuable for other filmmakers and might help shift the terms of the film/television debate in a fruitful way. In a number of the publicity events and interviews, it is possible to discern the collective work that went into the ten-year project that brought *Small Axe* into being. As executive producer, Tracey Scoffield speaks of McQueen with great admiration for his technical and creative skills: he is a director with 'the full skillset . . . he can do everything,' she says. But she also points out that McQueen wanted 'a collective way from the beginning' (Latymer), that he was good at letting others get on with doing jobs (NFT panel 2021) and evidences his ability to work with the huge number of people involved in the project: 'the cast and crew absolutely adored him . . . they will do whatever he asks' (Latymer). Olusoga's *Sight and Sound* interview pays attention to some of this in the discussion about the work done to get Black production staff into the crew. 'That was a job!' says McQueen, recounting how, when filming shifted to Wolverhampton, there was just one Black technician available: 'it was just because people don't feel welcome and it's just not good enough' (2020b: 35). Expanding on this in a number of interviews, Scoffield reports on the 'great effort to hire BAME cast and crew' (Ganatra, 11), on how heads of departments had to change the usual teams they called on (Latymer), on the difficulties caused by the length of the project ('The original West Indian people we'd wanted to be heads of departments were all busy, so we had to rethink it' (Clarke)) and on how they persuaded the BBC and Amazon to contribute to a trainee scheme so that a Black trainee could be working in every production department (Clarke).

BAFTA's fifteen nominations for *Small Axe* indicated the range of talents employed on the project over a long period of time. In praising the casting director Gary Davy, for instance, McQueen commented on how the length of the project affected his work: 'We were working with Gary for seven, maybe even eight years. I mean, we cast Letitia Wright . . . before she was in *Black Panther*, that's how far back it goes' (Ide). Scoffield recalls the dedication of costume designer Sinéad Kidao who worked on *Red, White and Blue* and 'collaborated with [Leroy] Logan to track down his original tailor from the 1970s so that he could help with the outfits' (Ganatra, 11). Going further back into the time of the project, McQueen and Scoffield describe the setting up of the Writers Room from which Courttia Newland and Alistair Siddons emerged as co-writers, with Alex Wheatle and Leroy Logan as advisors. Even before the Writers Room got going, a huge amount of early research went into the project. Scoffield found Helen Bart, an ex-BBC news journalist, who conducted 126 interviews over eighteen months from March 2014 which formed the basis of the early work in the Writers Room (Latymer). Bart was the first to interview

Logan, whose story is told in *Red, White and Blue*, and Scoffield says that it was only after Bart's research had been 'read, listened to and filtered' that it became clear 'that we were going to tell the true stories rather than creating fictional versions' (Ganatra, 10–11).

As more detail emerges on how *Small Axe* came to be made, it becomes possible to see how the film and television debate can be conceptualised in a different way. The stark choice that had to be made by those participating in the *Sight and Sound* poll can be reimagined as something more creative and fluid when its terms were being worked through in the making of *Small Axe*. As executive producer, Scoffield was a key figure in this and it is her commentary that offers information about working as an intermediary between television and film, between the BBC and 'a filmmaker, an artist' (NFT panel 2021). She felt that she had been approached by McQueen and the BBC to work on the project precisely because she had worked in both television production and feature film production and 'they are different' (Latymer); she had started with Channel 4 on Light Entertainment shows and spent ten years at the BBC first as a Script Editor, then as Head of Development and Executive Producer for BBC Films. She left the BBC to set up Rainmark Films and in 2018 was a founding director of Turbine Studios, the production company responsible for *Small Axe*.

Scoffield is adamant that McQueen is a filmmaker and that 'trying to get a director who is a filmmaker to do a standard television format was never going to happen' (Latymer). He was not used to working for television or making compromises: 'A lot of TV drama is made on very tight schedules,' she said. 'Steve is a film-maker obsessed with attention to detail and doesn't believe in making any compromises unless he has to – and then they'd be very creative ones' (Clarke). So, although they were working to a mini-series production schedule rather than that of a feature film, Scoffield put McQueen 'together with a group of people who were filmmakers in the form of Mike Elliott and Anita Overland', who were the two producers (RTS London Centre). From her own experiences in working on factual drama, she says that she shared McQueen's commitment to truth and accuracy; 'if you are telling a factual story, it should be as authentic as possible' (Ganatra). She was thus in a position to work with Bart on the research and McQueen felt that he could leave her to get the Writers Room going (NFT panel 2021) while he was away working on *12 Years a Slave* (2013) and *Widows* (2018). Scoffield thus seems to be positioned as an intermediary who can manage the film/television differences and is committed to getting McQueen's vision through the television processes and onto the screen (NFT panel 2021).

Understandably, sometimes the comments made by Scoffield and McQueen on the making of *Small Axe* reflect their very different roles and understandings. For instance, both recognise that the budget for *Small Axe* was nothing like the equivalent of five feature films. McQueen therefore told Aaron Hunt that 'This was made for a little bit of money. But one thing I know how to do as a British filmmaker is structure pound. We had to learn how to do that. It's incredible. When you find out the budget you won't fucking believe it.' Scoffield, on the other hand, continually asserts that the BBC contribution was 'a generous high-end BBC One contribution' (Ganatra, 11). Moreover, she stresses that the BBC was willing to go against standard television practice and provide financing before seeing the scripts, which Netflix and other streamers could not do (Latymer):

> Where we found it difficult was getting the funding for a concept, an idea, with Steve behind it but with no scripts. The BBC were prepared to develop it but Steve very much wanted to know that it would actually be made. We didn't want to be developing it for years and years and then not actually get it made.
>
> BBC Studios came on board to fully finance the production without scripts, which was exceptional and that's the nature of the BBC, to support an idea and to fund it, to make it happen. With them funding the project, we were able to go ahead. (Craig)

This was a particularly important commitment for McQueen, since in 2016 he had had a difficult experience working on a television project with HBO when a pilot, *Codes of Conduct*, had been cancelled before it was screened. Commenting on this experience, McQueen said 'he would not revisit that project. "I would never do it now . . . There's too much! . . . You need a situation where there's a little bit of curating going on"' (Travers). 'A little bit of curating' might describe Scoffield's role in the discussions that went on about financing; she worked to bring McQueen's need to have a firm commitment to making the programmes in line with BBC practices of funding.

We can find a similar interweaving of different approaches in the accounts of the creative practices in the making of *Small Axe*.[7] In terms of the differences between the films, Scoffield comments that these arise because McQueen is 'choosing what he believes to be the correct format for the story he wants to tell'. For instance, she describes how McQueen used different film stock because each episode has 'a different kind of painterly quality' (Latymer). Scoffield's accounts of these differences emphasise her aim of ensuring that they can be handled for television screening. She speaks of the cinematic aspirations of *Mangrove* with its letterbox-screen ratio filmed on 35 mm and of the referencing of 1970s television in *Education* which was shot on 16 mm film. This meant, as McQueen reported, that there were problems with the transmission of 16 mm, though he says that the 'BBC was very accommodating in the end' (Hunt). Scoffield gives more detail about this accommodation, explaining that there were extensive conversations with the BBC technical departments to make sure that *Education* could be delivered without buffering (RTS London Centre) and that the BBC agreed that it should not be transmitted in HD (Latymer).

In the case of *Lovers Rock*, the BBC itself almost seemed to be adopting the curating practices which McQueen had felt was needed. Scoffield recalls that the BBC, aware that this was going out on its mainstream family channel, was concerned not about the subject matter but that it 'had no obvious narrative' and 'not much dialogue'. This was resolved when a BBC Executive rang and formally advised her, speaking from what seemed to be a written statement, that *Lovers Rock* 'is a work of art by Steve McQueen and, as such BBC ONE will be proud to transmit it in its entirety' (Latymer).

The length of the different pieces was also the subject of intense discussion. Scoffield points out that they were neither a standard television length of an (approximate) hour for an episode nor a feature film length. This required 'uneven' scheduling which did not fit television's need to hit the 'rigorous junctions' when programmes stop and start at the hour. As an example of this, Scoffield describes the extensive discussions about the length of *Mangrove* at 2 hours 7 minutes. In the end, however, the head of BBC Content took it to the top, to the Director General, and as a result the BBC did what it almost never did and 'moved the news for *Mangrove*' (Latymer).

These detailed agreements which the BBC made with the *Small Axe* team might be explained through theories of convergence but these place more emphasis on audience choice, on 'how people want to see things' as McQueen had suggested to Alex Sepinwall, although actually most people had very little choice but to see *Small Axe* on television. On the other hand, these agreements, using Corless's rather aggressive metaphor, might be evidence of 'the clout wielded by Steve McQueen'. But it would seem to be more accurate to see the work of the executive producer here and to describe the process in a different way, as an interweaving of the different demands of cinema and television, pulling on one bit of material to stretch it out of its normal shape, reinforcing another bit to ensure that the texture can be felt. Taking up McQueen's notion of the need for 'a little curating', we might also take seriously, as Scoffield did in her work, his description of how the difficulties over *Education* were resolved: 'There was a conversation,' he said, 'but, of course, it's what the narrative wants. The narrative tells you what it wants to be, and 16 mm and the grade and everything else was very important' (Ide). In Scoffield's account, we can see how the BBC responded to the demands of the work itself – to the scope and scale of *Mangrove*, to the loose rhythms of the storytelling in *Lovers Rock*, the cramped, boxed-in framing of *Red, White and Blue*, the emotional punch of *Alex Wheatle*, the possibilities of the universe opening up in the gritty world of *Education* – and curated the *Small Axe* films for screening to mass audiences on broadcast television.

NOTES

With thanks to Charlotte Brunsdon, Ian Greaves and Roy Stafford, who discussed *Small Axe* with me. The conclusions and any mistakes are mine only.

1. The BBC supported the project from the beginning, as will be discussed later in this article. Amazon's commitment is less clear, though the *Los Angeles Times* reported that McQueen met Amazon's Studio Head Jennifer Salke in 2019 when 'filming was underway' (Yamato). Amazon then came on board to co-produce and distribute *Small Axe* in the USA and signed McQueen to a future deal.
2. See Greaves (2021), who notes that a previous attempt by *Sight and Sound* to cover television had been quickly dropped.
3. The others were Chloé Zhao, Sofia Coppola and Luca Guadagnino; each appears on one of four different covers.
4. Shabier, in his interview for the Kodak blog, discusses film stock and colour in some detail: 'The 500T 5219 and 7219 are probably my favorite film stocks.' He says that Poole 'did a fantastic job in not just enhancing the photochemical feeling in all of the films, but he has an incredible talent of making the beauty in black skin really shine' (Filmmaker Stories).
5. See the discussion about McQueen's position in a British context in R. Martin et al. 2021.
6. For further information about Black drama on television, see the information about the season 'Forgotten Black TV Drama' at the National Film Theatre in February 2019 (Forgotten Television Drama) and the article by Steve Rose (2019) about the season. In her analysis of the small number of BBC Plays for Today which have a non-white writer/director and/or deal with the experiences of Black and Asian communities, Eleni Liarou concludes that 'this rich tradition of TV single films and the developments in black British cinema in the 1980s and 1990s are important contexts' for *Small Axe*, 'which carries uncanny echoes of the plays explored here' (2022: 192).
7. I am not suggesting in what follows that Scoffield offers the definitive account of the production. I am exploring here the way she describes her understanding of what McQueen wants to do and how it can be achieved. The interview which Scoffield gave to Latymer Foundation is particularly interesting for the way in which she lays out the timetable for the project and the interaction of different elements.

CHAPTER 9

Small Axe and/as Cinematic Television

Hannah Andrews

Small Axe (BBC ONE, 2020) caused category confusion even before it was broadcast in December 2020.[1] It was presented using the rhetoric of cinema: individual dramas from the series were screened at the New York, Cannes and London film festivals; its BBC broadcast and simultaneous release on iPlayer were advertised as its 'premiere';[2] international partner Amazon Studios describe the episodes in their catalogue as 'a collection of five films'; and, perhaps most compellingly, during the promotion rounds for the series, director Steve McQueen repeatedly described it as 'cinema . . . films that happen to be on TV' (Winfield 2020).

There is a long history in the UK of 'films that happen to be on TV', from filmed television 'plays' of the 1960s and 1970s to the institutional bedrock for the UK film industry provided by television institutions such as BBC Films and Film4. The long-standing convergence between British cinema and TV has been met with efforts at rhetorical divergence, distinctions made between the media at the level of discourse (Andrews 2014). The positioning of *Small Axe* as cinema rather than television is a logical continuation of this decades-long process. However, the uncertain medial status of the series was exacerbated by the context of its distribution during 2020, the year that cinemas closed. Global Covid-19 lockdowns magnified the already tenuous distinctions between cinema and television in the age of streaming media, their boundaries now more visibly the result of discursive policing than ever before (Gray and Johnson 2021).

Small Axe was critically celebrated as McQueen's first foray into television. His prior career trajectory had been unusual for a British filmmaker for the absence of television work in its early stages.[3] This significantly supported the discursive framing of *Small Axe* as cinema: made by a filmmaker, these are, *de facto*, films. The application of this logic to the movement of other high-profile filmmakers, such as David Fincher, Martin Scorsese and Jane Campion, into television drama production, has been central to the development of a term that encapsulates the knotty relationship between these familial mediums: 'cinematic television'. The phrase has frustrated television scholars for almost two decades thanks to, among other things, its implicit cultural devaluation of television, its elitist use to 'legitimise' certain forms of television drama, and the essentialist assumptions about the medium specificity of cinema and television it entails (Mills 2013; Jaramillo 2013; Newman and Levine 2012). Nevertheless, outside of academe the notion of certain television programming as 'cinematic' retains a stubborn cultural currency, for example in the *Guardian*'s description of *Small Axe* as 'unapologetically cinematic' (O'Hagan 2020).

This chapter explores what it means for *Small Axe* to be conceptualised as 'cinematic television'.[4] It does so through attention to four elements that to cinema and television's intermedial relations. The first is the most disputed: the concept of 'cinematic' aesthetics, taken here to mean the medial features explicitly identified with cinema, but that can also be applied to other mediums to make them 'cinematic'. One way that some scholars have circumvented the inherent contradictions in aesthetic differentiation is to route discussions of the cinematic through affect theory, the second element examined here. Thirdly, the chapter examines *Small Axe*'s interpellation of a Black British audience, considering the politics of 'cinematic television's' address. The final feature is access, both in terms of McQueen's access to the means of production, and the public access to the films enabled by their broadcast on television (and availability on-demand). In reading the series through the lens of aesthetics, affect, address and access, the chapter assesses *Small Axe* as a case study of 'cinematic television' at a moment of crisis for medium specificity.

AESTHETICS

Speculating on *Small Axe*, then a project in development, in 2017, Clive James Nwonka suggested 'it will be interesting to see . . . if television drama, as it continues to become more cinematic itself, can become a more permissible space for McQueen's art film aesthetics' (Martin et al. 2021: 90). The implied equivalence here between the 'cinematic', contemporary television drama and 'art film aesthetics' is a familiar formulation in the re-evaluation of television style that has taken place in the twenty-first century, epitomised by debates around 'Quality Television'. Space does not permit a rehearsal of these often fraught discussions, though it is important to note that the emergence in the early 2000s of a wave of high-end (mostly) American drama series targeted at elite audiences and usually produced for premium cable channels like HBO prompted a new wave of intellectual interest in the aesthetics and criticism of television (McCabe and Akass 2008). This was typified by Jason Jacobs and Steven Peacock's valuable 2013 collection *Television Aesthetics and Style*, which features two chapters (by Brett Mills and Deborah Jaramillo) that provide a systematic unravelling of the concept of 'cinematic television' on technological, industrial and evaluative grounds. More recently, Rashna Wadia Richards has argued that 'aesthetic differentiation between overlapping media is ineffective from an analytical point of view' (2021: 26). She echoes the reservations of multiple scholars who have found the phrase frustrating in its vagueness and lack of 'conceptual rigour' (Restivo 2019: 5). Perhaps the most forceful of the aesthetic critiques of cinematic television comes from Jaramillo:

> The use of the term 'cinematic' to describe sophistication and beauty on television demands a critical examination for at least three reasons. First, it perpetuates an audio-visual media hierarchy that is hopelessly antiquated. Second, it does not advance our understanding of where the look and sound of television are going in any meaningful way. Finally, it implicitly argues that film has a clearly understood essence that can compensate for television's lack thereof. (2013: 67)

Her second and third arguments reflect the intrinsic dilemma of medium specificity theory and criticism in the age of media convergence, summarised in D. N. Rodowick's contention that, in the context of digitalisation, 'film's ontological anchors have come ungrounded', compelling us continually to question 'what is cinema?' (2007: 93).

The implication here is that pre-digital cinema's aesthetic status was a settled matter. A century's worth of squabbling over the essence of cinema suggests otherwise. Sergei Eisenstein's emphasis on montage, André Bazin's faith in photographic ontological realism or Christian Metz's framework of structuralist film language are just three of many contradictory examples in 'a genealogy of conflicting debates that sought the identity of film in medium-specific concepts or techniques' (Rodowick 2007b: 11). Media convergence has highlighted the extent to which materialist approaches to medium specificity tend to confuse 'cinema' with 'film'. By contrast, structuralist approaches, such as Metz's (1974), distinguish between the 'materially' and the 'systemically' cinematic, understanding the latter to be a plurality of codes that create a medium-specific signifying system. Beyond this, cinema has been defined in relation to modes of exhibition, such as in John Belton's claim that 'the cinema is the projection on a screen of life-size – or bigger than life-size – images before an audience; everything else is movies' (2014: 470). This seems to negate both the use of cinema space for the projection of non-cinematic materials (for example, live theatre or sporting events) *and* the intermedial co-option of cinema indicated by the term 'cinematic'. Whether cinema's identity is defined materially, semiotically or experientially, medium specificity approaches complicate the idea of the 'cinematic' when applied beyond film's medial boundaries.

Medium specific theorisations of cinema's materiality have been the most contended in recent years, thanks to the convergence between cinema and other media produced using digital methods (Mills 2013). The *Small Axe* films were made using different film materials: *Mangrove* and *Red, White and Blue* use 35 mm film, *Education* uses 16 mm film and *Lovers Rock* and *Alex Wheatle* were produced digitally. It is therefore not possible to make consistent aesthetic claims about the series' materiality, 'cinematic' or otherwise. Producer Tracey Scoffield notes that the choices of material were driven partly by budgetary restrictions.[5] *Lovers Rock*, for example, was restricted in location by a tight filming schedule that also drove the choice of digital production techniques, a filming challenge that is typical for television drama as well as low-budget cinema. She also notes that creative choices by McQueen and his director of photography, Shabier Kirchner, influenced the specific film materials selected, since film stocks have different 'painterly' qualities to them. The dramas are also made using varying aspect ratios, which affected the appearance of the series when presented on television. For instance, *Mangrove*'s 2.35:1 ratio requires a 'letterboxing' technique, the conventional presentation mechanism for television broadcasts of wide-screen feature films. This parallel may encourage a reading of the film as 'cinematic' at the level of aesthetic spectacle.[6] Scoffield attributes this creative choice to the needs of the story told, because the number of principal characters requires an image of scale. By contrast, *Education* is a more intimate, familial drama, presented in 16 mm cinematography and a 4:3 ratio that mimics the aesthetics of television films from the 1970s, the period in which it was set. Scoffield suggests that the film was 'their version of a Play for Today', the BBC's strand for single drama in the 1970s. In reproducing the style of a Play for Today, *Education* could be read as deliberately adopting televisual rather than cinematic aesthetics. However, this would be to ignore the extent to which filmed Plays for Today (as opposed to those produced using video-based studio techniques) were conceptualised in cinematic terms (Andrews 2014). An examination of the *Small Axe* films in terms of their material 'cinematic' quality therefore leads to inconclusive results.

Prior to *Small Axe*, McQueen's position on medium specificity has, like Belton, aligned cinema with the theatrical experience. He told journalist Mike Ryan 'there's no point in looking at a movie on your own at home', arguing that cinema is a communal experience, and its 'thrill' is located in the shared experience between viewers in the same space (Ryan 2018). Read by journalists as an implicit criticism of the intervention of streaming services like Netflix in the film industry (Sharf 2018), this objection to individualised cinematic experiences could similarly apply to television, though the question of 'communal' viewing experience is complicated by the broadcast mechanism. McQueen's critique of small screen viewing extends beyond the experiential dimension, and his statements on the medial status of *Small Axe* have made clear aesthetic contrasts between cinema and television at the level of production. He told *Sight and Sound*: '[for *Small Axe*], I did a television mix and a cinema mix, and the cinema mix informed the TV mix, which is a smaller and less sophisticated situation' (Aftab 2021). It is not uncommon for television aesthetics to be evaluated as unsophisticated by comparison with cinema, but it is noteworthy that McQueen's distinction relates here to sound. Sound is under-represented in discussions of cinematic television aesthetics, which tend to focus on the mediums' shared imagistic qualities and television's adoption of cinematic visual language. Sound has also historically been posited as a significant arena of distinction between film and television, for example, in John Ellis's influential argument that 'sound tends to anchor meaning on TV, where the image tends to anchor it with cinema' (1990: 129). In her analysis of his 2002 installation *Western Deep*, Tina Rigby Hanssen applies the concept of 'haptic audibility' to McQueen's art film work. She notes McQueen's prescriptiveness about how his work should be installed, focusing on how his manipulation of space 'brings sound closer' to allow listeners to 'become intensely involved with (and even physically touched by) the textures of sonic physicality' (2011: 137). If authorial control over the space of encounter between viewer/listener and screen is meaningful to McQueen, it is unsurprising that he views television sound as an inferior, 'less sophisticated situation'.

The example from *Small Axe* given by McQueen to illustrate the centrality of sound to the aesthetic experience of the films as cinema is the dance-floor sequences from *Lovers Rock* (Aftab 2021). He reports imagining audiences 'smashing up the cinema' during the scene in which Kunta Kinte Dub is played, a vision of audience identification that centres aesthetic appreciation in the body of the spectator. This mirrors the sequence's focus on embodiment. Long takes using a mobile camera create, according to Michael Gillespie, a 'sustained embeddedness in this spatiotemporality of the dance floor'. This in turn produces '"sonic bodies," people immersed in sound to such an extent that their embodiment of the music operates as a sounding of experience and desire' (2021: 48–9). In the sequence, the song's pulsating bassline creates an energy matched in increasingly frenzied movements by the dancers. The camera mingles with the bodies on-screen, its movements replicating the relentless rhythms of music and dancers, constructing a body of its own. Sound – the music combined with the whoops, whistles and shouts of the crowd – surrounds the viewer, supporting the 'embeddedness' Gillespie identifies. Individual vocalisations eventually converge into chanting 'Mercury Sound, this a Mercury Sound', and the song fades out, its beat replaced by the stamping of feet. The replacement of electronically produced music with the choral voice elevates the scene to one of spiritual sociality. This is intensified by the performances in the scene, the medium close-ups of swaying bodies, of enraptured, closed-eyed faces, of arms raised in solidarity. Rebecca Wanzo (2021) calls this a 'carnal cinema', one which emphasises the pleasures of Black embodiment via the construction of 'embodied' images and sounds. Sound is thus employed in *Lovers Rock* (and, as Wanzo points out, elsewhere in *Small Axe)* to enhance identification between a viewer's body and the 'cinematic' body of the camera.

Cinematic television has been most often understood as consisting of texts that appropriate the stylistic strategies associated with (certain kinds of) cinema. The location of cinema's essence in the medium's material or semiotic qualities is challenged by the existence of television that can adopt cinematic style. Experiential, site-specific definitions of cinema are logically incompatible with the intermedial expression 'cinematic television'. McQueen's alignment of the cinematic with embodied, experiential elements of the medium's aesthetics therefore complicates *Small Axe*'s status as cinematic television. His attention to 'haptic audibility' and the production of 'sonic bodies' is compromised by the assumed viewing environment of television. Small-screen viewing is positioned as a second-class engagement with the cinema, one that cannot match the emotional intensity of theatrical viewing. This alignment of cinema with shared emotional space can also be found in what Eugenie Brinkema (2014) terms the 'turn to affect' in film scholarship. Affect-led definitions of the cinematic may then provide an alternative route to understanding *Small Axe* as cinematic television.

AFFECT

Affect theory has frequently been applied to television, a medium Kristyn Gorton (2009) argues is particularly attuned to the capture and transmission of emotion. It has also been a central component in recent explorations of 'cinematic television'. Angelo Restivo's intervention in the debate, which focuses on the popular series *Breaking Bad* (2008–13), defines the cinematic as an 'interruptor within the regime of images', one that 'has the potential to introduce gaps, uncertainties and contradictions in the narrative of which they are a part' (2019: 7). His 'cinematic' stems from that of mise-en-scène criticism; he specifically accords to mise-en-scène the role of presenting the '*intensive* relations, the virtual "spaces in between"', alongside and against narrative's provision of *extensive* relations (34). Restivo claims that 'affect, which in the moving image is produced through formal aesthetic relations within and among images, has the potential to become that *interruptor* of narrative I have already claimed as the province of the cinematic' (11). Restivo's suffusion of the 'cinematic' with latency, immanence and intensity clearly aligns with affect, theorised as the 'connective thread between bodies and worlds, the immanent potential of matter that confirms one's Being-in-the-World' (Palmer 2020: 247).

There are many moments throughout *Small Axe* that can be interpreted as disrupting the momentum of narrative to produce uncertainties and to exploit immanent energies. An example appears in *Education*, in a short sequence in which Kingsley (Kenyah Sandy), who has just discovered he will be transferred to a new school for the 'educationally subnormal', takes a bath to quell his frustrated anger. (See Figure 9.1.) Filmed in a high-angle medium close-up of his upper torso and face, Kingsley is pictured with eyes closed, his thoughts troubled but inscrutable. The soundtrack combines sound effects of dripping water with Kingsley's heavy, anxious breathing. Non-diegetic electronic music, previously used in the film's opening sequence set at a planetarium, is introduced part way through the sequence. This recalls Kingsley's unbridled joy in the earlier scene, providing an implicit contrast with his despair in this one. The eerie quality of the music also contributes to this sequence's sense of unease, positioning both viewer and Kingsley out of place and time. Here, as elsewhere, the 4:3 aspect ratio creates a sense of claustrophobic enclosure to the image, the sensation of being captured in a situation from which there is no escape. Mise-en-scène and sound combine to generate an image that has limited narrative momentum but intense affective drive. The image of Kingsley suspended in the bath, neither awake nor asleep, neither quite still nor mobile, neither in nor out of place, suggests the indeterminacy Restivo associates with the cinematic.

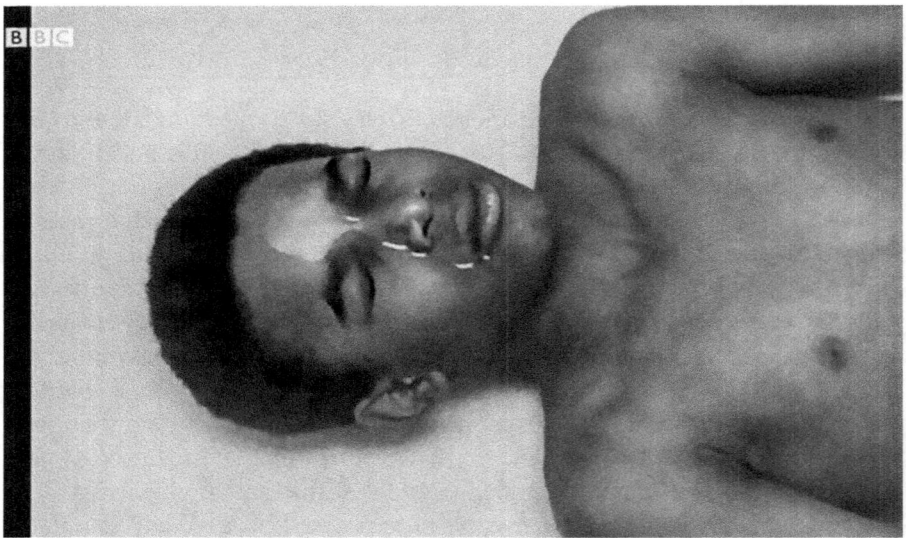

Figure 9.1. Kingsley (Kenyah Sandy) bathes, a moment of affective intensity in *Education*. (BBC ONE)

Like Restivo, Steven Shaviro centres affect in his definition of the cinematic, describing films as 'affective maps, which do not just passively trace or represent, but actively construct and perform, the social relations, flows and feelings that they are ostensibly "about"' (2010: 6). Brinkema (2014) argues that cinematic affect can be read as and for form, breaking away from the anti-formalist tradition in affect-led cinematic criticism. We can see manifestations of these 'affective maps' in the formal compositions used throughout *Small Axe*. For example, in *Red, White and Blue* a brief sequence depicts protagonist Leroy Logan's (John Boyega) final interview for the police force. Leroy is framed from behind in long shot as a small, dark figure in the foreground, against an imposing institutional backdrop dominated by large portraits on the wall, emphasised by the unusual bilateral symmetry of the image. (See Figure 9.2.) The panel of white faces opposite which Leroy sits includes those of the portraits, an image that maps the continuity between the nineteenth-century (patriarchal, colonialist, hegemonic) origins of the force and its contemporary legacy. By contrast, Leroy is denuded of individuality and autonomy in a mise-en-scène that conceals his face and magnifies his isolation. The semiotic excess of this image is affective in form, inasmuch as it both reflects and produces the intensity of this situation. The next shot presents a backlit profile of Leroy that creates a silhouette (see Figure 9.3), a framing that is reiterated several times and in different contexts throughout *Red, White and Blue*. This composition reflects the dichotomous position of Leroy as exceptional individual and anonymous avatar of his community within the racist police force. There is a narrative function here, as Leroy's character positionality between two incompatible worlds is the central conflict of the drama. But these images also map the uneven power dynamics of *Red, White and Blue*'s represented social world. These affective forms do not just represent Leroy's personal circumstances, but indicate a broader set of social relations, one that is legible not through direct signification, but, in Restivo's words, 'coaxed from the world' by the mise-en-scène (2019: 37).

In her critique of affect-led film criticism, Brinkema highlights the marked presence of the theorists' subjectivity, such that 'films *produce* something in the audience, or, sometimes, in the theorist, or, sometimes, in the theorist all alone' (2014: 31). She goes on to argue that 'affect is taken as being, in the end, *for us*'. This has the effect of conflating the personal experience of the theorist with the assumed 'us'. This generalises their subjectivity in a way that is logically inconsistent with affect as constitutive of intersubjective relations. This collapse of personal and universal is especially problematic when recent critiques of affect theory from the perspective of Blackness are taken into account. Colin Patrick Ashley and Michelle Billies argue that the consequence of affect theory's attempts to 'transcend' race has been a 'tendency of being race-avoidant [that] often reproduces and is productive of a universalizing "race-making"' (2020: 8). Tyrone Palmer calls out the 'unmarked whiteness' of affect theory, arguing that 'despite

Figure 9.2. Leroy (John Boyega) a small figure in the foreground as he is scrutinised by an interview panel. (BBC ONE)

Figure 9.3. Leroy (John Boyega) as a silhouette, robbed of individuality and agency in his placement between two incompatible worlds. (BBC ONE)

its pretenses toward universality, affect as force is tethered to the logics of raciality that create and sustain the World' (2020: 271). Elsewhere, he posits the logical impossibility of Black affect, given the position of Black not only as 'other' but as a theoretical negation of normative humanity in the 'onto-epistemological framework that structures civil society and the modern field of representation'

(2017: 32). Concepts of cinematic television that draw on affect theory derive from and work within philosophical traditions that poorly account for the historical meaning and position of Blackness. This radically compromises the applicability of affect-driven definitions of 'cinematic television' to *Small Axe*, or any other artwork that renders Black experience in audio-visual form.

For Restivo, the cinematic's affective drive is not an aesthetic end in itself but serves a distinct social and cultural purpose. The intensive force of cinematic mise-en-scène can 'interrupt the homeostasis of common sense' (2019: 39), forcing in the viewer a reckoning with the immanent and the indeterminate. Restivo modifies Walter Benjamin's argument about how cinema 'broke apart our habitual views of the world' (2019: 55), reprogramming the human sensorium to fit the conditions of life under capitalist modernity, suggesting that cinematic television can perform a similar function in the context of neoliberal political economic regimes. The 'our' in this statement is a similarly problematic, universalising gesture to the 'us' in affect theory critiqued by Brinkema. Restivo later argues that '[*Breaking Bad*] will thus assert the power of the cinematic to illuminate American life in the twenty-first century' (2019: 96). This assertion aligns the 'cinematic' specifically with American visual culture, seemingly precluding the possibility of a 'cinematic' that emerges from or resides elsewhere. If Restivo's 'cinematic television' is indeed a nationally specific one, then *Small Axe*'s determined address to Black British people renders the series incompatible with it.

Definitions of the 'cinematic' and 'cinematic television' that derive from affect theory provide answers to some of the logical inconsistencies in formalist aesthetic approaches. They rely not on the material, semiotic or experiential specificity of cinema to identify what is 'cinematic' and thus enable its application to intermedial contexts. The cinematic is defined by Restivo, following other affect-driven interpretations, as the disruption of surface meaning by immanence and indeterminacy to be found at the level of mise-en-scène. The *Small Axe* films regularly present sequences that possess these qualities, and therefore can be viewed as cinematic television on these terms. However, the theoretical incompatibility of Blackness with affect theory, and the national specificity of the series in relation to Black British experience, create a conflict between this version of 'cinematic television' and *Small Axe*. In both cases, impediments to affect-led interpretations of 'cinematic television' are less to do with the formal properties of the texts than they are with the identities of the filmmakers, the persons depicted and the interpellated audience. This requires us to consider the matter of address.

ADDRESS

Address is often overlooked in discussions of cinematic television, aside from an elitist, industry-driven presumption that these series target well-educated, high-income, high-status viewers in possession of superior levels of cultural capital to the undifferentiated 'mass' audience for 'regular' TV. Janet McCabe and Kim Akass (2008) argue that, in the case of HBO, the channel proposed that its address to a highbrow, niche audience licensed it to take the creative risks that are aligned with quality, and by extension with the 'cinematic'. There is a feedback loop of address: audiences are constructed through taste-centred channel branding as having the intellectual sophistication to desire challenging, high-quality content; therefore programme makers present themselves as possessing creative latitude to produce complex, beautiful television; and thus the texts are promoted and received as culturally superior. The implications of this kind of triangulation in terms of class, gender and racial politics have not gone unnoticed (Newman and Levine 2012). Cinematic television is produced and framed within these contentious cultural and industrial mechanisms of address.

In a radically different context, Clive James Nwonka and Anamik Saha (2021) posit an analogous 'triangulation of ownership' in relation to the circulation of Black British cinema, defined in relation not only to contexts and practices of production, distribution and exhibition, but also to critical and audience reception, each part bound by the prefix 'black'. For Nwonka and Saha, the 'Black' in Black British film permits it to exist as a 'unifying cinema of resistance' (2021: 5). Much as 'cinematic television' is putatively addressed to an audience for 'challenging' material, this is film addressed to an audience resistant to orthodox or mainstream audio-visual culture.[7] Nwonka and Saha foreground the complexity of relations between addresser and addressee, arguing that

> conceptualising black British film as a triangulation of ownership allows one to consider the tensions around black cinematic traditions and how institutions attempt to inorganically construct black images and stories, forgetting that they originate from an extremely rich and powerful visual and narrational tradition that constantly strives to alter the public orthodoxy. (2021:7)

In this analysis, the power to define Black British cinema does not rest in the hands of crude mechanisms of classification that serve industrial purposes of 'inclusion' and 'diversity', but in the hands of filmmakers and the audiences their work addresses. In this vein, McQueen highlighted the importance of *Small Axe*'s address to Black audiences:

> it was Black people seeing other Black people, feeling what they were feeling, and a Black director, a Black cinematographer, and the fact they could see each other and vibe off each other – and be each other, as you rightly said – that's what happened (Olusoga 2020).

Providing this level of visibility is a means for film (or television) to counterbalance the cultural marginalisation of Blackness. Nwonka and Saha suggest an investigation of Black film's efficacy in this political project depends not only on an examination of 'what black film is perceived and imagines itself to be' (2021: 6) but also a reappraisal of cinema as a concept and its relations with race, ethnicity, culture, politics and technology. One part of the reappraisal might include the spread of the 'cinematic' beyond the boundaries of cinema.

Small Axe has enjoyed a critical reception that offers a (qualified) celebration of its address to Black audiences (Naidoo 2021; Gillespie 2021; Wanzo 2021; Williams 2021), particularly its steeping in a heritage that is most meaningful to those with a strong familiarity with Black British culture. In relation to the cameo-like appearances of important figures from Black British culture throughout the series, Roshi Naidoo argues that '*Small Axe* rewarded the gaze trained to scan the background' (2021: 13). Naidoo's gaze is one that highlights the fleeting, ambivalent pleasure of recognition for Black audiences when their identity is confined to the margins of representation.[8] The mise-en-scène of *Small Axe* is awash with details of set design and composition that refer to cultural and social nuances of Black British life, from posters and record sleeves, to the surreal image of the cross-bearing traveller in *Lovers Rock* (Williams 2021: 57), to the large graffitied 'Powell for PM' that Frank Crichlow (Shaun Parkes) walks past at the beginning of *Mangrove*. Throughout *Small Axe* there is a repeated switching between foreground and background, usually achieved using a focus pull technique that manipulates the viewer's attention within the same shot. This aesthetic strategy is used most often to emphasise the harassment of the Black community by the police: examples can be found in *Red, White and Blue*, where the approach of a police car towards Kenneth Logan's (Steve Toussaint) van can be blurrily perceived in the background of a shot in which he occupies the foreground; in *Alex Wheatle*, where Alex's (Sheyi Cole) friend Breadstick (Khali Best) is approached and roughly detained by the police, framed from Alex's perspective down an alley; or in *Mangrove*, where the camera adopts the perspective of Frank, a passenger in a moving car from which he can see the bullying community police officer PC Pulley (Sam Spruell) harassing Benson (Shem Hamilton). These represent a reversal of the 'racist white gaze that patrols the series' (Williams 2021: 60); the gaze is not only trained to scan the background for traces of recognition but also for signals of risk. The repeated focus-switching not only provides a representation of Black community hounded by surveillance, but also rewards these specific viewing competences. This is an address to an alert, scrutinising audience.

Sarita Malik (2021) marks a distinction between Black 'film' and 'cinema', the latter identified with the practices of curation, programming, distribution and exhibition associated with the theatrical release. Malik's film/cinema distinction is a political one, in that 'cinema' can 'occupy the space of the more highbrow sounding, spectator-oriented industrial dimension of film' (Malik 2021: 24). She offers the example of titling the original *Black Film, British Cinema* book as a rhetorical device that claims space for Black representation within a culturally legitimated 'scopic regime', the kind that I have argued is also occupied by 'cinematic television'.[9] *Small Axe* may then be read in relation to a multiplied address: as Black film, and as British cinematic television. From one perspective, this can be seen as a positive reclamation of Black creativity, storytelling and representation within an increasingly visible and valued cultural form. This is undermined, however, by the dubious discourses of distinction employed in the process of legitimation, ones which depend on devaluing tastes that are implicitly raced, classed and gendered. It also ignores the 'television' side of cinematic television, especially the medium's democratising reach, its ability to offer broad, open access to important cultural touchstones.

ACCESS

While much of the discussion of cinematic television has centred on certain kinds of television programming adopting the aesthetics, affect and address of cinema, relatively little consideration is paid to what television has to offer cinema. Yet television has acted as a space of access for cinema throughout the intertwined histories of the mediums (Andrews 2014). Access can be conceptualised in two ways here, both of which are relevant to *Small Axe*. First, access can be conceived of as the access of filmmakers to the means of making cinematic material, via the developmental support of television institutions (see Geraghty in this volume). It is this kind of access that Malik speaks of when she describes the orientation in the 1990s of much Black British film towards public service broadcasters like Channel 4 and the BBC, such that 'national television broadcast was becoming a primary vehicle for Black film rather than the theatrical distribution to qualify as British cinema' (2021: 29). The expression 'vehicle' relates to the second sense of 'access': the use of the television medium to enable audiences access to materials they may not have otherwise been able to encounter. An access-led understanding of cinematic television may conceive of *Small Axe* as cinema *through* television, at the levels of production and reception.

In *Small Axe*, there is no clear separation between the two kinds of access described above. As Naidoo argues, *Small Axe* represents 'personal and communal agonies that need to be metabolised'. She goes on to argue that 'creative expression can help this process, which is why access to the means of *being* creative is so vital' (Naidoo 2021: 20). She speaks to the sense of responsibility endowed to the filmmakers who occupy positions in culture that enable this kind of representation and address. Kobena Mercer (1994) famously described this as the 'burden of representation' for Black artists, the assumption that their art speaks of, for or to their community. McQueen raised this in an interview with David Olusoga, when he affirmed 'give it to me, I want the burden' (2020). Whether the means of access to create moving-image art from Black perspectives is conceived as empowerment or burden, it nevertheless counteracts under-representation with visibility and audibility.

Television broadcast (and the affordances of streaming video on demand) magnifies this visibility, providing expanded access to cinema with limited barriers to entry. McQueen repeatedly emphasised the importance of this to *Small Axe*, stating one of his primary motivations for making the series as being that 'I wanted my mother to see these stories on TV' (Directors UK 2021). Elaborating on this point, he argued:

> From the start, I knew the stories I was telling about the British-West Indian experience had to be accessible to a wider audience, a mainstream audience. It's being broadcast on the BBC specifically so that everyone can have that access to it and see it for free. (O'Hagan 2020)

Applying Malik's (2021) and Nwonka and Saha's (2021) arguments about the politics of 'mainstreaming' for programmes for Black audiences might lead to a sense of suspicion about this aim for broadened access. As Saha (2017) argues, the machinery of television, especially the construction of audiences through television scheduling, has tended to marginalise programming by and for minorities, with only a select few that tend towards a consensual 'bourgeois Eurocentric worldview' broadcast in favoured time slots. The outcome is that 'scheduling effectively decides where the programmes of black and Asian filmmakers feature in the national conversation' (Saha 2017: 65). In the case of *Small Axe*, though, it was precisely the scheduling of the series during a peak time slot on the flagship channel of the national public service broadcaster which rendered it a noteworthy cultural event. Indeed, Scoffield pointed out how the varying length of the films in the series caused significant issues for schedulers.[10] She noted that the BBC showed willingness even to move the broadcast of the evening news to enable *Mangrove* to be shown in its entirety. Such a move is virtually unprecedented in contemporary scheduling strategy and can be understood as a statement of the BBC's commitment to *Small Axe* as a significant cultural milestone.

Further evidence of the televisual framing of *Small Axe* as culturally important can be found in the specially commissioned ident, created by McQueen and broadcast before the programmes. This consisted of brief images of the flags of West Indian nations, dissolving into one another, with reggae music as backing to the continuity announcements. Idents and interstitials, as John Ellis points out, are televisual mechanisms of framing, 'little instruction manuals on how to read TV' (2011: 60). This ident was therefore signalling a specificity of address for *Small Axe*. A socially – and televisually – marginalised audience are the primary addressees of *Small Axe* in a way that is rare for British television. The affective drive of the series then is not only to be found in the text itself, but paratextually in its scheduling, presentation and promotion. As Naidoo argues, emotions come into play when 'things hitherto considered niche, or belonging to one's private political, social or cultural world, are on view on Sunday night on BBC1' (2021: 13). While the imagery, composition and construction of affect in the *Small Axe* films may be 'cinematic', their political significance, according to this view, is profoundly televisual.

CONCLUSION

Television scholars have tended to resist 'cinematic television' as a textual descriptor because of both the aesthetic inconsistencies and elitist undertones of the term that have been highlighted here. However, at an industrial and broader cultural level, it is an expression that carries meaning and value, and therefore it is worth engaging with it, unravelling its potential applications and their cultural and aesthetic consequences. That is what this chapter has done by assessing the utility of applying the aesthetic, affective, address-led and access-driven definitions of 'cinematic television' to *Small Axe*, taking into consideration some of the specific complexities associated with its status as Black British moving-image text. Definitions of cinematic television driven by aesthetics have been found to have a number of logical contradictions, such that they do not offer a satisfying account for how television programming can be meaningfully 'cinematic'. Adopting definitions of the 'cinematic' based on affect theory offer an alternative route, especially attending to the abstract but commonly found idea of a 'cinematic feel'. This is complicated in relation to *Small Axe* and other Black cinematic television by the poor alignment between Black subjectivity and affect theory. The address of cinematic television to a cultural (elite) niche parallels, but is not equivalent to, the construction of audiences for Black cinema as resistant audiences. This may seem incompatible with the broad reach of television, a medium that constitutively provides open access to its content. *Small Axe*'s accessibility was manifested in a schedule pattern that centred it in the national cultural imaginary during (and after) its broadcast. While the series' 'cinematic' credentials can be – and have been – contested on aesthetic or affective grounds, it is its status as television that enabled *Small Axe*'s political, social and cultural significance.

NOTES

1. See also Christine Geraghty's chapter in this collection.
2. Individual episodes from the series also appear in the 'Film' catalogue of the iPlayer, an indicator of rhetorical divergence from other television content (Andrews 2014).

3. Ashley Clark rightly calls him 'incredibly atypical' in the context of the British film industry (Martin et al. 2021: 82).
4. The term 'cinematic television' is typically applied to serial dramas, though much of the discussion centres on aesthetic or stylistic matters rather than narrative. This chapter does not have space to analyse the narrative structuration of *Small Axe*, though it is worth noting that the arrangement of their stories into discrete feature-length dramas supports the claims that they are individual 'films'.
5. Scoffield was talking to the Latymer Foundation in an online event held in May 2021. A recording is available here: https://www.youtube.com/watch?v=4lZ9hBt4JLI&t=770s. Many thanks to Christine Geraghty for pointing me to this source.
6. Indeed, this reading was offered by Scoffield's conversation partner in the Latymer Foundation event, Charles Wijeratna.
7. This is not to suggest that either a) these are two entirely discrete audiences and that there is no overlap between them; or b) these audience constructions can be compared at the level of politics: an aesthetic taste for 'quality drama' is not equivalent to a desire for texts that aim to unsettle racial hegemonies.
8. McQueen also spoke of the thrill of recognition when Black people were encountered on television: 'I remember back in the day when a black person used to appear on television, you used to ring people, "There's a black person on TV," the whole family, people would be ringing you, "Oh, my god, did you see that?"' (Directors UK 2021).
9. Malik here borrows Metz's (1974) phrase. She speaks to Metz's argument that there are systemic distinctions between 'film' as material and content and 'cinema' as signifying system.
10. Scoffield at the Latymer Foundation event.

CHAPTER 10

Love in a Cold Climate: *Lovers Rock*

Thomas Austin

Lovers Rock, probably the most celebrated title in Steve McQueen's *Small Axe* pentalogy, has been characterised by Nadine Deller as 'a study in Black joy' (2020: 69).[1] She states: 'In this lovely film, Steve McQueen proudly declares that Black love rocks' (2020: 70). In this chapter I ask: what are the terms through which we can make sense of Black love as screened by McQueen? What are the political and aesthetic dimensions of its figuration in *Lovers Rock*?

In her book *Black Sexual Politics*, the American sociologist Patricia Hill Collins critiques 'the manipulation of sexuality and love by systems of power', and argues that 'oppression works by not only forcing people to submit [. . .] but also [. . .] by rendering its victims unlovable'. She elaborates:

> Once objectified in their own eyes and in those of their supporters, people police one another and all become more easily exploited and controlled. [. . .] In this context, resistance consists of loving the unlovable and affirming their humanity. Loving Black people (as distinguished from dating and/or having sex with Black people) in a society that is so dependent on hating Blackness constitutes a highly rebellious act. (2004: 250)

While Collins' work centres on the situation of African Americans, her insights are pertinent to McQueen's account of Black British experience in London in the early 1980s. *Lovers Rock* is an exception to the androcentric narratives that dominate McQueen's oeuvre.[2] Its heroine Martha (played by Amarah-Jae St. Aubyn) is confronted by a landscape of gendered expectations, risks and pleasures when she sneaks out from her parents' house to go to a blues party with her friend Patty (Shaniqua Okwok). McQueen moves to validate several dimensions of Black love: love between Black women and men, a love of reggae music, and a love of the West Indian diasporic community expressed through generations and genders coming together.³ In the process, *Lovers Rock* explores what Sachi Sekimoto and Christopher Brown call 'The sense of belonging to a community [which] speaks to an intersensorial and intercorporeal connectivity, producing bodies that feel responsively and harmoniously with each other' (2022: 23). To unpack this further, I focus on two scenes in particular: the 'Silly Games' dance sequence during the house party, and Martha's early morning bike ride with Franklyn (Michael Ward) after the party.

The binary logic of gender as it functions in a heterosexual culture is evident throughout the film, and this is reproduced more often than it is interrogated. The everyday, normative constitution of 'men' and 'women', and their positioning within social space, is channelled via the narrative vectors of desire and threat, but is first registered by shots of preparations for the house party, which install a gendered division of labour. Men move furniture out of the party room and set up the sound system. Some women are busy preparing food in the kitchen, and younger women are upstairs doing their hair and make-up. Those in the kitchen spontaneously start to sing 'Silly Games', Janet Kay's 1979 hit, which later provides the centrepiece of the party. In this context, the song's chorus suggests a female impatience with male failings: 'But I've got no time to live this lie. No, I've got no time to play your silly games.' Although brief, this moment also signals a celebration of female solidarity and mutual support, which also finds a parallel later in the film.⁴

A gendered polarity is reiterated when Martha and Patty enter the top deck of a bus on their way to the party. In this semi-public setting, the two women quietly move to sit near the front, while a group of young Black men hoot and call out to them from the back. Quotidian rituals of performance, display and mutual appraisal are intensified in the dance-floor scenes, which function largely according to a heterosexual logic. How do these scenes intersect with constructions of race, and in particular what Sianne Ngai (2005: 95) has called 'the notion of race as a truth located, quite naturally, in the always obvious, highly visible [Black] body'?

BLACK BODIES AND THE APPARATUS

In her work on the conversion to sound cinema in America, Alice Maurice has noted how transitional films 'emphasiz[ed] the hyper-presence of black bodies in order to deflect attention *away* from the apparatus and us[ed] those same bodies and their "inherent" talents to show off the prowess of the apparatus' (2013: 167, emphasis in original, cited in Raengo 2016: 194). A similar duality is evident in *Lovers Rock*'s dance sequences. Here audio-visuality offers the pleasures of a sonic and haptic immersion in the sounds, movement, heat and emotion of the party. One scene shows a succession of male hands gently reaching for female hands and elbows as the slow song 'Lonely Girl' by Barry Biggs plays. The hub of the party sequence is 'Silly Games', the song sung by the women preparing food in the kitchen. The DJ, Samson (Kadeem Ramsay), introduces the song on the mic by calling out 'Hold your ladies near. Fellas, just be fair and square.' In this way he appeals to male dancers and stresses male agency, but also implicitly echoes the song's injunction to treat women decently. Narratively, the tune brings together Cynthia and Bammy, slow-dancing for the first time, although the camera spends more time with Martha and Franklyn, who are held in an intimate framing and whose smooch almost feels like slow-motion.[5] As 'Silly Games' fades out, the dancers sing it all over again in unison, a capella for more than four minutes, their feet shuffling on the wooden floor.[6] The impact of the music, in conjunction with the tactility of Black bodies in close and rhythmic motion, of vivid synthetic fabrics (dresses and shirts in crimson, peach, pistachio, wine, navy and gold, shiny pink), and of condensation dripping down the walls, urges viewers to reach past the frame and engage corporeally with the scene.

McQueen has reiterated this elision of the filmmaking process in an interview with David Olusoga (2020: 32–5, emphasis in original):

> For me, it was about ritual. [. . .] To take you on that journey where it gets to the point where it transcends, even beyond the people in the room. It becomes church. Some people say the Holy Spirit or whatever, but you know, it did happen. [. . .] I became *invited* into that situation. It was an honour to be there. [. . .] It was a spiritual experience. It wasn't performative. Something happened in that room, and we happened to have a camera there to record it.

But Maurice's 'prowess of the apparatus' is also foregrounded in the evident deployment of multiple technical devices and inputs to embellish and relay the movements of the dancers. These include: intimate composition and tight framing, lighting, costume design and use of colours, and slow-motion. McQueen partially acknowledges this, and the significance, and difficulty, of shooting Black stories with Black actors and Black crew members, when he continues in the same interview: 'It was Black people seeing other Black people, feeling what they were feeling, and a Black director, a Black cinematographer [Shabier Kirchner], and the fact that they could see each other and vibe off each other [. . .] that's what happened.' In *Lovers Rock*, unlike the films that Maurice considers, Black bodies are recruited to tell a Black-centred, Black-authored and Black-filmed drama.

This audio-visual presentation of embodied Black joy and love stands in contrast to McQueen's prior spectacularisation of Black pain and suffering, most notably in *12 Years a Slave* (2013). In its preference for scenes of egregious brutality inscribed on suffering Black bodies, that film occludes the systemic dimensions of slavery as an economic and social regime and falls short in relation to Rabz Lansiquot's question: 'How do we deal with the realities of anti-Black violence through the audiovisual, without pandering to the desire for spectacle?' (2021: 95).[7]

MUSIC AND GENDER

To return to *Lovers Rock*, I now want to consider gender in a little more detail. Discursive constructions of gender function as a complex intertextual network, circulating as assumptions, tropes and contestations of 'masculinity' and 'femininity'. It is from this constellation of overt and covert codifications of gender, of more or less sanctioned models of behaviour, bodily comportment, dress, speech, etc., that repertoires of gender are lived out. The process is shaped by structural power and agentic choice, both conscious and unconscious, and is evident across everyday life and artistic practice, including film.[8] (Of course, such constructions also intersect in diverse ways with logics of race, class and sexuality, which carry their own norms and expectations.) So how exactly can we trace discourses of gender around the music that *Lovers Rock* mobilises so effectively in the party scenes?

Eighteen minutes into the film, Martha is talking to Franklyn on a sofa temporarily installed in the back garden:

Franklyn: So, you a Rude Girl or a Soul Head?
Martha: I listen Louisa Mark, Junior English, Gregory [Isaacs], Janet Kay.
Franklyn: Oh, see, see, Lovers, eh? [he drinks] Can I beg you a dance?

Lovers' rock, the musical genre which Martha listens to, and from which the film takes its name, flourished in the late 1970s and early 1980s. However, as Lisa Amanda Palmer (2011: 178) has noted:

> within scholarly, critical and historical reflections on reggae cultures, lovers' rock's fleeting if not invisible presence is often obscured by the predominance of the genre's more raucous reggae relatives, namely 'conscious' roots reggae and ragga 'slackness'. On the occasions when lovers' rock has been inscribed into the historical and cultural narrative of the reggae music scene in Britain, its romantic and erotic expressions are frequently seen as apolitical and antithetical to the 'conscious' political impulses of 'roots reggae'.

Significantly, this 'binary positioning of lovers' rock's soulful melodies against the hardcore political "toasting" and "chat" of "conscious roots"' is a gendered one. Thus, 'Lovers' rock is gendered as strictly black female territory, whereas the oppositional politics of conscious reggae is primarily assigned to the interests and concerns of black men' (2011:178). The latter is exemplified in *Lovers Rock* by several minutes of highly energetic male dancing and calling out to repeated plays of The Revolutionaries' 'Kunte Kinte Dub'.[9] During this sequence the women exit the dance floor, and Martha and Franklyn quietly leave the party.

Nevertheless, as Palmer argues, the genre of lovers' rock can disrupt and confound the binary division of (female) romantic reggae and (male) political reggae.[10] Dennis Bovell, the writer and producer of 'Silly Games', belatedly acknowledged this when he told the *Los Angeles Times* that by working with McQueen he had discovered a new perspective on the significance of the tune: 'The song became a kind of spiritual and a kind of protest: the authorities playing silly games with the people. I thought, Steve, how did you see that? I never saw that song as a protest' (Lynskey 2021).[11]

Small Axe, and especially *Lovers Rock*, met with almost unanimous praise in the mainstream (largely white) media in the UK. The series was also welcomed by many Black British commentators.[12] But ambivalence and elements of disappointment were also evident among some Black viewers and reviewers. For instance, on *The Conversation* website, Palmer (2020) wrote:

> The film is attentive to some of the various elements needed to hold a blues party in your 'yard'. The huge pots of rice and peas and curry goat. The removal of the carpet and furniture from your living room, as if you were moving house. The wiring up of the epic speaker boxes to balance the treble and the heavy baselines [sic] of the sound system. The eagerness to show off the latest style and fashion as you step into the party in shiny sateen dresses or your Gabicci shirt. [. . .] These details are important because it's very rare for them to be given such attention on British TV screens.
>
> However, because such representations are so rare, this attention to detail is also the film's weakness. The 'dub' scene, where we see a young Rastafari bredrin falling to the ground in a frenzied spiritual trance, missed the significance of dub as a deeply educational form of communication.[13]

Palmer also critiqued the film's extended deployment of Janet Kay's 'Silly Games' in the sequence discussed above:

> Sound system culture is about the selector's ability to 'rinse tune', meaning a sound system's credibility rests on demonstrating the unique depth and range of their music back catalogue. This means that no one song would have been playing for as long as 11 minutes.

For those who may be new to the sound system scene, these details may not matter at all. But for the folks who do remember, they mark the line between flashes of genuine insight and moments of contrived nostalgia.

Of course, neither *Lovers Rock* nor any of the other *Small Axe* episodes are documentaries, and they should not be evaluated against a notion of historical accuracy, despite the painstaking assembly of period details in their mise-en-scène. But Palmer's critique provides a pertinent reminder of the significant investments in, and demands made of, the series by Black audiences, particularly those of West Indian heritage.[14] At times like this, the burden of representation that McQueen has gladly shouldered can prove a heavy one (McQueen in Olusoga 2020: 29).

The blues party is clearly figured as a temporary respite from the everyday racism which Black people face beyond its walls. (This is personified by the four white youths who make monkey noises when they see Martha on the street, looking for her friend Patty.[15]) However, the threat of violence does erupt within this gathering, and it takes the form not of racist hatred, but of a sexual assault by a Black man on a Black woman. An argument develops when Martha's cousin Clifton complains that she missed his mother's funeral. He then mentions the domestic abuse that she and her mother have endured from her father: 'How long your daddy beat up you and your mama half to death before the two of you pick up and leave?' Moments later Martha finds Bammy, whose advances she has rejected twice already, forcing himself on Cynthia at the end of the garden. She interrupts Bammy by throwing a lighted cigarette at him, and tells Cynthia: 'Come stand by me, sis. Come sis.' She then warns Bammy off with a shard of glass held at his throat, and Cynthia runs back into the house. This assertion of female strength and solidarity, here against male violence, enlarges that adumbrated earlier in the kitchen scene, and also asks to be read as signifying Martha's intention to stand up to her father in the future.

Roshi Naidoo has celebrated *Small Axe* as an important opening up of 'creative spaces of candour' for Black people in Britain. Moving beyond the well-meaning but timid and ultimately limiting dead-end of positive representation, '*Lovers Rock* therefore could, for example, show Martha stopping a sexual assault in the garden, and could honestly depict the routine harassment of girls at the party and their confident ways of dealing with it' (2021: 20). The film thus critiques the gendered violence inherent in heterosexual culture, even while its narrative celebrates the formation of a heterosexual couple, that of Martha and Franklyn.

JUST ABOVE THEIR HEADS

Ten minutes from the end of *Lovers Rock*, Martha and Franklyn ride on his bicycle away from the blues party in the quiet of the early morning, laughing and sharing a cigarette. This brief but significant sequence confirms Martha's joy, trust and safety in the company of the right man (not Bammy, the inappropriate and ultimately violent suitor). The composition places the couple at the bottom of screen left, only visible from the chest up. While Martha and Franklyn remain in focus throughout the 37-second duration of the shot, the trees in the background take up most of the image. Through the sustained use of a mobile camera moving in front of them, the bicycle they are riding is kept out of shot, below the bottom of the screen. The effect of this is to lift the lovers slightly away from the earth, as if they are floating down the street. Their love has rendered the ride temporarily frictionless. (See Figure 10.1.)

In the final seconds of the scene, Franklyn calls out 'whoo-ee' and Martha, seated in front of him, laughs and spreads her arms as if flying. The image may fleetingly recall two other lovers, Jack (Leonardo DiCaprio) and Rose (Kate Winslet) on the deck of the *Titanic* in James Cameron's 1997 blockbuster. But more significantly, the scene offers a moment of self-citation by reworking a device that is central to McQueen's early short *Just Above My Head* (1996), and which he has also used, with variations, in *Hunger* (2008) and another *Small Axe* title, *Red, White and Blue* (2020).

Just Above My Head is a 16 mm film of nearly 10 minutes' duration that comprises a single mobile shot of McQueen walking while holding the camera. As T. J. Demos (2005: 69) notes, 'The location is undefined, for the camera, held by the artist, is positioned at belly level and is directed at the artist's head

Figure 10.1. Martha and Franklyn in *Lovers Rock*. (BBC ONE)

Figure 10.2. Steve McQueen, *Just Above My Head*, 1996 (still). 16 mm black-and-white film, transferred to video, no sound, 9 minutes 35 seconds, continuous projection. © Steve McQueen. Courtesy the artist, Thomas Dane Gallery and Marian Goodman Gallery.

and the sky above it for the film's duration.'[16] (See Figure 10.2.) In this short, the handheld camera has a limited mobility that is both comparable to, and also distinct from, the smooth tracking shot in the *Lovers Rock* bicycle ride. By contrast, in McQueen's two other deployments of comparable low-angle framing, the camera remains static. Other important differences also attend the three distinct iterations of this framing device.[17]

In his work on intertextuality in fiction film, Mikhail Iampolski argues that quotation within any film 'exposes its textuality'. This 'theatrical' rupturing of textual homogeneity operates as a further emphasis of the materiality of the filmic sign, in addition to that immanent in the framing of every image (Iampolski 1998: 29, 28, 257). But intertextuality also creates an accretion of new meanings, a '"piling" of one thing onto another' that Iampolski compares to the multiple significations of a hieroglyphic: 'Intertextuality too superimposes text on text, meaning upon meaning' (27, 28). Drawing on Iampolski, we can say that if a citation is recognised as such it will have three distinct but imbricating sets of impacts. It will rupture the narrative, such that it no longer appears as self-contained; it will provide an echo of another text that exists beyond the present one; and it will add some further depth to the present text, dependent upon the particularities of this echo. How might these processes take place in relation to the bicycle ride composition in *Lovers Rock*?

Much of McQueen's gallery work prior to his move into feature film was concerned with exploring the capabilities and limits of the recording apparatus, often in video format or 16 mm films transferred to video. These highly self-reflexive texts also constitute an inquiry into the tension between contingency and authorial control as played out in attempts to capture the profilmic event. At times McQueen cedes control to the autofocus, but in situations which are designed to push beyond the technology's capacity, as it struggles to cope with low light (in *Illuminer* (2002)) or attempts to find a point to focus on (when the video camera itself is thrown back and forth between McQueen and his sister, in *Catch* (1997)). Demos writes: 'if for McQueen video production becomes physicalized, so that the result indexes the body that creates it, its representation is also marked by what cannot be shown' (2005: 67). Delinda Collier (2014: 137) makes a similar point in relation to *Just Above My Head*:

> In *Illuminer*, the camera points toward McQueen lounging on the bed in a dark hotel room while he watches French television news coverage of the war in Iraq. In *Just Above My Head*, the camera points up from his waist and jerks around with the motion of McQueen's stride, his head bouncing in and out of the bottom of the frame. In both, the camera works independently of McQueen to attempt to focus its lens on his body. Both artworks dramatize the frustration and pleasure of autofocus that is conditioned by each camera's particular affordances.

However, in *Hunger*, McQueen's debut feature film, the contingent has been more or less eradicated.[18] The low-angle framing of *Just Above My Head*, which called attention to the limitations of the device but also to the jolts and movements of McQueen's body, has been replaced by a static camera and careful composition and blocking that enlarges and reasserts his authorial control over the profilmic event. Thomas Mulcaire's comments on McQueen's restaging in *Deadpan* (1997) of the celebrated falling-house stunt from Buster Keaton's *Steamboat Bill, Jr* (1928) are pertinent here:

> The difficulty for McQueen is that by framing or staging everything, the world that is represented is banished of all contingency – nothing can be other than it is. The scene is totally determined by its director. What began perhaps as a strategy of revelation passes into a strategy of control, in which nothing in the scene can depart by so much as an inch from its script. [. . .] This is the solipsism of narrative. What looks like the recording of an accident is no accident at all, it is a very calculated move. (Mulcaire 1998: 12)

So it is to narrative that we must turn to make sense of some of the impacts of the low-angle and tightly framed sequences in *Hunger*, *Red, White and Blue* and *Lovers Rock*. But these titles are emphatically not solipsistic, due to their critical engagement with social and political conditions in Britain in the 1980s. In each, the images' specificity of setting generates particular meanings. Indeed, Darby English has argued the same in a highly perceptive reading of *Just Above My Head*: its vague but significant rural location 'mitigates the abstractive tendencies structured into the work and privileged by McQueen's best commentators' (English 2013: 38).[19] However, unlike the original, *Hunger*, *Red, White and Blue* and *Lovers Rock* also mobilise self-citation as a further assertion of McQueen's authorial presence, reaching beyond the particularities of the diegesis to become a kind of stylistic signature.

The setting of *Hunger* is roughly coeval with that of *Lovers Rock*, but the film is strikingly austere, both formally and thematically. It centres on the 'dirty protest' by IRA prisoners at the Maze Prison in Northern Ireland, and the hunger strike of their leader, Bobby Sands (played by Michael Fassbender).[20] Just over 40 minutes into the film, following the noise and fury of uniformed officers' attacks on naked prisoners, the image cuts to prison officer Raymond Lohan (Stuart Graham) sitting silently in his Ford Granada. He is about to visit his mother in a nursing home. This brief mid-shot is followed by a 36-second static low-angle shot of a cloudy sky, which starts before Lohan opens the car door at the bottom of screen left, and continues as he climbs out of the car and reaches back inside to pick up a bunch of flowers for his mother. Much like McQueen's body in *Just Above My Head*, most of Lohan's body remains off-screen. At times only the top of his head is visible, at other moments he is framed from the chest up. A little more than a minute later he will be dead, shot in the head with a handgun, in what appears to be a revenge attack by a member of the IRA.

The use of the static low-angle shot as Lohan exits the car is more jarring than the framing in *Lovers Rock*. This off-kilter view of Lohan both isolates him and foregrounds the narrating agency that delivers this perspective. As a break from the conventional framing and continuity editing that is dominant in much of *Hunger*, this sequence stands out from the flow of images, and subtly puts the audience slightly on edge prior to the diegetic shock of the next scene, that of Lohan's murder.[21]

A very similar view askew is used in *Red, White and Blue*, which tells the true story of Leroy Logan, the son of Jamaican immigrants who left a career as a medical research scientist to join the Metropolitan Police in 1981. Logan has to cope with relentless racism from fellow officers, ostracisation by some members of the local Black community, and the vehement disapproval of his father, himself the victim of a brutal attack by white police officers. McQueen has said:

> I'm still struggling, to be honest with you [to understand Logan's choice] . . . he had so much going against him, being in the police force, the racism in the police force, as well as his father, who was attacked and beaten. [. . .] [Logan was] up against so much [. . .] the effort, mental, physical, emotional, is gigantic. [. . .] it's a titanic effort that he made to keep on going in that situation. (McQueen 2020)

Nine minutes in, a static low angle of a cloudy sky is held for 26 seconds as Logan's father Kenneth (Steven Toussaint) climbs down from the cab of his lorry and shuts the door. The framing is very similar to that used in *Just Above My Head* and *Hunger*, with Kenneth moving in and out of the bottom of the frame. In his pale brown work coat he walks across the road to buy a bag of chips from a mobile snack bar. Moments later a police Rover pulls up in front of his parked lorry. The significance of this is marked by a focus pull from Kenneth in the foreground of the shot to the Rover in the background.[22] When Kenneth returns to the lorry a white officer tells him he is parked illegally and has incurred a £50 fine. He protests, but is beaten by two officers who punch him, and kick him after he falls to the ground. Much like *Hunger*, the low-angle shot of the sky has been a preface to an outburst of violence. Any viewer familiar with *Hunger* would thus be receptive to a mechanism of anxiety and suspense here, generated by the echo of Lohan's murder.

Unlike the pale grey cloud in the comparable sequences in *Hunger* and *Red, White and Blue*, the background of the *Lovers Rock* shot is dominated by the green and orange of trees in what appears to be late summer or early autumn. And in contrast to the off-kilter framing in those two scenes, *Lovers Rock*'s mobile composition keeps Martha and Franklyn in harmony with their surroundings (the quiet morning street, with the verdant trees rising just above their heads) rather than alienating the couple from them. Nevertheless, in significant ways they remain constrained, tethered to a social and economic situation from which the blues party and the bike ride have offered only a temporary suspension.

The lovers are brought down to earth in the subsequent scene at the garage where Franklyn works as a mechanic, and to which he has taken Martha. 'My palace this, man,' he tells her. After he has put on some music and poured a drink, the pair embrace and start to kiss passionately. But they are interrupted when his young white boss Eddie (Frankie Fox) opens the door and turns on the striplights. Franklyn is immediately repositioned as an employee who has overstepped the mark. Eddie pokes him in the chest and tells him: 'Frank, this ain't a knockin' shop. You do not bring your Doris in here. All right? Good boy.' He then reminds Franklyn of an unfinished job that is due by tomorrow. The persistence of raced and classed structures of power force Martha and Franklyn to endure this moment of 'uncomfortable visibility' in the racialising gaze of a white man (Naidoo 2021: 17). Under Eddie's scrutiny, Franklyn's speech slips, as Deller (2020: 70) notes, 'from his usual musical [. . .] patois into a cockneyfied accent to appease his white boss'.[3] His code-switching and 'speaking white-while-black' (Sekimoto and Brown 2022: 101) is a response to his social subordination. In this white-owned space, Franklyn can only ever occupy the role of a non-white worker in service to another's enterprise. Far from being his 'palace', it remains the site of his labour, as Eddie makes clear.

While the garage remains resistant to Franklyn's attempts to remake it as a space of romance, the blues party instantiates a more successful refashioning of a quotidian setting into a space of Black joy and love. This is evidently only a bounded respite from the racism that persists beyond its walls, and it is still shaped by gendered pressures and violence within. But its provisional and insecure status magnifies its preciousness. And, like Martha and Franklyn, who agree to meet again, it too can be reconvened. In this way both the party and the romantic couple initiated there provide instances of 'joy disrupted and joy that disrupts' (Wanzo 2021: 55).

In bringing hitherto neglected stories of Black Britain to peak-time mainstream television, the *Small Axe* pentalogy has also showcased Black creative talent in acting, filmmaking and music. *Lovers Rock* in particular presents the strength and joy of a Black community and culture, a joy that is threatened by, but also works to actively disrupt and refuse, the everyday and systemic pressures of white majoritarian judgement, from implicit norms and expectations to overt racism. The lasting achievement of *Lovers Rock* is its dialectical celebration of the warmth of Black love in this cold climate.

NOTES

1. *Lovers Rock* was voted best film of 2020 in the annual *Sight and Sound* poll. *Sight and Sound*, 31:1 (2020–1).
2. For a critique of this tendency, see Patricia Francis's chapter in this collection.
3. Towards the end of the party, having escaped an attempted sexual assault by Bammy (Daniel Francis-Swaby), Cynthia (Ellis George) shares a kiss with her housemate Grace (Saffron Coomber). This gesture is not developed any further, and the scene remains ambiguous.
4. Thanks to Charlotte Adcock for pointing this out to me.
5. McQueen does deploy slow-motion for the next number, The Investigators' 'Turn out the Light'.
6. While most of the voices heard are female, the clearest male voice is that of seminal British reggae musician and producer Dennis Bovell, who wrote and produced 'Silly Games', and who plays Milton in the film. McQueen comments: 'Dennis Bovell is our Lee "Scratch" Perry, our George Clinton. [. . .] He had to be in the centre of the dance' (*Sight and Sound* 2020–1: 99).
7. See also Philip Kaisary's 2017 critique of *12 Years a Slave*, reprinted in this book as chapter six.

8. In his analysis of dance, Bryant Henderson (2019:1) argues that 'an individual's embodied performance of gender – one's corporeal presentation, performance, and lived understanding of their gender identity – can be recognized as an intertextual construct'.
9. See Kwame Phillips's analysis of this scene in chapter eleven.
10. Palmer (2011: 182) notes: 'By overlooking the cultural interdependence of political and erotic discourses that emerge within lovers' rock, critical interpretations of reggae dancehall cultures obscure the significance of complex discourses by black women that affirm the intersection of erotic and political identities.'
11. It is also worth noting, however, that in an interview with David Olusoga McQueen proposes a binary opposition between socially engaged art and 'love songs' as an exemplar of unengaged art. 'You get a lot of white people saying, "Oh Steve, the burden of this."' It's like, "The burden of what?" We have to talk about this. What would I do otherwise? Write love songs?' (McQueen in Olusoga 2020: 29).
12. In December 2020, *Sight and Sound* magazine devoted twelve pages to *Small Axe*, including positive reviews and comments by the following Black writers: David Olusoga, Kehinde Andrews, Gary Younge, Candice Carty-Williams, Kit de Waal and Jay Bernard.
13. For further discussion of this scene, see chapter eleven. See also the comments posted in response to a negative review of *Lovers Rock* on Youtube: https://www.youtube.com/watch?v=mXkY792xPaY.
14. The Black activist Leila Hassan Howe has suggested that McQueen 'used the eyes of today' in the party scene. She also noted the 'ahistorical' depiction of women such as Barbara Beese and Althea Jones-Lecointe in the *Mangrove* episode (Austin 2021).
15. As Malcom James (2019: 35) notes: 'With unofficial race bars operating on the doors of many clubs, sound systems were some of the only sites black young people had to congregate around. As focal points of black and working-class culture, these leisure sites were contingently seen as a threat to law and order; associated with a dangerous and culturally corrosive black culture.' On the devaluation of Black music as antisocial 'noise', see Stoever 2016. The three-part television documentary *Uprising* (2021), one of McQueen's spinoffs from *Small Axe*, paints a detailed picture of racist violence and police harassment of Black Londoners from the late 1970s to the urban uprisings of 1981.
16. Noting 'two fleeting views of trees (one of which closes the film)', Darby English (2013: 33, 39, 33) suggests that the work might be viewed as 'a kind of deconstructed pastoral' which 'withholds the view rather than divulging it'. He uses this reading to counter a well-established critical narrative of McQueen's early film and video installations that attempts to 'win McQueen's project for modernism: by seeing that all interpretive roads lead away from imagery and toward McQueen's "larger" criticisms of the film medium [and] its conventions'.
17. Of course, whether or not a viewer notices any of these citations depends upon their particular history and viewing repertoire.
18. Contingency may resurface in the performance of actors, but the extent to which this is subject to, or surpasses, McQueen's directorial control is beyond the scope of this chapter.
19. English is referring to the work of T. J. Demos and Okwui Enwezor in particular. He also suggests that *Just Above My Head* 'establishes McQueen in a notable isolation from accepted ways of using art to do "identity politics" [. . .] McQueen's primary activity is precisely not to exist for us as an image, marginal or otherwise, but to turn the camera away from whatever view he is taking in – so as to keep it for himself' (2013: 40).
20. See a more sustained analysis of *Hunger* by Eugene McNamee in Chapter three.
21. In *Hunger*, McQueen also breaks with convention through the use of some very long takes, particularly in the conversation between Sands and a Catholic priest (Rory Mullen), which runs without a cut for 18 minutes.

22. For further discussion of the uses of focus pull in *Small Axe*, see chapter nine by Hannah Andrews.
23. Courttia Newland, the co-writer of *Lovers Rock*, has pointed out that the film draws on a range of accents and speech forms from across the West Indian diaspora, including those originating in Trinidad and St Lucia, in addition to Barbados and Jamaica. Newland was talking at the Royal Television Society, 2021.

CHAPTER 11

A Different Kind of Dread: Dub, Ecstasy and Collective Memory in *Lovers Rock*

Kwame Phillips

WINDRUSH DUB

They came in their light-weight suits and straw hats and felt sombreros, teeth chattering, shivering in the draughty, freezing, alien, impersonal, busy atmosphere of the railway stations – Waterloo, Victoria, Charing Cross, or anywhere else they were dumped, together with their cardboard boxes, battered suitcases, and string-tied baskets. London had seen nothing like it before and Londoners were taken aback. A certain annoyance showed on the faces of the cockney porters, waitresses, cabbies, and policemen at this sudden onslaught on their quiet preserve. London's newspaper reporters, columnists, feature writers, and photographers had a field day or, to be more accurate, many field days at Waterloo station and London airport, covering the arrival of fresh contingents of West Indians. Their papers spread front, centre and back pages with an array of pictures, heavily spiced and peppery stories. The banner headlines described West Indians 'whose calypso flamboyance could not be chilled even by the frosty air of an English winter.' Actually, those gay West Indians were cold, hungry, miserable, and frightened. (Scobie 1972: 196–7).

For the approximately 300,000 Caribbean migrants that had made their way to the United Kingdom up until the early 1960s, Barbadian poet and novelist George Lamming describes England as coming to mean 'opportunity, horizons, success'. But Lamming also states that the colour of the West Indian's skin not only acted as 'a cage which betrays the bird within it', but also as 'a cage which was to keep [them] imprisoned in a social and economic strait jacket, denying [them] equal rights with the host population' (Hinds 1966: 152).

Despite the relationship of Britain to the former colonies, the reality of 'Mother England' was that English society was largely closed to migrants, and assimilation was deemed undesirable. Welcomes quickly became warnings that white, Christian culture was being polluted by 'dark, alien forces' and then became wailings by xenophobic nationalists that there was 'no black in the Union Jack' (Rex and Tomlinson in Palmer 1990: xvii). The result for West Indian people in Britain was a sense of both anomie and alienation, where they lived 'in a world of social acts taken for reality which [were] not of [their] own making', a problem that persisted into the immediate later generations (Littlewood and Lipsedge 1997: 238). In *Black Britain*, Chris Mullard (1973: 13–14) writes:

> A black man born in Britain is a shadow of a man. A form but no identity, because you are black. You are not a West Indian, Indian, Pakistani or African, because you were born in Britain and you know little or nothing about your parents' country. Even if you wished to, you cannot pretend you are a black immigrant, because embedded in your being is the knowledge that you are not . . . in the end you have no alternative but to remain alone, insecure, without an identity of your own making. Is it possible to be black and English? Does it necessarily follow that because a man is born and educated in a particular country that he should rightfully assume the identity of the nationals of that country?

Older generations had grown up in a colonised homeland, raised in the belief that as a colony they were essentially British, but after arriving on British soil, they faced racially motivated anger and resentment and unequal access to the benefits of citizenship. Figures such as Mullard argue that the situation was not any different for the legitimately British children of migrants, as they were still considered essentially alien and non-British. What emerged was either a rejection of Britishness completely or the complex adoption and co-opting of multiple national loyalties, a diasporic fluidity, especially for the offspring of these migrants. And while Eric Williams (1962: 279), Trinidad & Tobago's first Prime Minister, would say 'there can be no Mother India . . . no Mother Africa . . . no Mother England . . . A nation, like an individual, can only have one Mother. The only Mother we recognize is Mother Trinidad & Tobago', it might be argued that the Caribbean individual in the diaspora, though looking to belong and be accepted, had no one 'Mother' or no 'Mother' at all.

BLUES DUB

> Sometimes I feel like a motherless child,
> Sometimes I feel like a motherless child,

> Sometimes I feel like a motherless child,
> A long way from home, a long way from home
> (Traditional Negro spiritual, no date)

These motherless children of the so-called Windrush Generation are the subject of Steve McQueen's *Small Axe* anthology series, and the second story, *Lovers Rock*, specifically explores the ways in which this community sought to create an identity of their own making. The film depicts a 1980s all-night house party (often called 'blues parties') in West London, where Caribbean food, drink, music, dancing, languages and behaviours make visible their complex identity formation. Nadine Deller's review in *Sight and Sound* cites the film as 'a study in Black joy, [that] submerges the audience in an alcohol- and weed-fuelled, sweat-soaked snapshot, against the backdrop of Thatcher's London, of a Black Britain where love, music and dance reign' (Deller 2020). The films of *Small Axe*, and *Lovers Rock* in particular, are anchored by the songs that served as a soundtrack for an era of resistance, resilience and coming of age. As Ivie Ani (2020: 4) states, music has served as a backdrop to movements – from the Civil Rights era to the current Black Lives Matter period – operating as soundscapes of 'the soul and the spirit of periods and places defined and defied by Black people [that] help translate what is often left unspoken'. Redmond (2013: 8) further argues that 'these sonic productions were not ancillary, background noise – they were absolutely central to the unfolding politics because they held within them the doctrines and beliefs of the people'.

The harmonies and heavy basslines heard at the house parties depicted in *Lovers Rock* became a soundtrack for the West Indian diaspora communities who carved out their own social and cultural practices on the margins of British society (Lowndes 2020). Alex Wheatle, subject of one of the other films in the anthology, speaks specifically to this role of music for identity, especially so for second-generation Black British people. Wheatle recalls:

> Those of us who were born in the UK adopted Jamaican style. I've got Jamaican parents, but I do not speak like them. Everyone wanted to dress like a Jamaican and everyone wanted to speak like a Jamaican. We all tried to imitate that because we saw ourselves as more Jamaican than British. We felt that the British did not accept us. My parents' generation, when they came over in the late '40s and '50s, were not accepted. They were not allowed into the clubs in central London, so they had parties. (Ani 2020: 4)

Known as 'blues parties', these house parties were late-night sound system dances held in a private residence, where Caribbean people sought 'spiritual "refuge" in the blues against a backdrop of discrimination and riots in the 1950s', transforming domestic spaces in 'rebellious ways' (Henry and Worley: 190). Ani (2020: 4) argues that for this Black British community, blues parties were 'an escape into a world within a world – a world of their own'. As depicted in *Lovers Rock*, the audience is immersed within this world within a world. As Deller (2020) describes it, 'the camera follows bodies moving across the dancefloor, men and women holding each other close, hips swaying to the rhythm of reggae, [creating] a sense of blissful communion'. She argues that this kind of filmmaking is characteristic of McQueen's work, where 'the intimacy with which the camera lingers on a couple's embrace, the energetic writhing of men dancing, or the minutiae of silent communication through dance and body language is reminiscent of certain sequences in *Shame* (2011) and *12 Years a Slave* (2013)', though in this film focusing not on trauma. Rather, 'McQueen gazes on in wonder, and marvels at the ordinary, everyday Black experience.' But I would argue that the depiction of ordinary, everyday Black experience is a depiction of trauma, or at least the consequences of trauma for a marginalised population in the UK. This I find in one scene in particular, the 'Kunta Kinte Dub' scene near the end of the film, a scene that shows how dub music, with its deconstructed form, has a role in articulating and giving testimony to what Gilroy refers to as '*unspeakable* (historical) terrors' (Veal 2013: 205, emphasis in original). In this way, the film puts itself in conversation with films like John Akomfrah's *Handsworth Songs* (1986), which uses filmic language to reveal an otherwise incommunicable 'malaise at the heart of British society, one that was rooted in the inner contradictions of its imperial past' (Eshun and Sagar 2007: 22).

The dub scene in *Lovers Rock* begins in an extreme close-up, as the DJ slowly lowers the needle onto the vinyl record. The inimitable whistle and melody of The Revolutionaries' 'Kunta Kinte Dub' begins to play. A montage of the hands of the partygoers begins to beat the kitsch wallpapered walls of the room in excitement. As the bassline starts to play, the group of men start to dance feverishly, skanking, jumping, bodies contorting in rhythm. There is a freedom to their movement, a harmony of excitement and exhilaration, a fraternity of motion that builds to a collective imploration to start the song again. The rewind. 'If the timing is right, a rewind will bring excitement to the dancefloor, a celebration of the music being played, an energy charge for the place and the people' (Fintoni 2015). The wheel up. The needle hurtles across the vinyl's grooves as the DJ's hand frantically spins the record back. Music writer Laurent Fintoni (2015) describes the rewind as 'the most democratic musical practice of modern times', allowing the audience to have a conversation with the performer and ensuring the discourse of music does not flow just one way. In a wide shot, the DJ restarts the vinyl record, this time the deck and system lost within the crowded dance floor. The inimitable whistle and melody of The Revolutionaries' 'Kunta Kinte Dub' begins to play. A long take of the bodies of the partygoers shows them swaying in anticipation of the beat of the bassline, blending into the kitsch wallpapered walls of the room. Some hold their fists aloft, as if accessing power, celebrating power, anticipating power. As the bassline starts to play, the group of men start to dance feverishly, vibrating, thrashing, bodies contorting in rhythm. There is a liberation to their movement, a harmony of exaltation and elation, a fraternity of motion that builds to a collective ecstatic moment of shouting, stomping, writhing on the floor until the song starts again. The rewind.

It is not a surprise that this moment of the film is accompanied by a dub soundtrack. Another dub classic, 'Minstrel Pablo' by Augustus Pablo, plays immediately before 'Kunta Kinte Dub' in the party's playlist. Dub, pioneered by recording studio engineers such as Osbourne 'King Tubby' Ruddock (1941–89), Lee 'Scratch' Perry (1936–2021), and Errol 'Errol T.' Thompson (1941–2005), flourished during the era of Roots Reggae that ran from the late 1960s into the 1980s. Michael E. Veal's *Dub: Soundscapes and Shattered Songs in Jamaican Reggae*, a comprehensive overview of dub's history and development, is a crucial text for understanding the aesthetics and social significance of the music form. Veal (2013: 2) states that dub's significance as a style lies in the deconstructive manner in which these engineers remixed reggae songs, applying sound-processing technology in unusual ways to create a unique pop music language of fragmented song forms and reverberating soundscapes that would go on to influence popular electronic music (such as hip-hop, techno, house, jungle, ambient and trip-hop) across the world.

Although dub is a fluid process with no set rules, a key characteristic of dub music is an emphasis on reverb and delay (echo). Dub engineers used reverb and echo to 'reunify fragmented songs' and disorient the listener, often producing psychedelic results that gave the music a 'trippy' reputation, such that 'good dub sounds like the recording studio itself has begun to hallucinate' (Sullivan 2014: 3). This hallucinatory feature is a critical component for the functioning of dub as a memory device, and consequently as a means for fostering shared identity through collective memory. Veal (2013: 198) argues that much of the genre's compositional tension is generated through subversion of the listener's expectations, based on the vocal song with which they are previously familiar, such that 'in the sonic culture of humans, the sensation of echo is closely associated with the cognitive function of memory and the evocation of the chronological past; at the same time, it can also evoke the vastness of outer space and hence (by association), the chronological future.'

Discourse around dub consistently evokes ghosts and memory, the past and the future, the living and the unliving. This metaphorical and metaphysical application of dub music, with sonic tropes of reverb, delay, heavy bass and distorted vocals, artistically situates the form in a liminal space as 'not an instrumental, nor a version, but both and neither at the same time', abstracting sound, subverting speech, echoing and reverberating the ghosts of the original track, becoming a 'simulacrum, a cave, where one sees the shadows of the story upfront, but always undefined' (Navas 2014: 43). As Ian Penman states in his article for *The Wire*, 'Dub messes big time with . . . notions of uncorrupted temporality. Wearing a dubble face, neither future nor past, Dub is simultaneously a past and future trace: of music as both memory or futurity, authentic emotion and technological parasitism.' He further states that dub's 'tricknology is a form of magic which does indeed make people disappear, leaving behind only their context, their trace, their outline' (Penman 1995: 39). Kodwo Eshun (1998: 64) describes the perception and sensation of listening to dub as having to have '[y]our ear . . . chase the sound. Instead of the beat being this one event in time, it becomes a series of retreating echoes, like a tail of sound. The beat becomes a tail which is always disappearing around the corner and your ear has to start chasing it.' Fisher goes as far as to describe the dub producer as 'a manipulator of sonic phantoms detached from live bodies', where 'dub time is unlive, and the producer's necromantic role – [their] raising of the dead – is doubled by [their] treating of the living as if dead, the way that [they transform] the voice of the living into the "ghosts of ghosts of effects"' (2013: 53, citing Eshun 1998).

Three geographical spaces haunt in dub of the period: the immediate remembered Caribbean home, the oppressive European exile migrant home and the mythical African home to return to. Dub's trace reverberated across all these spatial and temporal dimensions. It is not a coincidence that a group named The Revolutionaries had a song called 'Kunta Kinte Dub', named after an enslaved protagonist in Alex Haley's 1976 novel and 1977 mini-series *Roots*. Veal (2013: 198) argues that 'the sensation of echo during a period when the symbol of Africa was being consciously revitalized in diasporic consciousness, [meant that] the creators of dub managed to evoke a cultural memory of ancestral African roots through heavy use of the reverb and echo effects and various musical strategies of African origin'. Paul Sullivan (2014: 3) argues that 'Jamaica's dub pioneers used echo . . . to provoke a sense of Jamaica's ancestral African roots, while at the same time invoking the infinity of the cosmos – and the future – by creating cavernous spaces within the music.'

Dub record producer Augustus Pablo once stated that 'Everybody used to say our music is "unfinished"' (Veal 2013: 220). But this deconstructed nature of dub, this unfinishedness of dub, shouldn't be grounds for criticism, but instead taken as a critical value, because inherent in that unfinishedness is the continued conversation with the past and the future, with ancestors and dreams. Inherent in that unfinishedness is potential and possibility, something that British society often didn't give to these Black populations. Gilroy (1993: xi) argues in *The Black Atlantic* that the movement of people back and forth across the ocean creates a 'dynamic intercultural identity that is beyond the scope of national borders and ethnic classifications', such that these politicised identities are 'always unfinished, always being remade' and ethnicity is an 'infinite process of identity construction'. As such, dub, characterised by being an inherent unfinished form, is a soundtrack for this making and remaking. *Lovers Rock* is a snapshot of this making and remaking process.

VIRAL DUB

Sullivan (2014: 1) evocatively describes dub as being 'ethereal, mystical, conceptual, fluid, avant-garde, raw, unstable, provocative, transparent, postmodern, disruptive, heavyweight, political, enigmatic . . . way more than "a riddim and a bassline", even if it is that too . . . a genre and a process, a "virus" and a "vortex"; it draws the listener into a labyrinth, where there are false signposts and "mercurial" trails that can lead to the future, the past . . . or to nowhere at all.' Which leads back to *Lovers Rock*, and the experience of dub as presented in the film.

Goodman (2012: 27), in *Sonic Warfare: Sound, Affect and the Ecology of Fear*, describes the experience of a Jamaican sound system as follows:

> On either side of the room, the walls are lined by gigantic stacks of speakers of erratic assembly. Some look as if they have been repurposed from wardrobes, others from TV cabinets, their electrical and cathode ray intestines ripped out to be replaced by cone-shaped woofers resembling black eyes, a visual dead end. The air hangs heavily with a pungent smoke, rippling with pulses of intensity that oscillate from one wall to the other. A chemical clock waiting to switch. Lungs constricted, chestplates rattling, the throbbing body of the crowd holds its collective breath as one pressure wave after another surges through, jogging on the spot to mobilize the momentum in dance. Spectral voices of the DJ are echoed, reverbed into ghosts – lost in the viscous blobs of bass, the magnetic vibrations of a body snatcher. This is the masochism of the sound clash and its active production of dread.

Again, the language use is evocative and poetic, an attempt to place the reader in the space. McQueen uses cinematic language to be more direct in portraying the house party dance floor. In that space, with the camera largely positioned below eye level, pointing up from below, immersed within the dancing crowd, the audience is not so much a member of the party, as much as they are submerged within its vortex, unable to escape the bodies. The notion of a virus resonates here, as the various waves of motion move from one body to the next, increasingly frenetic, increasingly intense. It is not unlike spirit possession, and thus more akin to traditional practices within Protestant Christian branches like the Baptists, or hybrid African-Christian forms like Revivalism (often referred to as Pocomania or Pukumina), than it would be for the Rastafari faith that is predominantly implied in *Lovers Rock*. Indeed, one of the criticisms levelled at the film has been that a Rasta falling to the ground in a frenzied spiritual trance is incongruous with Rastafari practice and comportment. But all performances of identity in *Lovers Rock* and in the community that it portrays are incongruous with a strict measurement against 'authenticity'. Earlier in the film, this is addressed explicitly when Franklyn (played by Micheal Ward) has an introductory conversation with Martha (played by Amarah-Jae St. Aubyn) that serves to confirm what their identity is in that space:

Franklyn: Where you people dem come from?
Martha: Jamaica. Mile Gully.
Franklyn: Country gyal.
Martha: Not me. Born right here so.
Franklyn: Ah Portmore me come from, you know. Wha you family name?
Martha: Trenton. Yours?
Franklyn: Cooper.
Martha: We no have Cooper in the family.
Franklyn: Alright. So . . . you a Rude Gyal or Soul Head?
Martha: I listen Louisa Mark, Junior English, Gregory, Janet Kay.
Franklyn: Seen, seen. Lovers, eh?

Here, in an adopted Jamaican patois that drops in and out, they quickly establish their Jamaican heritage, where exactly they can reference in the homeland, if they are related, and what cultural groups they belong to. It is clear that these presented identities are performed in a Butlerian sense, where performativity means an act that not only communicates, but also creates and constructs an identity through repetition. Later in the film this is seen again when Franklyn's boss discovers him and Martha in the garage where Franklyn works, and Franklyn quickly code switches back to a deep London accent, all while Lee 'Scratch' Perry's 'Dreadlocks in Moonlight' continues to play from the interrupted love scene. Again, this is identity performativity in action.

The dub scene depicts the ghost of a reality, echoes of Rasta, reverberations of Reggae, memories of the Caribbean. Expecting to find a consistent truth, a stable cultural identity, is to ignore the simulacrum that this space is, its dynamic unfinishedness and its disruptive function. This is consistent with Veal's (2013: 199) articulation of how this dub space functions. He states, 'the condition of simultaneously yearning for and being alienated from a cultural homeland that can never be fully experienced as home, and also from the very *history* of connection to that homeland, allows us to interpret dub as a cultural sound painting of a type, vividly dramatizing the experience of diasporic exile'. Exile in this way evokes Said (2000: 173), who characterised exile as the 'unhealable rift forced between a human being and a native place, between the self and its true home.' It evokes James Clifford (1994: 307), who notes that the narratives of diaspora are binary in composition, drawing upon idealised images of a past in the construction of a cultural 'safe space' in a hostile present. It is echoed in the words of Jamaican poet Kwame Dawes (2001: 203), who surmised that in Jamaica, 'the Africa that is constructed is mythic and defined in terms of the current space of exile'.

The dub scene then, viewed through the lens of how a Revivalist religious space might operate, where rituals are characterised by drumming, dancing, and spirit possession, depicts not this community in truth, but rather the truth of this community. As Zaibi (2014: 5) describes spirit possession in Revivalist/Pocomania rituals, 'the dancer conjures spirits, revives the dead and recreates the realm of ancestors which, in a sense, is a re-enactment and revival of lost bonds. As such, the dance becomes a site of collective memory fraught with a psychic dimension; it is a moment of liberation from the wounds and traumas of the past.' Fanon (1968: 57) explains this force of the possession dance as a 'permissive circle [in which] may be deciphered as in an open book the huge effort of a community to exorcise itself, to liberate itself, to explain itself'. As Penman (2001: 107) articulates, the dub 'virus' operates on the extended timescale of a postcolonial clash of civilisations, in which the ghosts of slavery and forced migration return to haunt the European spirit.

Veal (2013) invokes Gilbert Rouget's 1985 study of the relationship between music and induced states of altered consciousness, which proposes two such states, one of *possession* and one of *ecstatic contemplation*. Dub music can be seen as a catalyst for both states. Despite not being liturgical or devotional music, dub – 'infused with the religious passion of Rastafari-influenced reggae, overtones of Euro-American psychedelia, and political passion' – functions to 'induce states of pseudo-possession and/or contemplative ecstasy in conformity with procedures ultimately rooted in traditional African music' (Veal 2013: 200). Exploring the dub scene in the film, the intense spatial manipulations of the dancing can be interpreted as 'functioning to liberate the body and mind from the physical rhythms of oppression by providing a convulsive glimpse of abandon'. Lee 'Scratch' Perry describes this 'convulsive ecstasy of possession' induced by dub in a 1995 interview:

> When you hear dub you fly on the music. You put your heart, your body and your spirit into the music, you gonna fly. Because if it wasn't for the music, oppression and taxes would kill you. They send taxes and oppression to hold you, a government to tell you what to do and use you like a robot. So they will torment you to death. So when you hear dub you hide from the fuckers there. (Martin 1995: 29–33)

The dance floor, that constructed cultural safe space, is both where the people hide and fly, what Fisher (in Eshun and Sagar 2007: 17) calls a 'chiasmus of past and future', where 'the present is pure becoming; it *is not*, but it *acts*. The past . . ., no longer acts but it has not ceased to *be*.' Filtered through Deleuze, the insertion of dub into this space puts 'everything into a trance', where the music is 'a kind of agitation' of memory, where 'memory is the invention of a people . . . not the myth of a past people, but the story-telling of a people to come' (Fisher in Eshun and Sagar 2007: 25).

LOVERS ROCK DUB

Me:
    Just got an idea to make a dub version of *Lovers Rock* somehow
    Like completely remix the film
    But a dub version
    Now need to figure out what the dub version of a film is
Them:
    You in some creative juice!
Me:
    Just popped in my head all of a sudden
                                 (Instant message with a friend)

In discussing the filmic structure of work by influential British art group the Black Audio Film Collective, Fisher (2007) comments that time is not spatialised into a conventional narrative logic and is instead dislocated, folding and refolding like a dreamscape. Visually, McQueen in *Lovers Rock* is not doing that. The film is lush and intoxicating. Sonia Saraiya of *Vanity Fair* describes it as 'achingly beautiful' in its detail and composition. That is not to say that it does not utilise non-conventional devices in its narrative structure. Firstly, two significant party scenes in the film are improvised, unplanned in advance and filmed as it unfolded – the contrasting Janet Kay Silly Games scene that ends in an a capella singalong and the Kunta Kinte dub scene. McQueen states, 'They would have happened with or without me . . . The party became a reality because the actors were willing to go somewhere. What happened in those scenes was real and it transcended the period, the acting, everything. There was some deep shit going down in those scenes, I can tell you that. It was like I was invited to go along with them' (O'Hagan 2020). Secondly, as Saraiya (2020) points out, much of the story is wordless, 'conveyed via look or gesture or the shift in mood when one record is swapped for the next'. But the dreamscape that is portrayed (and potentially produced) is done so because of the role of music in that wordlessness. And if notions of home and community are formulated in this dreamscape, it is done so by having these notions passed on generationally and generated collectively, such that 'there are no stories . . . only the ghosts of other stories' that 'provoke a sense of [ancestral roots and] the infinity of the cosmos' (Eshun and Sagar 2007: 58; Sullivan 2013: 3). In the dreamscape of *Lovers Rock*, dub provides an ephemeral space for ecstatic liberation from racial trauma.

Enwezor (in Eshun and Sagar 2007: 113) states that 'the ghosts of . . . stories inform the notion of a historically inflected dub cinema whose spatial, temporal and psychic dynamics relays the scattered trajectories of immigrant communities'. This leads to the question: what would a dub cinematic version of *Lovers Rock* look like? What would dub music's sonic tropes of reverb, delay, heavy bass and distorted vocals that echo and reverberate the ghosts of the original look like in a visual form? How would one (re)articulate and (re)inscribe the unfinishedness of dub back onto McQueen's work? From these questions came the idea to create *Lovers Rock Dub: An Experiment in Visual Reverberation*, an audio-visual dub version of McQueen's *Lovers Rock* that used dub music as an inspiration to explore the 'lingering and tugging resonances, echoes, hauntings, associations [and] traces' of diasporic memory (Vidali and Phillips 2020: 69), and explore how the echo and reverb of the music mimic the spectral nature of collective memory and cultural identity formation, where being and belonging are intimately connected to nostalgic notions of home and community. To do this, I activated Veal's (2013: 198) words that 'dub is about memory in the immediate sense that it is a remix, a refashioned version of [the] already familiar', deriving its power from its manipulation of the audience's prior experience of the film.

What does it mean to feel theory rather than read it and to be guided by the demands of the subject matter and the requirements of a particular medium? The *Lovers Rock Dub* project allows for a visual articulation of the descriptive and evocative language used to explain dub. But it also uses the ideology and aesthetic of the mixtape, where material is manipulated, mixed, remixed, reordered, resequenced, added to, put in conversation with other material, to create an entire 'sound/image-scape' that is connected to a history of subversion and 'do-it-yourselfness' that operates outside and on the margins of dominant power structures. In what I call 'mixtape scholarship', I am trying to convey multimodal narratives of the disenfranchised, the under-represented and the marginalised in a manner not bounded by academic tradition or traditional form. Glennon (2018) defines the mixtape as having a set of four characteristics: hybridity, distribution, intervention and labour. All four of these characteristics inform mixtape scholarship as I implement it, and as I implemented it in the production of *Lovers Rock Dub*.

Glennon (2018) explains hybridity as the unique form of the mixtape as being part composition and part compilation, combining elements from

DUB, ECSTASY AND COLLECTIVE MEMORY IN *LOVERS* 169

multiple sources, media and timeframes and frequently blurring lines between read and write cultures, and cultural consumption and production. He goes on to explain intervention as being the ability of the creator of a mixtape to intervene in the recording process and to attain control over what is heard, to affect where sounds begin and end, to overlay material, and to combine elements from multiple sources. Labour as a characteristic of mixtapes is defined as involving time, effort and investment of labour, such that it is differentiated from the process of creating a playlist, mix CD or disc drive filled with MP3s, all of which often simply require dragging and dropping file references from one window to another or via algorithmic selection.

Lovers Rock Dub condenses the 70-minute runtime of *Lovers Rock* to a roughly 17-minute project. The main story narrative is removed to leave a concentrated and re-edited narrative focus on the dance party; the sound for the session is set up, the partygoers arrive, and the party starts. Over the course of the 17 minutes, what is heard is an actual audio mixtape that mixes reggae and dub songs, audio excerpts from the footage in *Lovers Rock*, and audio excerpts from John Akomfrah's *Handsworth Songs* and from a 2010 Dub Summit at Dubspot in New York City that featured dub pioneer Scientist. The tracklisting is shown at the end of the visual mixtape:

Robin Hood – Cry Tuff & The Originals
Handsworth Songs – John Akomfrah
Darling Ooh – Errol Dunkley
How Long Dub – Pat Kelly & King Tubby
Turn Out the Light – Investigators
Dub Games – Janet Kay & Dennis Bovell
What is Dub? – Dubspot
Kunta Kinte Dub – The Revolutionaries

Over the course of the 17 minutes, what is seen is a mix of manipulated, mixed, remixed, reordered, resequenced footage from the original McQueen film put into conversation with intertitles of quotations from Eduardo Navas, Linton Kwesi Johnson, Paul Sullivan, Debra Vidali Spitulnik and myself, and Kodwo Eshun and Anjalika Sagar. The original footage from *Lovers Rock* is then also 'dubbed', that is, made to echo and reverb by applying a number of video effects using Adobe Premiere Pro (primarily the echo video effect and Gaussian blur video effect) to mimic that dub music characteristic. (See Figure 11.1.)

Glennon (2018) characterises mixtape distribution as happening via non-mainstream methods, typically via personal exchange, mail order, downloading from non-corporate/commercial websites, purchasing from merch stands at gigs or via non-mainstream formats. At present, *Lovers Rock Dub* is hosted on Vimeo, but its ideal distribution method would be installation/projection in a

Figure 11.1. *Lovers Rock Dub* screenshot.

large- screen format to the actual size of the actors, so as to best create immersion. The goal is to provoke and extend the dub impact in an embodied way, and to broadly call forth that liminal space that abstracts what is heard and what is seen, in order to make palpable (and hopefully tangible) those ghosts of ghosts of effects (now both sonic and visual).

As a visual mixtape or a 'dub film', *Lovers Rock Dub* is also in conversation with both the philosophical and the artistic tradition of hauntology. Hauntology, first introduced by Derrida in his 1993 book *Spectres of Marx*, is a concept referring to the return or persistence of elements from the past, as in the manner of a ghost. It describes a situation of temporal and ontological disjunction in which presence is replaced by a deferred non-origin (Buse and Scott 1999: 11). The concept is derived from his deconstructive method, in which any attempt to locate the origin of identity or history must inevitably find itself dependent on an always-already existing set of linguistic conditions (Fisher 2013: 45). Ultimately, hauntology is 'about memory's power (to linger, pop up unbidden, prey on your mind) and memory's fragility (destined to become distorted, to fade, then finally disappear)' (Reynolds 2012: 335). Artistically, the aesthetic application of hauntology has been used to explore ideas related to temporal disjunction, retrofuturism, cultural memory and the persistence of the past. But hauntology often looks at these ideas in connection with horror and unease, linking those ghosts to terror and dread. Dub ghosts are a different kind of dread, and Black connections to spirits have a different history. There's a kind of tragic coincidence and harmful harmony in Black people having been derogatively called 'spooks' and 'shadows', but even with a historical connection to trauma, dub is perceived as joyful and jubilant in its haunting. And as Alexander Weheliye highlights in *Phonographies* (2005: 102), the term 'dub' itself not only 'indicates a doubling or copying but carries homonymic overtones of duppy (the Jamaican word for spirit and/or ghost) so that the dub version of a song provides not only its shadow but also its spectral other'. Aesthetically and artistically, this was my aim in *Lovers Rock Dub*, to bring forth a 'duppy' from the film, or to paraphrase Veal, to create a cultural sound-image painting of a type, vividly (re)dramatising the experience of diasporic exile.

Despite the 'tricknology' of dub (and dub cinema), the magic of *Lovers Rock* (and the dub scene in particular) is not in how it makes people disappear, as Penman discusses, but rather it is in what it reveals of the Black Caribbean community that it portrays. The party space provides a locus for shared memory making and memory reinforcement, and for identity formation and affirmation. The oppressed bodies dance freely with the traces and outlines of joy and sorrow, of trauma and triumph. Riddims girder raw emotion, basslines bolster hopefulness, virus and vortex transmit and twist collective understanding and overstanding. And as McQueen himself states in the aptly titled article 'It's rebel music that moves me' for *The Guardian*, 'In its DNA, a blues dance was a form of resistance and release. People were working for the weekend when they could let loose, come out of themselves. To be surrounded by people like themselves was, in itself, important, because it allowed them to feel comfortable enough to let go and lose themselves – and be understood without question' (O'Hagan 2020). As Kew (2021) highlights, the dub-fuelled blues party as a site of both refuge and rebellion evokes Niaah's Fanon-inspired concept of an 'occult zone', a redemptive, transformative place of simultaneity, 'emphasising the transcendent, spiritual benefits of congregating and "crystallising" a collective bond' (Henry and Worley 2021: 195). An inside for outsiders. A darkened space of light. A dread-filled refuge from dread.

CHAPTER 12

The Burden of Expectation: Where are the Women in Steve McQueen's *Small Axe* Films?

Patricia Francis

INTRODUCTION: BLACK WOMEN AND THE HIERARCHY OF EXISTENCE

In 1986 in *Sisterhood: Political Solidarity between Women*, bell hooks contended that 'Women are the group most victimised by sexist oppression. As with other forms of group oppression, sexism is perpetuated by institutional and social structures; by the individuals who dominate, exploit, or oppress; and by the victims themselves who are socialized to behave in ways that make them act in complicity with the status quo' (1986: 127). Similarly, nearly thirty years later in 2015 Katherine Smits argued that '[i]n the twenty-first century the legal barriers to women's public speech have been eliminated, but, many feminists argue, persisting social, cultural and economic structures continue to silence and discount their voices' (2015: 165). Women continue to challenge systemic practices that endeavour to hush their voices, and in this chapter I will discuss how the silencing and discounting of women's voices that Smit refers to is amplified in the Steve McQueen pentalogy *Small Axe*. It is important to first explain my use of 'silence' and 'silencing' as a means of describing the exclusion of the plurality of women's voices in particular, in their experiences and actions of dissent as they challenge patriarchal and colonial forces. In suggesting that the women are 'silenced', I do not conceive of them as being submissive or compliant, nor does the suggestion of the women being 'silenced' characterise them as defenceless victims. Instead, I refer to the idea of 'silence' and 'silencing' as a means of describing a social and political marginalisation that women encounter, where there is an absence of their equal presence within a social, political and economic sphere and where still, the authority of patriarchy and hegemony subsequently and successfully undermines them as women. In this chapter I will discuss how the *Small Axe* series consistently neglects to conceive of a space from which the dominant ideology of the Black British woman is undermined, even if momentarily, and instead offers a narrative where her existence is positioned within a sociological, historical, patriarchal and familial framework that too often confines and defines her as a stereotypical presence.

Broadcast between November and December 2020, the *Small Axe* pentalogy affirms the necessity for a repositioning and reimagining of Black women as separate to and independent of Black men and white women. Indeed, Akasha Hull et al.'s book *All the Women are White, All the Blacks are Men, But Some of Us Are Brave* (1982) offers innumerable examples of the inequity Black women encounter with regards to health, education, racism and sexism, and it remains a valuable contribution to Black women's studies. Hull and Smith wrote:

> Merely to use the term 'Black women's studies' is an act charged with political significance. At the very least, the combining of these words to name a discipline means taking the stance that Black women exist – and exist positively – a stance that is in direct opposition to most of what passes for culture and thought on the North American continent. To use the term and to act on it in a white-male world is an act of political courage. (1982: xvii)

While the book's focus is on African American experiences, many of the issues address, as its title signals, the courage of speaking about Black women's realities. In Britain, Black feminists put women at *The Heart of the Race* (1985, 2018), the title that Beverley Bryan, Stella Dadzie and Suzanne Scafe took for their collective study of Black women's lives in Britain. However, Black women are still not perceived or portrayed on equitable terms as their white counterparts, as can be evidenced by, for example, the disproportionate amount of social media abuse Hackney Member of Parliament (MP) Diane Abbott was subjected to during the run-up to the 2017 General Election. Abbott is the United Kingdom's first Black female MP and, at the time of writing (May 2022), is the MP for Hackney North and Stoke Newington. An Amnesty International UK investigation into online abuse against women MPs revealed that Abbott experienced a 'disproportionate amount of abuse and was the target of almost a third (31.61%) of all abusive tweets . . .' (2019). A more recent example that proposes a hierarchy of Black women's social value in the UK can be demonstrated by the Metropolitan Police response to the tragic killing of sisters Bibaa Henry and Nicole Smallman in 2020, which differed from the appalling killing of Sarah Everard in the same year, by a Metropolitan Police officer. It was a family search, and not that of the Metropolitan Police, that resulted in the sisters being found. When asked during a BBC interview why she felt her case had not received the level of outrage as Sarah Everard, Mina Smallman, the mother of the sisters, said: 'Other people have more kudos in this world than people of colour' (BBC 2021). Smallman explained that police officers were sent to guard the scene where her daughters' bodies lay, and instead they took photos of the women, which they then shared on social media. These are not isolated incidences but act to suggest a commentary that exposes an enduring intersectional inequity experienced by Black women. The recent findings from the review of the case of Child Q act to underline this. A fifteen-year-old school pupil referred to as 'Child Q' was, in 2020, taken out of a school exam by police officers in London. Quoting a safeguarding report, the 'Independent Online' wrote that Child Q was 'strip-searched by officers – who knew she was menstruating – after teachers suspected that [she] was in possession of cannabis [. . .] Child Q's mother was not informed of the search, while teachers remained outside the room while it took place' (White 2022). It could be argued that neither Child Q's mother nor Child Q herself were considered by these agents of government institutions to deserve any level of respect, dignity or ascendency. Implicit in this is the suggestion that even Black women's civil rights can be denied. Nearly forty years after *Sisterhood: Political Solidarity between Women*, Black women and girls in Britain continue to encounter a marginalisation that they must persistently challenge if they are to achieve economic, social and political parity.

SMALL AXE: THE SOCIAL AND POLITICAL CONTEXT

It is important to offer context to the period leading up to and during which the five Steve McQueen films are situated, as this will enable insight into the limitations and social barriers that existed during that time and in particular for Black communities, and expose the nuanced intersectionality of the Black female experience. The 1980s were a politically charged period, in which racialised communities were disproportionately affected by the social policies and political decisions made by the Conservative government led by Margaret Thatcher. High interest rates, public spending cuts and a recession followed by high unemployment fuelled widespread civil unrest. A 2014 investigation carried out by Professor Yaojun Li found that when the recession was at its highest in 1982, Black and Pakistani/Bangladeshi men's unemployment rate reached nearly 30 per cent as compared with only 12 per cent for white men (Li 2014). The economic situation was impacting racialised communities, who were also being targeted because of their ethnicity. The far-right National Front had a visible presence on Britain's streets. Intimidating in appearance, they presented a real threat to those from Black and Asian communities they came into contact with, terrorising and causing them physical harm. Similarly, the incidences of Black deaths in police custody and other institutional settings continued to rise (Athwal 2002) against a backdrop of racialised communities experiencing disproportionately high levels of social deprivation, poor housing and poor educational achievement. In addition, the use of the 'Sus' law by the police (a law that permitted police officers in England and Wales to stop, search and potentially arrest people on suspicion of loitering with the intent to commit an arrestable offence) (Jefferson 2011) had the effect of aggravating an already fraught relationship with Black communities. In April 1981 'Operation Swamp' saw the Metropolitan Police arrest one thousand people in ten days. This inflamed already unstable tensions within the racialised communities and triggered uprisings in Brixton and Tottenham in London, which then spread around the country to cities including Liverpool, Manchester and Nottingham (John 2006).

Hostility towards racialised groups in Britain was enduring. It was Margaret Thatcher who, in a 1978 television interview for the ITV investigative current affairs programme *World in Action*, suggested that 'people are really rather afraid that this country might be swamped by people with a different culture, and you know the British culture has done so much for democracy, for law and done so much throughout the world, that if there's any fear that it might be swamped people are going to react and be rather hostile to those coming in' (*World in Action* 1978). Such alienating proclamations were not the first to be publicly expressed by a Conservative Member of Parliament. In April 1968 Enoch Powell delivered another during his infamous 'Rivers of Blood' speech at a Conservative Association meeting, in which he suggested that in parts of Great Britain, those arriving from Commonwealth countries (in response to the British government's recruitment campaign)[1] would 'have the whip hand over the white man'. Powell's statement was provocative. Migrants were characterised as a threat to society, ideological outcasts, and perceived as enemies to an enduring white British culture. Indeed, while two of McQueen's five films, *Lovers Rock* (2020) and *Education* (2020), may be perceived as fictional in their narrative approach, they offer true accounts of what the West Indian population and their descendants were encountering as a result of the physical and verbal, racial and discriminatory assaults they were experiencing – a social reaction to their non-white Caribbean presence. In consequence, a defiant Black population was determining their future as they continued to work, buy their own homes, raise their children and navigate the periodic discord and unrest that occurred as a result of the social, political and economic inequity they continued to face as marginalised and racialised groups (Francis 2013).

REVEALING AND CENTRING WOMEN'S VOICES

Women have been both active and proactive in that process of determination and in confronting socio-economic, political, colonial and patriarchal barriers to their own progress and that of their community. Indeed, women have played major roles in civil unrest, which is often underplayed, hinted at or ignored. For example, the Grunwick Dispute in 1976 was led by Jayaben Desai, a South Asian woman who, along with other factory workers, walked out of the Grunwick film-processing laboratory in London in 1976 in protest over low pay and poor working conditions.

Similarly, the women's role in the 1984 Miners' Strike is often considered only in their setting up of soup kitchens, compiling food parcels and ensuring that the men and children were fed. However, the women, particularly those involved in the Nottinghamshire strike, are seldom acknowledged for their activism on the picket lines, in fundraising and raising awareness of the issues by speaking at rallies. The oral history interviews I have undertaken bring this out. One contributor asserted that the women's involvement influenced the longevity of the strike: 'The strike wouldn't have stayed on as long as it did without the women ... I think the men would have given up and went back' (Francis 2019). The wives and partners of miners were defiant in their actions and their intention to defeat Margaret Thatcher and her government's denunciation of the strike. Indeed, the women's boldness and audacity to persist with what was considered a working-class fight is scarcely accorded due acknowledgement. Their voices were seldom given volume then and were often drowned out by political noise and picket-line battles.

Black women were also dissenting, and while their activism shouted of a racial and gendered inequity and assertion for change, their voices remained almost inaudible, overpowered by their communities' concern over the poor educational achievement of young Black boys, the disproportionately high numbers of Black men and boys being stopped and searched by the police (Jefferson 2012), and the number of Black people, mainly men, dying in unexplained or mysterious circumstances when in police, hospital or prison custody (Athwal 2002). But the women were finding their own voices, voices with shared experiences that were independent of other feminist or patriarchal structures. For example, in 1958 Claudia Jones set up the *West Indian Gazette*, a Black campaigning newspaper which was a means of communicating with her community and was considered to be 'a catalyst, quickening the awareness, socially, and politically' (Bryan, Dadzie and Scafe, 1982, 2018: 137). Similarly, Olive Morris in 1973 co-founded the Brixton Black Workers Group (BWG), and OWAAD (Organisation of Women of Asian and African Descent) in 1978. Black women were organising separately from the white feminist movements and were talking about issues specific to them. The authors of *Heart of the Race* acknowledge the rise of Black women activists during the seventies and explain that, '[it] was a time when Black women were becoming increasingly visible and active. We were involved in tenants' and squatters' campaigns, in the struggles of our community against the abuses of the education system and in a variety of defence campaigns which arose out of our daily battles with the police' (Bryan, Dadzie and Scafe, 1982, 2018: 155). That Black women have contributed significantly to their community's fight for social and economic parity is often given little significance despite their actions having tangible impact, and it is this general absence of the women's presence and effectiveness that is also evident in Steve McQueen's *Small Axe* pentalogy.

THE BURDEN OF EXPECTATION: THE PORTRAYAL OF WOMEN IN STEVE McQUEEN'S *SMALL AXE* FILMS

McQueen has created a series of films that offer insight into the lived experience of those from African-Caribbean and Asian communities during 1970s and 1980s Britain. The narrative in each film is established within a social context that implores reminiscence or comprehension with the period under view. McQueen uses his films to speak of the Black African-Caribbean/British experience, to critique a social system that undermined Black achievement and Black progress, and to show a resilience and fortitude that has endured across the generations. These are commendable films for many reasons, in particular because they contribute to the historical legacy of Black Britons and to British social history. That these films are not documentaries is irrelevant here. What matters is that they exist and offer testament to the shifting and ongoing battle that racialised people encounter in their attempt for racial and social parity. Sir Steve McQueen, now perceived as a member of a British order that operates to oppress and marginalise, has used his position and voice to 'speak' of that marginalisation and oppression that the social system perpetuates. In doing so McQueen positions himself firmly within and, it might be suggested, critiques the emerging and unfolding characteristics of an enduring and deviating social and political arrangement that endeavours to preserve itself. But there is insufficient self-reflection in these films and an absence of female consciousness as, at the heart of each film, there is a desire to centre the story around Black men, despite women having many competent and combatant stories to contribute to Britain's historical legacy. On initial appraisal, that women are not given prominence in McQueen's films might be challenged, as there is welcome representation of Black female defiance in *Mangrove* (2020), the first of the *Small Axe* films, when student Altheia Jones-LeCointe says: 'We need to challenge the system . . . We mustn't be victims but protagonists of our stories and what better way of representing ourselves but self-representing ourselves.' A bold, incisive statement then and now. Indeed, Black women are seen in multiple roles across the *Small Axe* films. They are mothers, teenage girls, lesbian as well as heterosexual, educators and nurses, and operate within an oppressive socio-economic and political system that restrains them as members of the Black community and confines and defines them as Black women. But the emphasis is on the women as carers, nurturers and sexual beings.

In *Alex Wheatle* (2020), the women provide food and sustenance for the men, which is affirmed when Dennis's mother questions Alex: 'yu mudda nuh cook fi yu?' Implicit in her inquiry is the Burden of Expectation – that it is the duty of women to care for, to nurture and be resilient for their family. She confronts Dennis for being late, from the kitchen where she is anchored, preparing the Christmas dinner alongside someone we perceive to be her daughter. Rather than apologising, Dennis's response is to ask her to 'fix up a drink' for Alex. The social presumption of women's role belonging in the kitchen is not only unchallenged in the film but is reinforced as the son walks away from his mother, to take a seat in the living room where he waits for the drink. Similarly in *Red, White and Blue* (2020), new recruit Leroy Logan is conscientiously supported by his wife, who is also the mother of his baby. Indeed, her obligation as a wife undermines her own anxiety about being left alone in her advanced stage of pregnancy. He asks for her 'support' as he is about to leave to attend a six-week police training course and it is given unconditionally. A pattern of compliance is suggested with regard to the women; they are seldom heard. The only conversation between them that is heard and given volume is when they share cooking tips, and even here there is a blatant effort to please the 'man of the house' as Leroy's mother takes a quick glance at her husband when she states that she does not put sugar in the oil she cooks with.

Viewing McQueen's films through a feminist lens reveals a pentalogy that does not offer a challenge to the dominant social and political positioning of Black women. Instead, in the process of constructing films around Black male protagonists, McQueen risks reinforcing traditional, patriarchal and racist conceptions. Altheia in *Mangrove* might be considered a contradiction to this notion. This tenacious female character is clearly confident and assertive, but she is also pregnant and with this knowledge the viewer's perceptions shift from her activism to her impending role as nurturer and carer for her newborn child and the danger that activism might pose to that. The Burden of Expectation is again accentuated as the two female Mangrove activists console each other's maternal anxieties – their concerns should they be given a prison sentence. They are bonded in sistah-hood as they share, understand and accept the burden. This minute-and-a-half sequence, allocated to Altheia and Barbara, might have been used to demonstrate their indomitable characters, but instead it acts to suggest and amplify the idea of women's primary purpose as mothers and carers. So, *Mangrove* too reinforces the burden. Indeed, despite her dominance, Altheia is not the main character in the film. The story is not about her, it is about Frank Crichlow and the bullying and brutality he endures from the Metropolitan Police in his effort to safeguard his restaurant.

Closer observation exposes a pentalogy in which not one of McQueen's films tells a progressive story about a steadfast Black British woman who, for example like Leroy Logan or Frank Crichlow, was also required to challenge the socio-economic and/or political system. *Education* (2020) is about a nurse and a mother striving for the best education she can achieve for her son. *Red, White and Blue* (2020) is based on the true story of retired superintendent Leroy Logan and his navigation of a racist Metropolitan police force. *Alex Wheatle* (2020) is based on the true story of the male author of young adult fiction, and his experiences before achieving success in that role. These selected stories are based on true events and tell of Black male protagonists' subversions of racial discriminatory practice. The women play supporting roles. Absent from the choice are depictions of the Black female experience. The films fail to position women as leads, or in compelling, dominant roles. *Lovers Rock* (2020) is a dramatisation of blues parties in the 1980s, held as a consequence of Black people not being admitted into mainstream clubs. Martha, a teenager, is seen climbing down a drainpipe, defying her parents in order to attend one of these parties. As she throws her white, virgin, unscuffed shoes out of her bedroom window, this young woman betrays her family's expectation of her as a daughter and sabotages societal assumption of her as a woman. The Burden of Expectation is summonsed, and the audience is asked to make a judgement on Martha's integrity. This is more than a film about Black youths finding freedom and the music that enabled them to escape the ideological structures that undermined their social position. The Burden of Expectation is provoked, as Martha attempts to untether her Black female self from social and family constraints, her actions becoming a comment on her morality as a woman. A Black man is seen carrying a white cross, his presence acting to remind Martha of the pure Christian values she is betraying as she 'strays' from the patriarchal fold. Few of McQueen's five films devote much time to the female experience and this one risks portraying Black women as deceitful and promiscuous, as Martha abandons piety and fidelity for the subversive and immoral act of attending a blues party and for having awareness of her own agency. A counterargument might be that *Lovers Rock* is a celebration of Martha's self-determination and of her fortitude; she confronts Bammy as he attempts to sexually assault a woman at the party and his resulting aggression towards her for the disruption is met with equal defiance. Martha instructs the Black sistah she rescues to 'come and stand by me sis'. But the sistah does not stand by Martha's side against this male aggressor; instead she thanks Martha and quickly flees the scene, leaving Martha alone to face the perpetrator. Where *Lovers Rock* might have depicted camaraderie among women and represented the historical legacy of Black women working in unity and defending each other, it characterises instead a woman who ultimately needs a man to protect her. The two women do not resist the offender in solidarity; instead the victim escapes the danger and Franklyn arrives in time to 'protect' Martha from Bammy's aggressive advance.

The nature of Martha's liberty and agency must be acknowledged within the patriarchal confines from which this film is constructed. Franklyn and Martha leave the blues dance and Franklyn takes her to his workplace; he puts music on, offers her 'tea' and then pours spirit into a glass. Martha removes her coat. This action perhaps describes her new-found autonomy, but her power is limited. Rather than feminine sovereignty, masculine prowess is being celebrated here as the camera stays long enough on Franklyn to discern his intention. He sips the 'tea' and lingers momentarily to 'gaze' at Martha's form before he makes his move in her direction. The narrative speaks of an intended sexual conquering, which is reinforced when Franklyn's boss arrives, switches the light on in the workshop, and interrupts their amorous embrace. He insultingly comments on the lack of light and in response Franklyn says, '. . . it's the big light . . . you know how it's usually too bright.' This suggests his level of familiarity with this type of activity, which is confirmed when Franklyn informs his boss that they were not stopping and that they 'just popped in on their way home'. What Martha fails to then see is the meaningful stare Franklyn gives his boss. Words are not required between men who understand sexual conquest as a mark of virility and manhood; Franklyn assumes consensus with his boss in his endeavour with Martha, and although it is not reciprocated, in that moment Martha is stripped of control. In the exchange that occurs between the men, power and authority become their preserve and Martha's autonomy has no function. Once again, the opportunity to conceive of a narrative about Black women as self-governing and assertive is lost.

Singer Janet Kay's 1979 hit 'Silly Games' features significantly and repetitively in *Lovers Rock*, as it did on the reggae scene at that time. Viewers are transported back to the claustrophobic racist control of the state, and the words '*You're as much to blame, 'cos I know you feel the same . . .*' have profound social and political relevance here as Black men and women whine and entwine, moving as one to the reggae rhythm. But they are not as one. McQueen acknowledges systemic racism and portrays it, yet in his *Small Axe* films he fails to advocate for 'Black sistahs'. Not one of the five *Small Axe* films is dedicated to any of the many Black women active in the struggle for equality and change in the UK. They existed and they were visible. Women such as Moira Stuart, Britain's first Black female newsreader who was regularly on British screens reading the BBC news. Diane Abbott, Britain's first Black British female MP, the longest-serving Black MP in the House of Commons, who has subsequently set up a number of initiatives supporting Black women, men and children in the UK (Abbott 2022). Indeed, Turner Prize-winner Lubaina Himid was central to the British Black Arts Movement in the 1980s and wrote about the challenges of being a Black female artist in the '80s in Margaret Thatcher's Britain. Aurella Yusuff wrote of Himid:

[i]t was not only her work as a practising visual artist which was of importance, but her writing and curatorial practice which was key to the visibility of Black women artists in Britain at a time when they were marginalised from group shows. Exhibitions of women artists almost exclusively featured white women, while Black art exhibitions predominantly focused on male artists [. . .] Himid was responsible for organising several groundbreaking exhibitions, including *Five Black Women* (Africa Centre, 1983), *Black Woman Time Now* (Battersea Arts Centre, 1983) and *The Thin Black Line* (Institute of Contemporary Art, 1985), which presented emerging Black and Asian women artists, providing a much-needed outlet for the public presentation of their work (Yusuff 2021).

There are also less visible women who are still worthy of note, such as Professor Shirley Thompson, the first woman in Europe to have composed and conducted a symphony within the last forty years. They all, it can be argued, offer compelling narratives. Surely a woman's story could have qualified as a leading story for at least one of the five *Small Axe* films. It was disappointing that dramatisation and documentation of the Burden of Expectation could not have extended into the multiple experiences of Black women in Britain in any detail.

More should be expected from a Black Writers' Room that is creating stories about injustice and racial discrimination in the 1980s. Black men were not alone in being turned away from nightclubs, it was not only Black men who were assaulted or experienced direct violence by the police. Black women were involved in the nationwide uprisings and activist struggles in the fight for equality. However, it would seem that the men in this writing arena did not consider Black women's stories could be sufficiently engaging for a prime-time BBC ONE audience. A Royal Television Society article suggested Helen Bart, 'a former West Indian BBC News journalist was busy uncovering the stories of everyday people in the 1960s, 1970s and 1980s' as possible topics for *Small Axe* (Ganatra 2020). Of the 126 interviews she conducted, is it really conceivable that not one of them was strong enough to inspire a narrative retelling with a woman at the centre, as protagonist not victim, nurturer or deceiver? In an online interview in the magazine for men *Esquire*, McQueen named Alistair Siddons and Courttia Newland as co-writers of *Lovers Rock* and *Red, White and Blue* and Alex Wheatle and Alistair Siddons as co-writers of *Alex Wheatle*, *Education* and *Mangrove* (*Esquire* 2020). All men. By this account, Black British women were not even present in that creative space to write and develop stories alongside them. When society is being admonished for under-representation in boardrooms, on recruitment panels, in the media and at the Oscars, for example, how could there be such an oversight? In 2020, the same year that the *Small Axe* films were broadcast, 'Diamond', the industry-wide system for monitoring and reporting diversity in broadcasting, collected data relating to more than

740,000 television and production contributions, and reported 'very low contributions being made in the roles of Writer and Director by those who are disabled or from Black, Asian and Minority Ethnic groups. 3.5% of Writer contributions and 4.9% of Director contributions are by those who are disabled; 6.5% of Writer contributions and 8.4% of Director contributions are by those who identify as Black, Asian and Minority Ethnic' (Creative Diversity Network 2020). In not providing a chair for Black women around that *Small Axe* writers table, the Black male writers, who demonstrate through the films their cognisance of the resultant impact of discriminatory practice on racialised lives, silence Black women's voices, and in so doing contribute to their enduring sexualised and racialised marginalisation. The writers failed to offer Black women an opportunity to tell their own stories, and so have perhaps unwittingly contributed to the normalisation of Black women's continued absence from positions both in front of and behind the camera.

In his study of Black popular cultural forms in *Welcome to the Jungle* (1994), Kobena Mercer noted:

> The impact of black women's voices in the early eighties heralded the pluralization of black identities that would become a key theme throughout the decade. From autonomous organisations formed in the late 1970s, such as the Organization of Women of Asian and African Descent (OWAAD), to AWAZ (meaning 'voice'), and Southall Black Sisters, to C. L. R. James' 1981 lecture at the Riverside Studios, urging us to read Alice Walker, Toni Morrison and Toni Cade Bambara . . .
> (Mercer 1994: 11)

Nearly three decades ago, Black women's contribution to the social and political struggle was being acknowledged, a contribution that continues today as evidenced, not least, by the Black Lives Matter movement, set up in 2013 by three Black women in response to the acquittal of George Zimmerman for the killing of Black teenager Trayvon Martin in Florida in 2012.[2] By 2016, the first Black Lives Matter chapter in Europe was set up in Nottingham. Indeed, Black women have and continue to challenge neocolonial and patriarchal systems that marginalise communities. They bore and continue to bear the Burden of Expectation and are inclusive in their actions. In 1988, five years before Steve McQueen made his film *Bear* (1993), Ngozi Onwurah made *Coffee Coloured Children* (1988), a film that featured her brother and poetically described the emotional trauma of racial harassment growing up with dual heritage in Britain. In 1986 Maureen Blackwood co-directed *The Passion of Remembrance* as part of Sankofa Film and Video Collective. It imaginatively explores race, class and gender and speaks of the plurality of the Black experience. The 1980s saw the Black Arts Movement that included artists such as Lubaina Himid, Sonia Boyce, Keith Piper and

Eddie Chambers, who were creating works inspired by anti-racist and feminist discourse. Himid's *We Will Be* in 1983 and Boyce's *Big Women's Talk* in 1984 used art to conceive a space that represented and re-presented Black women's experiences. Such opportunity to have a voice was limited then, as noted by the character Maggie in *The Passion of Remembrance* (1986). Referring to under-representation on British television during the 1980s, she said:

> Every time a Black face appears we think it has to represent the whole race. We don't have the space to get it wrong, that's the problem. (Blackwood and Julien 1986)

Maureen Blackwood co-directed the film with Isaac Julien. Cooperation and collaboration was key in their construction of this visual work that confronts gender, race, class and sexuality from a Black British and patriarchal perspective. The cultural complexities discussed in the film demonstrate the value gained in a collaborative process that enables a space for challenge and candour. The female speaker in the film says '. . . forget trying to pigeon hole me. Forget trying to end the conversation because you've decided that I'm a feminist, not worth talking to. Forget trying to shut me up!' Here the writers' conscious and insightful script offers a narrative that speaks to the heart of the issue. Both female and male voices are present and centred in this film that confronts issues that were concerning Black communities in the 1980s, and Blackwood and Julien demonstrate the richness in discourse that can evolve when both voices are given equal volume. An approach that was unfortunately lacking in the *Small Axe* pentalogy.

CONCLUSION

In *Mangrove*, when Frank Crichlow asks Altheia 'What are we fighting for?', she responds defiantly, '*For my unborn child . . . It counts beyond us here . . . I'm not just here defending myself but trying to defend all of us.*' The burden Black women bear has not been and is not limited to their gender. It is borne for their communities, demonstrated by the actions of Black women. For example, the Black Lives Matter movement is a women-led movement, founded with the purpose of intervening 'in violence inflicted on Black communities by the state and vigilantes'.[3] They gained worldwide support as depicted in the international and national response to the killing of George Floyd, where Black women in cities around England mobilised the public to march in protest (Francis 2021). Similarly, the United Families and Friends campaign group, originally a coalition of Black families, now includes families from varied ethnicities and cultures affected by deaths in police, prison and psychiatric custody (United Families and Friends Campaign). Marcia Rigg is a prominent campaigner for the group and is the sister of Sean Rigg who died in police custody in 2008. The group work with and for communities. Indeed, these women, just as Claudia Jones, Olive Morris, Diane Abbott and others, are not the first pioneering Black women working for their communities in an effort to affect change. While this understanding is evident specifically in the script for *Mangrove*, it is unfortunate that McQueen and his writers did not consider more fully, and in the wider social and political context, the importance and need to establish a space within the pentalogy for Black British women alongside that of the Black male protagonists.

Prime-time Sunday evening viewing across five weeks offered McQueen the opportunity to give volume to Black women's voices; to offer an account that countered stereotypical, racist and sexist narratives. He did not take it. In these films the voices of Black British women remained virtually silent. The five films offered wonderful insights into aspects of the lived experiences of Black Britons. However, by not offering a place from which the plurality of Black British women's voices could resonate, and failing to imagine or construct a narrative that aligns more closely with their realities, McQueen bore 'the burden' for Black men only.

NOTES

1. An example is the *Empire Windrush* landing at Tilbury Docks in Essex in Britain in 1948, carrying passengers from the Caribbean who made the journey in response to the British government carrying out campaigns in their countries inviting them to work in England. On arrival, the new migrants experienced hostility, discrimination and violence and were considered a threat to British culture. Documentaries and news items have broadcast the accounts of many, and the Steve McQueen films offer a fictional representation of the reality of living and growing up in Britain during the 1970s and 1980s. The BBC offers an overview up to the present day of the Caribbean migrants and the challenges they still encounter at <https://www.bbc.co.uk/news/uk-43782241>.
2. Patrisse Cullors, Alicia Garza and Opal Tometi were the founding members of the Black Lives Matter Movement in America that became a global network of Black Lives Matter chapters.
3. Black Lives Matter UK are registered in the UK under the name of the Black Liberation Movement UK and are operating to end racial discrimination and fighting for racial equality, equity and justice. More about the movement can be found here – https://blacklivesmatter.uk/

CHAPTER 13

Boy with Flag and Black British Experience in *Handsworth Songs* and *Red, White and Blue*

Thomas Austin

Vanley Burke's photograph *Boy with Flag, Winford in Handsworth Park, 1970* appears in films by two of the most important figures in British cinema of the past thirty-five years. *Handsworth Songs*, directed by John Akomfrah of the Black Audio Film Collective, was first broadcast on Channel Four in 1986 during the channel's experimental phase, and *Red, White and Blue*, directed by Steve McQueen, was released as part of the *Small Axe* series on BBC ONE in 2020. What parallels and contrasts are evident across these two deployments of Burke's image, and what do they tell us about the aesthetic and political strategies of Akomfrah and McQueen, and their particular engagements with Black British experience?

THE PHOTOGRAPH

Often called the godfather of Black British photography, Burke emigrated from rural Jamaica to the UK in 1965 at the age of fourteen to join his parents, who ran a grocery shop. Kieran Connell notes: 'Within two years [he] had begun taking photographs in Handsworth, Birmingham, making a "conscious decision to document the lives and experiences of black people"' (Connell 2012, citing his own interview with the photographer). Burke has stated:

> History is normally written by the victor, and [. . .] as a group of people we were complaining about the way our history was written and I felt it was important that I, having the opportunity to take photographs, should do something to document our own history [. . .] the history of the Black community in Handsworth. (Burke, nd)

Figure 13.1. *Boy with Flag, Winford in Handsworth Park, 1970* by Vanley Burke.

The photograph under discussion depicts a Black boy, Winford Fagan, aged about eight, standing with his bike in the park, with a Union Jack flying from the handlebars. Burke comments:

> It evoked a strange feeling in you. This whole thing about belonging and identity was very strong at the time, and here is this young kid, just bold, cutting across all those arguments with his bicycle and his flag, and I just thought it was so brave and wonderful of him, so I took the photograph. (Burke, nd)

In a 2015 interview, Fagan asserted his identification as British, even while he was the victim of racist abuse as a child:

> I had that flag on my bike for as long as I had the bike. A union jack was something you would have then, not just for bunting. People asked me, 'Why not a Jamaican flag?' but I didn't know about Jamaica. I was born here. [. . .] At the time, there was a lot of racial hatred and gang violence. I remember being chased by skinheads, most of them a lot older than me, but some my age. [. . .] There were certain hours of the night when

you couldn't be on the road in case you were beaten up or stabbed. It was frightening. It wasn't just skinheads who gave us abuse: it was English people in general. They saw us being in their country as an invasion. ('Winford Fagan', 2015)

Fagan's statement chimes with W. E. B. Du Bois's influential concept of 'double consciousness', an attempt to capture the 'two-ness' of African American experience developed in his 1903 book *The Souls of Black Folk*. In his posthumously published autobiography, Du Bois wrote of 'that dichotomy which all my life has characterized my thought: how far can love for my oppressed race accord with love for the oppressing country? And when these loyalties diverge, where shall my soul find refuge?' (1968: 169). A similar social and psychological investment in the 'oppressing country' (here Britain), even in the face of everyday and institutional racism, is traced in both *Handsworth Songs* and in McQueen's portrayal of the Black police officer Leroy Logan in *Red, White and Blue*. But there are also salient formal and political differences between the two texts, which an inquiry into their respective remediations of Burke's photograph helps to clarify.

HANDSWORTH SONGS

Black Audio Film Collective's most celebrated production, *Handsworth Songs* interrogates and reworks mainstream television and press coverage of three days of violence in September 1985, in which police were attacked and shops damaged in Handsworth, Birmingham. It does this in part by splicing such material with archive footage of Afro-Caribbean immigrants arriving in the UK and building new lives there, thus tapping into intertwined currents of optimism, melancholy and foreboding. Akomfrah has said: 'one of the things I'm obsessed with [is] archives, because on the one hand they're repositories of official memory, but they're also phantoms of other kinds of memories that weren't taken up' (Corless 2012: 45). Of the footage of the 'riots' and their aftermath, he noted:

> [we] needed to slow it down, open it, stretch it out. Because although you might say this happened in one afternoon, actually what happens in one afternoon has decades in it. We were going to open it up and show you how there are five decades there. (Power 2011: 61, cited in Highmore 2017: 109)

Boy with Flag appears 17 minutes into the film as the final image in a short montage of five of Burke's black-and-white photographs showing Black children on the streets, or, in one instance, at school with a white teacher. The sequence is accompanied by musique concrète, and follows on from a clip of a Black woman complaining to journalists about unemployment and police harassment of Black youth in the months preceding the uprising. An earlier montage of images from the 1950s and 1960s includes new immigrants' wedding photographs, along with footage of them at home, going to work and dancing on a night out. Ratik Asokan has commented on the impact of this assemblage: 'Now it is impossible for us to watch the crass television coverage of the riot, which is introduced later in the film, without thinking of the previous generations that settled in Handsworth and tried to make a life there' (Asokan 2018). Another consequence of this use of bricolage is to capture a sense of disappointment among the first generation of immigrants, which Ben Highmore has compared to unrequited love: 'The secret history of disappointment is freighted with the unrequited love of migration' (Highmore 2017: 116). By the time of the civil unrest of the 1980s, the offspring of those post-war immigrants were confronted with unemployment, everyday racism and police harassment. Situated within this historical framework, Burke's image of Fagan and his Union Jack becomes a challenge to the racialised stereotype of the 'black bomber' (Connell 2012), and is instead redolent of the complex subjectivation of the young (male) Black Briton, who is both at home and never at home in the country.

Akomfrah has commented on the difficulty of trying to escape reductive racist expectations of what Black people in the UK can and cannot be:

> [there is] that mirror moment when you suddenly realize that actually, this figure, this ghost that you've been trying to run away from [. . .] the fiction of the black figure, was in fact, and is in fact, you [. . .] You suddenly realize that all the news accounts and the TV reportage – about a young man or woman who is causing trouble, and who you were trying to avoid because you were trying to be a good British subject – were talking about you. (Akomfrah in Asokan 2018)

Akomfrah's account here echoes Frantz Fanon's seminal analysis of the accretion of racialised constructions, and their impact on the Black self when subjected to a white person's gaze, in *Black Skin, White Masks*:

> I was responsible at the same time for my body, my race, my ancestors. [. . .] I discovered my blackness, my ethnic characteristics; and I was battered down by tom-toms, cannibalism, intellectual deficiency, fetishism [sic], racial defects, slave-ships, and above all else, above all: 'Sho' good eatin'. (Fanon [1952] 1986: 112)[1]

Asokan glosses Akomfrah's experience and his filmmaking response thus:

The trauma, as it were, comprises growing up black in a racist country. The (self)diagnosis is the belated recognition that this society made you want to escape your skin color. Having understood that escape is impossible, and indeed misguided, you then search for a therapy. Here's where the archive comes in. The visual history of imperialism serves as a master key to your complexes. By deconstructing the archive you reframe your relationship to society. (Asokan 2018)

It is instructive to compare and contrast the use of *Boy with Flag* in *Handsworth Songs* to an untitled image of a young Black boy in a cowboy hat in Raoul Peck's documentary on James Baldwin. *I Am Not Your Negro* (2016) is a film which also deals with the liminal social positioning of Black citizens in a racist country, in this case the United States. Baldwin's words in the film are either read in voiceover by the actor Samuel L. Jackson, or recorded in his television appearances and public speeches. The following passage is taken from footage of Baldwin's speech to students at Cambridge University in 1965:

At the moment you are born, since you don't know any better, every stick and stone and every face [in dominant media] is white, and since you have not yet seen a mirror, you suppose that you are too. It comes as a great shock at the age of 5 or 6 or 7, to discover that Gary Cooper killing off the Indians when you were rooting for Gary Cooper, that the Indians were you. It comes as a great shock to discover the country which is your birthplace and to which you owe your life and your identity has not in its whole system of reality evolved any place for you.

Twice Peck cuts away from archival black-and-white film of Baldwin at Cambridge. The first shift is to an image of a young Black girl looking at white mannequins of children in a clothes shop window; the second is to the boy in the cowboy hat. The latter matches the last sentence of the speech, which lasts for 15 seconds. A slow zoom in to the photograph ends with the boy's head and face occupying the majority of the frame as he looks directly at the camera. (See Figure 13.2.)

In this and many other sequences in *I Am Not Your Negro*, words and images are organised in a mutually supportive logic in order to secure meaning. Baldwin's verbal eloquence is illustrated by stills and clips from the archive, such as the boy in the cowboy hat. At the same time, the significance of these images is clarified, their meanings delimited and anchored, by his words.

By contrast, *Handsworth Songs* employs Burke's photograph metonymically, rather than 'underwriting' it with spoken text. Akomfrah elaborates on the process in a discussion of metonymy in his later film, *The Nine Muses* (2010):

Figure 13.2. *I Am Not Your Negro* (Velvet Film, Artémis Productions, Close Up Films, 2016).

> I work to find poetry in the metonymic, to work with images that have authority and autonomy and value in their own right. So [in one sequence from *The Nine Muses*] it's a horse in a field, it is free, it's running around, and at some point it approaches the camera. But its meanings free float, they can be commandeered, not just as magic or mystery, but also from the juxtaposition of images. [. . .] Here is an image of a creature, a horse, it's roaming free, it's 'wild', no saddle on its back, so the viewer knows in some way that you are working with ideas of freedom. But the trick is not to state it, not to underwrite it. Then it merely becomes symbolic. There is a value in the metonymic, a vitality, a truth. [. . .] So we have images that have a value and an autonomy in their own right, and an aura at the same time. But one is not being forced to see a meaning. (Akomfrah in Austin 2016b)

In *Handsworth Songs*, Burke's image functions as one of several figurations of the complex social positioning of Black Britons but, like the horse in *The Nine Muses*, it still retains some autonomy, with meanings floating free. Its polyvalence is neither simply self-evident nor entirely contained within the armature of the film's argument.[2]

RED, WHITE AND BLUE

The second deployment of *Boy with Flag* that I want to discuss occurs in Steve McQueen's *Small Axe* pentalogy. *Red, White and Blue* tells the true story of

Leroy Logan, a second-generation immigrant who left a career as a medical research scientist to join the Metropolitan Police in 1981. Logan, played by John Boyega, has to cope with relentless racism from fellow officers, ostracisation by some members of the local Black community, and the vehement disapproval of his father, himself the victim of a brutal attack by white police officers. McQueen has said:

> I'm still struggling, to be honest with you [to understand Logan's choice] . . . he had so much going against him, being in the police force, the racism in the police force, as well as his father, who was attacked and beaten. [. . .] [Logan was] up against so much [. . .] the effort, mental, physical, emotional, is gigantic. [. . .] it's a titanic effort that he made to keep on going in that situation. (McQueen 2020)

In his career as an artist and filmmaker McQueen has worked across diverse modes and registers, from the experimental to popular genres, and the *Small Axe* series is certainly closer to the popular end of this spectrum. Compared to the essayistic and experimental techniques of *Handsworth Songs*, *Red, White and Blue* offers a far more conventional narrative, one that is realist, immersive and character-centred.[3] The drama is clearly aiming for a much larger audience, but it, like the other *Small Axe* titles, remains utterly political in both intent and impact, by calling attention to relatively neglected histories of Black people in Britain. McQueen has said: 'I wanted to make *Small Axe* for my mother, in a way that you could turn on the telly and have it accessible to her' ('Lovers Rock', 2020).

Following the final scene of Logan and his father sharing a drink in the kitchen, and the subsequent end credits, Burke's photograph is the last image of *Red, White and Blue*. Here it takes on a summative function, condensing the complexity of Logan's preceding journey. It is never made clear whether or not viewers are to think of this image as that of the young Leroy. However, as a result of the photograph's positioning, it remains tethered to the story of Logan, a loyal public servant who quotes Robert Peel ('the police are the people and the people are the police'), but by the end of the narrative has not been allowed full entry to the state he sets out to serve.

To this extent, *Boy with Flag* reiterates Logan's liminality as one seeking inclusion but repeatedly excluded and discriminated against due to his racialisation as a Black man. This process has been foregrounded throughout the drama, not just through events such as the micro-aggressions and isolation he endures from white colleagues at the station, but also through the texture of mise-en-scène. The latter registers the 'environmental press'[4] of white institutional spaces, including his superior's office and the training facility at Hendon College, that are adorned with pictures of Queen Elizabeth II and 'great white men'. Logan's persistence in the face of institutional and everyday racism is both signalled and validated by the Union Jack that adorns Winston Fagan's handlebars in Burke's image. But the photograph still operates metonymically, with a degree of autonomy that exceeds the narrative of *Red, White and Blue*, and without the verbal underwriting provided in the sequence from *I Am Not Your Negro* discussed above.[5]

In his contribution to the 1993 collection *Vanley Burke: A Retrospective*, Stuart Hall cautions against simplistic assumptions about the transparency and neutrality of photography:

> 'Making visible' [. . .] cannot be simply documenting what is already there. [Instead] framing 'fixes' what is not elsewhere fixed [. . .] a whole way of life, largely unrecorded (and undervalued) *acquires* a value, a surplus of meaning, a 'representativeness' it did not know it had. (Hall 1993: 14, emphasis in original)[6]

The multiple resonances of *Boy with Flag* as both a recognition of and an active intervention in the complex and often embattled social positioning of second-generation Black immigrants in the UK have been further extended and amplified by the image's filmic remediations considered here. As Evelynn Hammonds has argued, 'visibility in and of itself does not erase a history of silence nor does it challenge the structure of power and domination, symbolic and material, that determines what can and cannot be seen' (Hammonds 1994, cited in Keeling 2007: 11). Nevertheless, Burke's photograph and its productive reframings by Akomfrah and McQueen make a contribution to this (still) urgent and ongoing confrontation by claiming space from which to articulate something of Black British experience.

NOTES

1. The original 'petit-nègre' phrasing of the marketing slogan which ends this litany of stereotypes is: '*Y a bon banania!*' Banania is a French cereal comprising banana flour, cocoa and sugar. For an excellent analysis of Fanon's argument, along with racist tropes in the promotion of Banania, see Gordon 2015: 50–2. On 'petit-nègre', 'a form of simplified French developed by the French military overseeing Senegalese soldiers', see Gordon 2015: 159, n6.
2. Perhaps the most striking instance of metonymy in *Handsworth Songs* is derived from archive footage of a foundry. The screen fills with a monochrome image of a huge pile of chains, on which is superimposed the single word 'CHAINS', then 'For Workshop and Factory' and 'For those who go down to the Sea in Ships'. Reframed and repurposed, these found images and words resonate with the spectre of slavery, without mentioning it explicitly.
3. Nevertheless, in this and other *Small Axe* titles, McQueen occasionally holds shots longer than is strictly necessary for narrative purposes. For example, when Leroy, now in uniform, leaves the youth club that he used to attend as a teenager, the camera cuts to

a flock of pigeons in flight and the image is held for 20 seconds. The birds are implicitly from Leroy's point of view, and so gesture to his interiority, but their exact meaning is not entirely clear. That is, they function metonymically, not unlike another shot of birds in *Handsworth Songs*.

4. I have borrowed this concept from gerontology, where it refers to 'psychosocial stressors' in the built environment. 'The environmental press theory is a theory of adaptation that focuses on person variables (competencies), environmental variables (environmental press), and the interaction between the two variables' (Adler nd; Lichtenberg et al., 549). I suggest that this model could be reworked to register something of the naturalisation and reproduction of whiteness as a dominant force in the built environment of the UK and beyond.

5. Photographs are also inserted into two other *Small Axe* titles, *Mangrove* and *Alex Wheatle*. In the former, a rapid 20-second montage of images of the construction of the Westway in London visualises the passing of time during the trial of the Mangrove Nine in 1970. In the latter, 45 minutes into the 65-minute episode, McQueen cuts to a 4-minute montage of black-and-white photographs of the 1981 New Cross fire, in which thirteen young Black people died, and subsequent protests, accompanied by Linton Kwesi Johnson's poem 'New Crass Massakah'. This sequence initially disrupts the diegesis, temporarily shifting its visual register from screen drama to documentary photography, and its soundtrack to a solo spoken word performance. As Wheatle's story continues, the material is partly reintegrated within the narrative, motivated as a gesture to his growing politicisation and understanding of himself as a Black Briton. But both the photographs and the poem retain some autonomy as cultural artefacts in their own right.

6. Hall writes of Burke's later images of Handsworth: '[T]he variety of ways of "being black in Britain" which these images re-present cannot be defined or placed any longer *solely* in relation to racism. [. . .] Racism persists, but the black people in Vanley Burke's photographs cannot be defined by, or their value exhausted through the relationship to, racism alone' (1993: 15, emphasis in original). This reading is also applicable to the *Small Axe* series, insofar as it celebrates Black community, resilience and creativity as 'hard-won victories in the face of racism', but also as something more than this (*Small Axe*, nd).

CHAPTER 14

Small Axe is a Start: An interview with Bernard Coard

Thomas Austin

This chapter is based on an interview of 100 minutes' duration with the renowned Grenadian activist, politician and author Bernard Coard.[1] Our discussion revisits his seminal 1971 work on institutional racism in British education, *How the West Indian Child is Made Educationally Sub-normal in the British School System*, and explores his response to the dramatisation of the scandal he uncovered in the *Small Axe* episode *Education*.[2] The interview also considers Coard's involvement in the spinoff BBC ONE documentary *Subnormal: A British Scandal*, and his critique of the current state of UK education.

In 1967, having gained a Masters degree in comparative politics at Sussex University, Coard began a PhD in development economics. He also worked as a youth leader in Deptford, and then, from 1969, as a teacher in two London schools for the 'educationally subnormal'.

I never met a middle-class or upper-class kid in any of those schools. Neither in the seven that I did youth clubs for, nor the two where I taught full time. Not one middle-class or upper-class kid. [They were] all white working-class and Black from the Caribbean. The schools were both co-educational. I would say that most of the teachers were good people. [But] They can't do the good work that they are capable of because the system is not constructed for that. The curriculum they have to work with, the expectations that are laid down for them [. . .] that is a social crime in itself. [. . .] [In *Education*] it would have been just as valid for McQueen to have a classroom where there is a sympathetic, empathetic teacher who is trying his or her best, but constrained by what [. . .] level is expected of the children. That would have been another way to do it, but what he did [with a bored and disengaged teacher] was perfectly authentic because a quarter of my experiences were like that.

How did you feel your book and your own intervention was represented in Education?

My wife and I had been married for less than two years and we went to this party, this fete, in Tulse Hill, south of the Thames. Grenadian guys and their families. They were quite Caribbean oriented, so they had people from the Bahamas and everywhere in between [. . .] And at these fetes [they played] Mighty Sparrow, Lord Kitchener, the most famous calypsonians from Trinidad and Tobago, music from the latest carnival. [. . .] My wife and I were on the dance floor about eight o'clock and that's very early for a fete, most people don't get on the dance floor until ten. People are there eating and drinking and chatting, and this couple dancing next to me, the husband said, 'excuse me, but I hear you're one of the teachers at these schools'. There were very few Black teachers in general, and even less in these ESN schools, in fact I never met another one. And he said, 'Tell me what's going on in these schools, because my kid and some of these other guys' kids are at these schools and come home after years, they can't read, they can't write, they can't do simple arithmetic.' So he asked me a lot of questions, his wife asked me questions. Next thing I know, people come off the dance floor and join in asking questions. And the next thing I know they turn off the music. There was no fete! People just gathered around and they had a million questions. I had to answer all their questions. This went on for two or three hours! And at the end of that time, they said, 'You have to write a paper, we have a conference in three months' time.'

A lot of them were community activists. They were aware that things were wrong but they didn't know all the details. I said, 'Hold on, let me make one thing clear. I am a student doing development economics. I have come here to do my degree and then return to serve my people in Grenada' [. . .] Between working full time and studying (in theory part time but also really full time), I had no time for anything else. I had no links with the Caribbean community, no links at all because I had no time on my hands. Going to a fete three times a year was my only link. It was the only place they could have caught me. They said, 'Make yourself an expert [in education], you have three months. London University has a School of Education [. .] go there.'

So I had to do a lot of reading. I looked at stuff from France, Germany, Australia, America, Jamaica. I tried to see what research had been done on the things I had observed in the classroom. I could describe what I had seen but it's not just me. Other people have researched this and they have found the same thing. So [my intervention] is a polemic, but it's also academic. So I do this thing and I write about 20 pages, and I present it at the conference, to community activists and parents as well. And at the end of it, almost everybody in the hall surrounded me and said, 'You have to publish it now [. . .] This is what we need, and you have three more months now to turn it into a book. Go and make yourself an expert on this. We don't want any excuses.' [. . .]

So I write this thing, the initial thing is 210 pages long. But then I say to myself no, no, no. Caribbean parents working in factories on shift systems have minimal sleep, with kids to look after. They don't have time to read 210 pages. So I cut out three-quarters of the chapters, just focus on the most important things, bring it down to 50, 55 pages, make it a pamphlet or a booklet, not a book. [*How the West Indian Child is Made Educationally Sub-normal in the British School System*] The other parts were published in other places. [. . .] And then we tried to get a publisher. Nobody would publish it. And they would all tell me, 'Listen, Caribbean people are a tiny fraction of the British population, a small market. And more than that, they don't buy books.' [. . .]

One night I'm invited to a meeting. Twenty-six Caribbean organisations are meeting from all over Britain, meeting in London. They say, 'We will raise the money to have it printed.' But then no distributor would take it. WHSmith and others said, 'We don't have room on our shelves, and nobody's going to buy it.' [. . .] So, these same twenty-six organisations said, 'Don't worry. Once it's published we'll go door to door and sell it.' Sold 10,000 copies in the first few weeks, door to door. We had to reprint. And of course now [there have been] five separate editions: '71, '91, 2005, 2007 and now, 2021.

[The Caribbean organisations also said:] 'We will organise. You say we need supplementary schools.' There were already a few, but what I said was, this thing has to be nationwide. We really have to get going with supplementary schools on a big scale because it improves our self-image, self-concept, self-belief, self-confidence. This is fundamental. So I gave an impetus to that, I didn't start it. [. . .] Parents' groups, youth groups, supplementary schools all over the place, Saturday classes and so on. All of that took off in a big way because of the book. When people laud me with all kinds of praise, I have to remind them it's not about me. I am not a mover and shaker. I did not leave Grenada to write a book on education. I claim no credit whatsoever for that. That is the community, genuinely, it takes all the credit.

Do you think Small Axe *and* Subnormal *have helped revive interest in the book?*

The fifth edition of my booklet was published in February of this year, 2021, as a fiftieth anniversary edition. [. . .] The book is addressed to Black parents, to them directly: this is what's going on, this is what you can do about it. [But] lo and behold, the reaction of many white teachers [in 1971] was very positive. The media [radio, television, newspapers] was also sympathetic. So I got a very receptive media. I personally have been sent half a dozen PhD theses taking sections of the book and working out theses. [. . .] It has been widely circulated and quoted and referenced in works of education and sociology textbooks. [. . .] But that's different from the wider public. [. . .] When *Education* came out, because of the emotion that was captured, the drama of it all raised a whole new light [on the issue].

With *Education*, from the halfway point, tears were coming to my eyes and I cried for the rest of the programme because I'm reliving what I witnessed all those years ago. It's just very emotional, and the fact that the film was powerful enough to have me, [with] knowledge of the thing, still crying without control is the highest praise, in my view, of the quality of the film.

The [2021] relaunch on Zoom of the fifth edition [of the book] had 2,600 people register. But unfortunately the organisers weren't expecting that, they only had room for 500 people online. [. . .] A few people lost their internet access for a minute or two and somebody else got in and they couldn't get back on the programme. Jeremy Corbyn was supposed to speak at the launch but he couldn't get in! So it was oversubscribed massively, and unquestionably the *Small Axe* series and in particular *Education* is responsible for that renewal of interest among a wider audience.

What was your opinion of Subnormal?

The one criticism that I've heard from a number of Caribbean people [living in Britain] who I've spoken to [. . .] everybody sing its praises [but] they say one thing is that it should not have been done [just] in that hour. It's not possible to do more than was done in that hour. But there should have been a second hour a few weeks later [. . .] that says, 'OK, this is what happened then. Now, how has it changed? What's happening now?'

[Director Lyttanya Shannon] did a fantastic job. You need to have a human interest, listen to what happened to these kids, [who were] basically warehoused. This is powerful. [. . .] Of course that's high praise for McQueen and his other executive producers, because they chose her. They chose somebody young but with the talent to pull it off. [. . .] So it's not a criticism of what they did at all to say, 'There needs to be a sequel, [because] all Caribbean parents, virtually without exception, are saying, very little has changed. [. . .] Why? And what ideas are there to achieve a change?'

In 2021, you wrote in The Chartist: *'The [continuing] disproportionate exclusion of Caribbean-origin children from schools mirrors a more deep-seated and profoundly damaging exclusion of these children and their parents' identity, history, culture, and contribution to Britain from the curriculum of the British school system'* (Coard 2021). *What role can media productions like* Small Axe *play in challenging these exclusions? What else needs to be done in the UK?*

There has not been enough written about how Black children in schools are doubly excluded. Everybody talks about exclusions, and condemn it rightfully, because any serious education system knows that a child that misbehaves, whether at home or at school, is a cry for help. [. . .] So that's one form of exclusion, everybody has condemned it, and it must be brought to an end. But exclusion starts before that. Imagine you're a Black kid and you're in school and you know that Blacks have lived in Britain since Roman times. [. . .] And there's nothing [taught] about them, right? Eric Williams's book *Capitalism and Slavery* shows that Britain's industrialisation was in fact born of, created from, slavery, the Caribbean and sugar.³ [. . .] So the fact is that the Caribbean built industrial Britain. And on top of that, Caribbean people helped in the First and Second World Wars. [. . .] [But] this is not integrated into the history of the country. So you're whitewashed out of British history, you're whitewashed out of world history. [. . .] Exclusion of identity, culture, history, contribution. That exclusion starts from day one of school. And before school, media. Even before you go to school, exclusion starts, from the moment you can watch the TV. That's the background, that's the context. And therefore the power of those two films [*Education* and *Subnormal*]. What the *Small Axe* series does is shine a powerful and positive light on Caribbean people's presence [in the UK]. It's a start. [Now] there will have to be other films, dealing with Black people in Elizabethan times, Black people in Roman times, drama prior to the slave trade, Black people's contribution to the First and Second World Wars, and things like that.

NOTES

1. The interview took place via Zoom on 25 November 2021.
2. The protagonist of *Education*, twelve-year-old Kingsley (Kenyah Sandy), has dyslexia but is placed in a school for the 'educationally subnormal', where expectations are far lower than at his previous school. In one excruciating scene, Kingsley and his classmates have to endure their teacher singing 'The House of the Rising Sun' and accompanying himself on the guitar. McQueen told the *Washington Post* that the scene was based on his own childhood experience (Hornaday 2020).
3. Eric Williams's groundbreaking study *Capitalism and Slavery* was first published in the US in 1944. The book argues that profits from the slave trade financed Britain's industrial revolution in the eighteenth and nineteenth centuries, and that slavery was only abolished by the British government once the system had become uneconomic.

Films and Television Programmes

Alex Wheatle, dir. Steve McQueen (2020).
Amazing Grace, dir. Michael Apted (2006).
Ashes, dir. Steve McQueen (2002).
BBC News (2021), Mina Smallman: 'I know what Sarah Everard's parents are experiencing'. 26 March, online <https://www.bbc.co.uk/news/av/uk-56450969> (last accessed 19 March 2022).
Bear, dir. Steve McQueen (1993).
Black Power: A British Story of Resistance, dir. George Amponsah (2021).
Breaking Bad (2008–13).
Burn!, dir. Gillo Pontecorvo (1969).
Caribs' Leap, dir. Steve McQueen (2002).
Catch, dir. Steve McQueen (1997).
Charlotte, dir. Steve McQueen (2004).
Choke (dir: Clark Gregg, 2008, USA).
Codes of Conduct, dir. Steve McQueen (2015).
Cold Breath, dir. Steve McQueen (1999).
Deadpan, dir. Steve McQueen (1997).
Diary of a Sex Addict (dir: Joseph Brutsman, 2001, USA).
Django Unchained, dir. Quentin Tarantino (2012).
Don Jon (dir: Joseph Gordon-Levitt, 2013, USA).
Drumroll, dir. Steve McQueen (1998).
Education, dir. Steve McQueen (2020).
Exodus, dir. Steve McQueen (1992–7).
Girls, Tricky, dir. Steve McQueen (2001).
Gravesend, dir. Steve McQueen (2007).
Handsworth Songs, dir. John Akomfrah, of Black Audio Film Collective (1986).
Hunger, dir. Steve McQueen (2008).
I Am a Sex Addict (dir: Caveh Zahedi, 2005, USA).
I Am Not Your Negro, dir. Raoul Peck (2016).
Illuminer, dir. Steve McQueen (2001).
Just Above My Head, dir. Steve McQueen (1996).

Lincoln, dir. Steven Spielberg (2012).
Lovers Rock, dir. Steve McQueen (2020).
Manderlay, dir. Lars von Trier (2005).
Mangrove, dir. Steve McQueen (2020).
Many Rivers to Cross, dir. Patricia Francis (2013), online film recording, available on YouTube at <www.youtube.com/watch?v=Fp76muFTDIk> (last accessed 7 April 2022).
Mees, After Evening Dip, New Year's Day, 2002 (dir. Steve McQueen, 2005)
New York, New York (dir: Martin Scorsese, 1977, USA).
Nymph(o)maniac (dir: Lars von Trier, 2013, Denmark).
The Passion of Remembrance, dir. Maureen Blackwood and Isaac Julien, of Sankofa Film and Video Collective (1986).
Pressure, dir. Horace Ové (1975).
Prey, dir. Steve McQueen (1999).
Red, White and Blue, dir. Steve McQueen (2020).
Sex and the City (1998–2004).
Shame, dir. Steve McQueen (2011).
Small Axe, dir. Steve McQueen (2020).
Steamboat Bill, Jr., dir. Charles Reisner, Buster Keaton (1928).
The Story of Lovers Rock, dir. Horace Ové (2011).
Subnormal: A British Scandal, dir. Lyttanya Shannon (2021).
The Tallest Tree in Our Forest, dir. Gil Noble (1977).
Taxi Driver (dir: Martin Scorsese, 1976, USA).
Thanks for Sharing (dir: Stuart Blumberg, 2012, USA).
12 Years a Slave, dir. Steve McQueen (2014).
Tremé (2010–13).
Uprising, dir. Steve McQueen and James Rogan (2021).
Welcome to New York (dir: Abel Ferrara, 2014, France/USA).
Widows (1983–5).
Widows, dir. Steve McQueen (2021).
World in Action: Thatcher Interview, ITV, 30 January 1978, online video recording, <https://www.youtube.com/watch?v=JR9X6FkkOeY> (last accessed 4 August 2021).

Bibliography

Abdurraqib, H. (2021), *A Little Devil in America: in Praise of Black Performance*. New York: Random House.
Abbott, D. (2022), 'Diane Abbott MP Hackney North and Stoke Newington', at <https://www.dianeabbott.org.uk/projects#:~:text=London%20Schools%20and%20the%20Black%20Child%20(LSBC)%20is%20an%20initiative,attainment%20amongst%20London's%20Black%20students.&text=Together%20we%20discuss%20the%20obstacles,attainment%20in%20London%20and%20beyond> (last accessed 15 January 2022).
Abrams, A. (2022), 'Steve McQueen's "Sunshine State" illuminates the cavernous halls of Milan's Pirelli HangarBicocca', *Wallpaper**, 8 April, online at <https://www.wallpaper.com/art/steve-mcqueens-sunshine-state-illuminates-the-cavernous-halls-of-milans-pirelli-hangarbicocca> (last accessed 13 July 2022).
Adams, G. (1996), *Before the Dawn: An Autobiography*. Oxford: Heinemann Publishers Ltd.
Adams, R. (2020), 'Fewer than 1% of university professors are black, figures show', *The Guardian*, 27 February, online at <https://www.theguardian.com/education/2020/feb/27/fewer-than-1-of-uk-university-professors-are-black-figures-show> (last accessed 13 July 2022).
Adler, J. (nd), 'Environmental press: Revisiting the concept in current research', at <https://cuny.manifoldapp.org/read/environmental-press-revisiting-the-concept-in-current-research/section/1c4610b6-ebce-47af-b302-e2b05b384dcb>.
Aftab, K. (2021), 'Steve McQueen on the future of film', *Sight and Sound*, (September), 31: 7, 45.
Aitkenhead, D. (2014), 'Steve McQueen: My hidden shame', *The Guardian*, 4 January, online at <https://www.theguardian.com/film/2014/jan/04/steve-mcqueen-my-painful-childhood-shame> (last accessed 19 July 2022).
Åkervall, L. (2018), *Kinematographische Affekte. Die Transformation der Kinoerfahrung*. Munich: Fink.
Akyildiz, S. G. (2021), 'Disgraced of the West, deserted of the East: Men in the films *Shame* and *Issiz Adam*', *Cinej Cinema Journal*, 9: 1, 425–55.
Alberti, J. (2013), '"I Love you, man": Bromances, the construction of masculinity, and the continuing evolution of the romantic comedy', *Quarterly Review of Film and Video*, 30: 2, 159–72.

Allyn, D. (2001), *Make Love Not War: The Sexual Revolution, An Unfettered History*. London: Routledge.
Altman, R. (1989), *The American Film Musical*. Bloomington: Indiana University Press.
Altman, R. (2019), *Film/Genre*. London: British Film Institute.
Amnesty International UK (2019), 'Black and Asian women MPs abused more online', at <https://www.amnesty.org.uk/online-violence-women-mps> (last accessed 19 March 2022).
Anderson, E. (2022), *Black in White Space: The Enduring Impact of Color in Everyday Life*. Chicago and London: University of Chicago Press.
Anderson, M. (2013), 'Image conscience', *Art Forum*, 17 October, at <www.artforum.com/film/id.43508> (last accessed 19 March 2017).
Andrews, H. (2014), *Television and British Cinema: Convergence and Divergence Since 1990*. Basingstoke: Palgrave Macmillan.
Andrews, K. (2020), 'Mangrove', *Sight and Sound*, (December), 30: 10, 27.
Andrews, W. L., 'North American slave narratives: autobiographies listed chronologically.' *Documenting the American South*. University Library, University of North Carolina, Chapel Hill <docsouth.unc.edu/neh/chronautobio.html> (last accessed 19 March 2017).
Ani, I. (2020), 'Black power through music: What spirit sounds like', *Small Axe Zine*, Amazon, at <https://www.vanityfair.com/sponsored/story/black-power-through-music-what-spirit-sounds-like> (last accessed 5 September 2022).
Apostolidis, P. and J. A. Williams (2017), 'Sex scandals, reputational management and masculinity under neoliberal conditions', *Sexualities*, 20: 7, 793–814.
Arthurs, J. (2003), 'Sex and the City and consumer culture: Remediating postfeminist drama', *Feminist Media Studies*, 31, 83–98.
Ashley, C. P. and M. Billies (2020), 'Affect & race/blackness', *Athenea Digital*, 20: 2, e2323 <https://doi.org/10.5565/rev/athenea.2323> (last accessed 17 March 2022).
Asokan, R. (2018), 'Memories of underdevelopment', *Art in America* (1 October), online at <https://www.artnews.com/art-in-america/features/memories-of-underdevelopment-6356>.
Athwal, H. (2002), 'Black deaths in custody', 11 November, available on the *Institute of Race Relations* website at <www.irr.org.uk/article/black-deaths-in-custody> (last accessed 25 March 2022).
Austin, T. (2016a), 'Interiority, identity and the limits of knowledge in documentary film', *Screen* 57: 4, 414–30.
Austin, T. (2016b), 'Temporal vertigo: An interview with John Akomfrah', *Senses of Cinema*, 79, online at <https://www.sensesofcinema.com/2016/feature-articles/john-akomfrah-interview/>.
Austin, T. (2021), telephone interview with Leila Hassan Howe, 15 November.
Bailey, C. (2012), '*Survival*, *Hunger* and *Shame*', in 'A conversation with Steve McQueen', in I. Friedli (ed.), *Steve McQueen Works*, Basel: Laurenz Foundation, Schaulager, 184 (exhibition catalogue).
Baldwin, J. (1985), 'The Fire Next Time: My dungeon shook', in *The Price of The Ticket: Collected Nonfiction 1948–1985*, New York: St. Martin's Press, 338–87.
Baldwin, J. (1998a), 'The Devil Finds Work', in *Collected Essays*, edited by T. Morrison. New York: The Library of America, 477–572.
Baldwin, J. (1998b), 'The Price of the ticket', in *Collected Essays*, edited by T. Morrison. New York: The Library of America, 830–42.
Baldwin, J. (1998c), 'Stranger in the Village', in *Collected Essays*, edited by T. Morrison. New York: The Library of America, 117–29.
Balsom, E. (2013), *Exhibiting Cinema in Contemporary Art*. Amsterdam: Amsterdam University Press.

Baptist, E. E. (2014), *The Half Has Never Been Told: Slavery and the Making of American Capitalism*. New York: Basic Books.
Barnard, J. (2020), 'Alex Wheatle', *Sight and Sound*, (December), 30: 10, 34.
Baughan, N. (2020/21), 'Education', *Sight and Sound*, (Winter), 31: 1, 130.
Bazin, A. (1960), 'The ontology of the photographic image', translated by Hugh Gray, *Film Quarterly*, 13: 4, 4–9.
Beckert, S. (2004), 'Emancipation and Empire: Reconstructing the worldwide web of cotton production in the age of the American Civil War', *American Historical Review*, 109: 5, 1405–38.
Beckert, S. (2014), *Empire of Cotton: A Global History*. Knopf.
Bell, C. (2003), 'Dealing with the Past in Northern Ireland', *Fordham International Law Journal*, 26: 4, 1095–1126.
Bell, C. (2008), *On the Law of Peace: Peace Agreements and the Lex Pacificatoria*. Oxford: Oxford University Press.
Bell, J. (2018), 'Thieves like us', *Sight and Sound*, (November), 28: 11, 22–6.
Bell, J. (2020/21), 'Television of the year', *Sight and Sound*, (Winter), 31: 1, 101–2.
Belton, J. (2014), 'If film is dead what is cinema?', *Screen* 55: 4, 460–70.
Benjamin, W. (1968), *Illuminations: Essays and Reflections*. New York: Harcourt.
Bew, P. (2007), *The Making and Remaking of the Good Friday Agreement*. Dublin: The Liffey Press.
Bew, P. and Gordon G. (1999), *Northern Ireland: A Chronology of the Troubles, 1968–99*. Dublin: Gill & Macmillan Ltd.
'BFI At Home, Subnormal: A British Scandal Q&A with Steve McQueen', 13 May 2021, online at <https://www.youtube.com/watch?v=DxwQljY_3Yo>.
Bishop, C. (2005), *Installation Art: A Critical History*. London: Tate Publishing.
Black Lives Matter, 'Black Lives Matter Herstory', at <https://blacklivesmatter.com/herstory> (last accessed 30 March 2022).
Blackett, R. J. M. (2013), *Making Freedom: The Underground Railroad and the Politics of Slavery*. University of North Carolina Press.
Blum, A. (2015), 'Each night in rapture: the silent sound of *Shame*', *Studies in Gender and Sexuality*, 16: 2, 123–8.
Bourdieu, P. (1998), 'The myth of "globalization" and the European welfare state', in *Acts of Resistance: Against the New Myths of Our Time*, translated by Richard Nice. Cambridge: Polity Press.
Bourne, S. C. (dir.) (1999), *Here I Stand*, WinStar Home Entertainment.
Boyea, C. L. (2021), 'BFI presents *Small Axe* a collection of five films', National Film Theatre Programme, (October), 40.
Bradley, R. (2015), 'Reinventing capacity: Black femininity's lyrical surplus and the cinematic limits of *12 Years a Slave*', *Black Camera*, 7: 1, 162–78.
Bradshaw, P. (2014), '*12 Years a Slave* – Review', *The Guardian*, 9 January, at <www.theguardian.com/film/2014/jan/09/12-years-a-slave-review> (last accessed 19 March 2017).
Braid, B. (2014), '"You force me into the corner and you trap me": The crisis of hegemonic masculinity in Steve McQueen's *Shame*', in A. Pilinska and H. Siganporia (eds), *All Equally Real: Femininities and Masculinities Today*. Oxford: Inter-Disciplinary Press, 9–18.
Braid, B. (2014b), 'Fassination, fandom and the crisis of hegemony: Michael Fassbender's performance of masculinity and the female gaze', in A. Chauvel, N. Lamerichs and J. Seymour (eds), *Fan Studies: Researching Popular Audiences*. Oxford: Inter-Disciplinary Press, 73–84.
Brinkema, E. (2014), *The Forms of the Affects*. Durham, NC: Duke University Press.

Brody, R. (2013), 'Should a film try to depict slavery?', *The New Yorker*, 21 October, <www.newyorker.com/culture/richard-brody/should-a-film-try-to-depict-slavery> (last accessed 19 March 2017).
Brown, K. J. (2017), 'At the center of the periphery: Gender, landscape, and architecture in *12 Years a Slave*', *The Global South*, 11: 1, 121–35.
Brunsdon, C. (1997), 'Men's genres for women', in H. Baehr and G. Dyer (eds), *Boxed in: Women in Television*. New York: Pandora, 184–202.
Bryan, B. Dadzie, S. and Scafe, S. (1985, 2018) *The Heart of The Race Black Women's Lives in Britain*. London: Verso.
Buchanan, R. and R. Johnson (2009), 'Strange encounters: exploring law and film in the affective register', *Studies in Law, Politics, and Society*, 46, 33–60.
Bukatman, S. (2003), 'Syncopated city: New York in musical film (1929–1961)', in S. Bukatman, *Matters of Gravity: Special Effects and Supermen in the 20th Century*. Durham, NC: Duke University Press, 157–83.
Burchell, G., C. Gordon and P. Miller (1991), *The Foucault Effect: Studies in Governmentality*. University of Chicago Press.
Burke, V. (nd), interviewed on video, online at <http://www.vanley.co.uk/about-vanley>.
Buse, P. and A. Scott (1999), *Ghosts: Deconstruction, Psychoanalysis, History*. London: Macmillan.
Butler, J. (1990), *Gender Trouble*. New York: Routledge.
Campbell, C. and F. Ní Aoláin (eds) (2003), *Fordham International Law Journal*, special edition, 'Transitional Justice – Northern Ireland and Beyond', 26: 4.
Carty-Williams, C. (2020), 'Lovers Rock', *Sight and Sound*, (December), 30: 10, 31.
Cavell, S. (1996), *Contesting Tears. The Hollywood Melodrama of the Unknown Woman*. Chicago: The University of Chicago Press.
Cavell, S. (2005), 'Philosophy the day after tomorrow', in S. Cavell, *Philosophy the Day after Tomorrow*. Cambridge; Belknap, 111–31.
Chambers, E. (2012), *Things Done Change: The Cultural Politics of Recent Black Artists in Britain*. Amsterdam and New York: Rodopi.
'*Charlotte*' (2013), in *I Want the Screen to be a Massive Mirror: Lectures on Steve McQueen*. Schaulager Basel: Laurenz-Stiftung, 170.
Chen, T. M. and D. S. Churchill (eds) (2007), *Film, History and Cultural Citizenship: Sites of Production*. New York and London: Routledge.
Clark, A. (2020), 'In *Small Axe*, Steve McQueen explores Britain's Caribbean heritage', *New York Times*, 11 November <https://www.nytimes.com/2020/11/11/arts/television/steve-mcqueen-small-axe.html> (last accessed 15 April 2022).
Clarke, S. (2021), 'Key people in the creation of BBC One's *Small Axe*', *Production Focus*, Royal Television Society, 10 June <https://rts.org.uk/article/creation-steve-mcqueen-s-anthology-small-axe> (last accessed 15 April 2022).
Clifford, J. (1994), 'Diasporas', *Cultural Anthropology*, 9: 3, 302–38.
Clover, C. (1992), *Men, Women and Chainsaws: Gender in the Modern Horror Film*. London: BFI Publishing.
Coard, B. (2021), 'Black children still underachieving', *The Chartist*, 20 May, online at <https://www.chartist.org.uk/black-children-still-underachieving/>.
Coates, T.-N. (2014), 'The Case for Reparations', *The Atlantic*, June <www.theatlantic.com/magazine/archive/2014/06/the-case-for-reparations/361631/> (last accessed 19 March 2017).
Cobb, J. N. (2014), 'Directed by himself: Steve McQueen's *12 Years a Slave*', *American Literary History*, 26: 2, 339–46.
Collier, D. (2014), 'Steve McQueen', *Nka: Journal of Contemporary African Art*, 25, (Fall), 136–9.
Collins, P. H. (2004), *Black Sexual Politics: African Americans, Gender, and the New Racism*. New York: Routledge.

'Congratulations, Steve McQueen', *Sight and Sound*, 31: 1, (Winter, 2020–1), 99.
Connell, K. (2012), 'Photographing Handsworth: Photography, meaning and identity in a British inner city', *Patterns of Prejudice*, 46: 2, 128–53.
Connolly, M. (2009), *The Place of Artists' Cinema: Space, Site and Screen*. Bristol and Chicago: Intellect Books.
Consultative Group on the Past (2009), *Report of the Consultative Group on the Past*. Belfast, Northern Ireland <www.cgpni.org/fs/doc/Consultative%20Group%20on%20the%20Past%20Full%20Report.pdf> (last accessed 28 June 2009).
Corless, K. (2012), 'One from the heart', *Sight and Sound*, (February) 22: 2, 44–6.
Corless, K. (2020/21), 'The Best 50 films of 2020', *Sight and Sound*, (Winter), 31: 11, 50–3.
Cox, D. (2008), 'Hunger strikes a very sour note', *The Guardian*, 3 November <www.guardian.co.uk/film/filmblog/2008/nov/03/hunger-bobby-sands> (last accessed 28 June 2009).
Craig, D. (2020), 'Steve McQueen: It took "a lot of effort" to get *Small Axe* made', *Radio Times*, 10 November <https://www.radiotimes.com/tv/drama/steve-mcqueen-small-axe-struggle-news/> (last accessed 15 April 2022).
Creative Diversity Network (2020), 'Diamond The Fourth Cut', October, *Creative Diversity Network* website at <www.creativediversitynetwork.com/wp-content/uploads/2021/01/CDN-Diamond4-JANUARY-27-FINAL.pdf> (last accessed 2 April 2022).
'Danny Glover says producers told him his Haiti film lacked "white heroes"', *Miami Herald*, 28 July 2008 <www.miamiherald.com/news/nation-world/world/americas/haiti/article1929662.html> (last accessed 19 March 2017).
Dassanowsky, R. von (2007), 'A Caper of one's own. Fantasy female liberation in 1960s crime comedy film', *Journal of Popular Film and Television*, 35: 3, 107–18.
Dawes, K. (2001), *Talk Yuh Talk: Interviews with Anglophone Caribbean Poets*. Charlottesville: University of Virginia Press.
De Certeau, M. (1984), *The Practice of Everyday Life*. Berkeley: University of California Press.
de Cuir Jr, G. (2020/21), 'Alex Wheatle', *Sight and Sound*, (Winter), 31: 11, 126.
de Waal, K. (2020), 'Education', *Sight and Sound*, (Winter), 30: 10, 33.
Dean, M. (2010), *Governmentality: Power and Rule in Modern Society*. London: Sage Publications.
Deleuze, G. and F. Guattari (1987), *A Thousand Plateaus. Capitalism and Schizophrenia II*, translated by Brian Massumi. Minneapolis: University of Minnesota Press.
Deller, N. (2020), 'Lovers Rock', *Sight and Sound*, (Winter), 30: 10, 69–70.
Demos, T. J. (2005), 'The Art of darkness: on Steve McQueen', *October*, 114, 61–89.
Demos, T. J. (2013), 'Indeterminacy and bare life in Steve McQueen's *Western Deep*', in Demos, *The Migrant Image: The Art and Politics of Documentary during Global Crisis*. Durham, NC: Duke University Press, 34–53.
Denby, David (2013), 'Fighting to survive: *12 Years a Slave* and *All is Lost*', *New Yorker*, 21 October <www.newyorker.com/magazine/2013/10/21/fighting-to-survive-2> (last accessed 19 March 2017).
Derrida, J. (2012), *Specters of Marx*. Taylor and Francis.
Directors UK (2021), '*Small Axe* – Steve McQueen in conversation with Asif Kapadia', 4 June, online at <https://directors.uk.com/news/podcast-small-axe-steve-mcqueen-in-conversation-with-asif-kapadia> (last accessed 25 March 2022).
Doane, M. A. (1982), 'Film and the masquerade: theorizing the female spectator', *Screen*, 23: 3–4 (September–October), 74–88.
Doane, M. A. (2003), 'The Close-up: scale and detail in the cinema', *Differences*, 14: 3, 89–111.
Doherty, T. (2013), 'Bringing the slave narrative to screen: Steve McQueen and John Ridley's searing depiction of America's "peculiar institution"', *Cineaste*, 39: 1, 4–8.

Douglass, F. (1845/2014), *Narrative of the Life of Frederick Douglass, An American Slave*. Penguin.
Du Bois, W. E. B. (1968), *The Autobiography of W. E. B. Du Bois: A Soliloquy on Viewing My Life from the Last Decade of Its First Century*, edited by H. Aptheker. New York: International Publishers.
Duncanson, K. (2008), 'Embodiments of the English constitution in the romanticised narratives of the funeral of Diana, Princess of Wales and *Four Weddings and a Funeral*', *Australian Feminist Law Journal*, 28, 121–47.
Dyer, R. (1997), *White: Essays on Race and Culture*. London: Routledge.
Dyer, R. (2005), *Only Entertainment*. London: Routledge.
Dyer, R. (2012), *In The Space of a Song: The Uses of Song in Film*. London: Routledge.
Eakin, S. and J. Logsdon (1968), 'Introduction', *Twelve Years a Slave, by Solomon Northup. 1853*, edited by Eakin and Logsdon. Louisiana State University Press, ix–xxiv.
El-Enany, N. (2020), *(B)ordering Britain: Law, Race and Empire*. Manchester University Press.
Ellis, J. (1990), *Visible Fictions: Film, Television, Video* [second edition]. London: Routledge.
Ellis, J. (2011), 'Interstitials: how the "bits in between" define the programmes', in P. Grainge (ed.), *Ephemeral Media: Transitory Screen Culture from Television to YouTube*. London: BFI, 59–69.
Ellison, R. (1941), 'Recent Negro fiction', *New Masses*, 5 August, 22–6.
Engell, L. (2021), 'Foreword', in L. Gotto, *Passing and Posing between Black and White. Calibrating the Color Line in U.S. Cinema*. Bielefeld: Transcript, 9–14.
English, D. (2013), 'Somewhere in Devon', in S. E. Hauser (ed.), *I Want the Screen to be a Massive Mirror: Lectures on Steve McQueen*. Schaulager Basel: Laurenz-Stiftung, 31–43.
Enwezor, O. (2012), 'From screen to space: Projection and reanimation in the early works of Steve McQueen', *Steve McQueen: Works*, edited by I. Friedli. Schaulager Basel: Laurenz-Stiftung, 20–35.
Enwezor, O. (2015), 'Okwui Enwezor: All the world's futures – statement by the curator of the 56th International Art Exhibition', online at <https://universes.art/en/venice-biennale/2015/tour/all-the-worlds-futures/curatorial-statement> (last accessed 6 April 2022).
Equiano, O. (2003), *The Interesting Narrative and Other Writings* [revised edition]. Penguin.
Eshun, K. (1998), *More Brilliant Than the Sun: Adventures in Sonic Fiction*. London: Quartet Books.
Eshun, K. and A. Sagar (2007), *The Ghosts of Songs: The Film Art of the Black Audio Film Collective, 1982–1998*. Liverpool: Liverpool University Press.
Esquire with B. Brietling Townhouse (2020), 'Steve McQueen on George Floyd, racist inequality in the UK and his new series, *Small Axe*', 11 November, available on the *Esquire UK* website at <www.youtube.com/watch?v=ySnOSrQeDLU&t=4s> (last accessed 2 April 2022).
Fanon, F. [1952] (1986), *Black Skin, White Masks*, translated by Charles Lam Markmann. London: Pluto Press.
Fanon, F. (1968), *The Wretched of the Earth*. New York: Grove Press, Inc.
Farred, G. (2014), *In Motion, At Rest: The Event of the Athletic Body*. Minneapolis: University of Minnesota Press.
Fay, J. (2022), 'Hollywood's white privacy: Stanley Cavell and James Baldwin', *Screen*, 63: 1, (Spring), 100–6.
Featherstone, M. (2016), 'Carnotopia: the culture of sadism in *Nymphomaniac*, *Shame* and *Thanatomorphose*', in J. Gwynne (ed.), *Transgression in Anglo-American Cinema: Gender, Sex, and the Deviant Body*. Columbia University Press, 25–41.
Ferrer, A. (2014), *Freedom's Mirror: Cuba and Haiti in the Age of Revolution*. Cambridge: Cambridge University Press.

Film at Lincoln Center (2021), 'In Conversation with Steve McQueen on *Small Axe*', 10 June <https://www.filmlinc.org/daily/in-conversation-with-steve-mcqueen-on-small-axe/> (last accessed 15 April 2022).

Filmmaker Stories (2020), 'DP Shabier Kirchner used Kodak . . .', 22 December <https://www.kodak.com/en/motion/blog-post/small-axe-anthology> (last accessed 15 April 2022).

Fintoni, L. (2019), 'Wheel it up: History of the rewind', *Medium*, 14 February <https://medium.com/cuepoint/wheel-it-up-history-of-the-rewind-21fdcff243d9> (last accessed 13 June 2022).

Fisher, J. (2013), 'Themes and variations in the work of Steve McQueen', in S. E. Hauser (ed.), *I Want The Screen To Be A Massive Mirror: Lectures on Steve McQueenin*, Schaulager Basel: Laurenz Stiftung, 73–82.

Fisher, M. (2013), 'The Metaphysics of crackle: Afrofuturism and hauntology', *Dancecult: Journal of Electronic Dance Music Culture*.

Fisher, M. (2014), *Ghosts of my Life: Writings on Depression, Hauntology and Lost Futures*. Zero Books.

Fleetwood, N. (2011), *Troubling Vision: Performance, Visuality, and Blackness*. Chicago: University of Chicago Press.

Forgotten Television Drama (2019), '"Forgotten black TV drama" season at BFI Southbank' (February) <https://forgottentelevisiondrama.wordpress.com/2019/01/10/forgotten-black-tv-drama-season-at-bfi-southbank-february-2019/> (last accessed 20 April 2022).

Foulkes, J. (2015), 'Seeing the city: The filming of *West Side Story*', *Journal of Urban History*, 41: 6, 1032–51.

Fox, A. (2016), 'The New Anglo-American cinema of sexual addiction', in J. Gwynne (ed.), *Transgression in Anglo-American Cinema: Gender, Sex and the Deviant Body*. New York: Columbia University Press, 9–23.

Francis, P. (2019), oral history interview with an anonymised participant, 1 February.

Francis, P. (2021), 'Black Lives Matter: How the UK movement struggled to be heard in the 2010s', 7 June, available on *The Conversation* website at <https://theconversation.com/black-lives-matter-how-the-uk-movement-struggled-to-be-heard-in-the-2010s-161763> (last accessed 30 March 2022).

Ganatra, S. (2020), '*Small Axe*: The real Black British experience', November, *Royal Television Society* website at <https://rts.org.uk/article/small-axe-real-black-british-experience> (last accessed 2 August 2021).

Gates, Jr., H. L. (1988), *The Signifying Monkey: A Theory of African-American Literary Criticism*. Oxford: Oxford University Press.

George, N. (1988), *The Death of Rhythm and Blues*. New York: Pantheon Books.

George, N. (2013), 'An essentially American narrative: A discussion of Steve McQueen's film *12 Years a Slave*', *New York Times*, 11 October <www.nytimes.com/2013/10/13/movies/a-discussion-of-steve-mcqueens-film-12-yearsa-slave.html> (last accessed 19 March 2017).

Gerstle, G. (2022), *The Rise and Fall of the Neoliberal Order: America and the World in the Free Market Era*. Oxford: Oxford University Press.

Gill, R. (2007), 'Postfeminist media culture: elements of a sensibility', *European Journal of Cultural Studies*, 10: 2, 147–66.

Gillespie, M. B. (2016), *Film Blackness. American Cinema and the Idea of Black Film*. Durham, NC and London: Duke University Press.

Gillespie, M. B. (2021), 'Pressure drop: a "Small Axe" introduction', *Film Quarterly*, 74: 4, 48–50.

Gilroy, P. and McQueen, S. (2021), 'Transcript: In conversation with Steve McQueen', *Sarah Parker Redmond Centre Podcast*. Available online at <https://www.ucl.ac.uk/racism-racialisation/transcript-conversation-steve-mcqueen> (last accessed 2 September 2021).

Gilroy, P. (1993), *The Black Atlantic: Modernity and Double Consciousness*. Cambridge Mass: Harvard University Press.
Gilroy, P. (2013), '*12 Years a Slave*: In our 'post-racial' age the legacy of slavery lives on', *The Guardian*, 10 November <www.theguardian.com/commentisfree/2013/nov/10/12-years-a-slave-mcqueen-film-legacy-slavery> (last accessed 19 March 2017).
Gledhill, C. (2000), 'Re-thinking genre', in C. Gledhill and L. Williams (eds), *Reinventing Film Studies*. London: Arnold, 221–43.
Glennon, M. (2018), 'Mixtapes v. playlists: Medium, message, materiality', *Sounding Out!* <https://soundstudiesblog.com/2018/06/25/mixtapes-v-playlists-medium-message-materiality/> (last accessed 13 June 2022).
Glitre, K. (2006), *Hollywood Romantic Comedy: States of the Union 1934–1965*. Manchester: Manchester University Press.
Golden Globes (2021), <https://www.goldenglobes.com/winners-nominees/2021> (last accessed 2 May 2022).
Gonzalez, E. (2013), '*12 Years a Slave*: review', *Slant Magazine*, 13 September 2013 <www.slantmagazine.com/film/review/12-years-a-slave> (last accessed 19 March 2017).
Goodman, S. (2012), *Sonic Warfare: Sound, Affect, and the Ecology of Fear*. Cambridge, MA: MIT Press Ltd.
Gordon, L. R. (2015), *What Fanon Said: A Philosophical Introduction to His Life and Thought*. London: Hurst and Company.
Gorton, K. (2009), *Media Audiences: Television, Meaning and Emotion*. Edinburgh: Edinburgh University Press.
Grandin, G. (2015), 'Capitalism and Slavery', *The Nation*, 1 May <www.thenation.com/article/capitalism-and-slavery/> (last accessed 19 March 2017).
Grandin, G. (2014), *The Empire of Necessity: Slavery, Freedom, and Deception in the New World*. Metropolitan.
Gray, J. and D. Johnson (2021), *Television Goes to the Movies*. New York and London: Routledge.
Greaves I. (2021), 'Television is not just for Covid', *CST Online*, 30 April <https://cstonline.net/television-is-not-just-for-covid-by-ian-greaves/> (last accessed 17 April 2022).
Grosz, E. (1994), *Volatile Bodies: Towards a Corporeal Feminism*. Bloomington: Indiana University Press.
Grotkopp, M. and H. Kappelhoff (2012), 'Film genre and modality: The incestuous nature of genre exemplified by the war film', in S. Lefait and P. Ortoli (eds), *In Praise of Cinematic Bastardy*. Newcastle: Cambridge Scholars Publishing, 29–39.
Gwynne, J. (2021), '"Not conducive for sobriety": Sex addiction and neoliberal masculinity in *Don Jon* and *Thanks For Sharing*', *Cinej Cinema Journal*, 9: 1, 181–99.
Hall, S. (1993), 'Vanley Burke and the "desire for blackness"', in M. Sealy (ed.), *Vanley Burke: A Retrospective*. Lawrence and Wishart.
Hammond, P. (2021), 'Steve McQueen says "Small Axe" films were designed for TV', *Deadline*, 12 May <https://deadline.com/2021/05/small-axe-steve-mcqueen-interview-contenders-tv-1234757588/> (last accessed 15 April 2022).
Hammonds, E. (1994), 'Black (w)holes and the geometry of Black female sexuality', *differences: A Journal of Feminist Cultural Studies*, 6: 2–3.
Hanich, J. (2020), 'On pros and cons and bills and gates: The heist film as pleasure', *Film-Philosophy*, 24: 3, 304–20.
Hanssen, T. R. (2011), 'The ambient soundscape of gold mining: Noise, sonic physicality and affect in Steve McQueen's *Western Deep*', *International Journal of Performance Arts and Digital Media*, 7: 2, 127–39.
Hansen-Miller, D. and R. Gill (2011), '"Lad flicks": Discursive reconstructions of masculinity in popular film', in H. Radner and R. Stringer (eds), *Feminism at the Movies: Understanding Gender in Contemporary Popular Cinema*. New York: Routledge, 36–50.

Harari, Y. N. (2011), *Sapiens: A Brief History of Humankind*. London: Vintage.
Harvey, D. (2005), *A Brief History of Neoliberalism*. Oxford: Oxford University Press.
Hayward, S. (2006), *Cinema Studies: The Key Concepts* [third edition]. London: Routledge.
Hebdige, D. (2015), *Cut 'n' mix: Culture, Identity and Caribbean Music*. London: Routledge.
Henderson, B. (2019), 'Intertextuality and dance: An approach to understanding embodied performance of gender in dance discourses', *Journal of Dance Education*, 19, 1–9.
Henry, W. and M. Worley (2021), *Narratives from Beyond the UK Reggae Bassline: The System is Sound*. Palgrave Macmillan.
Highmore, B. (2017), 'City of strangers (qualities of disappointment)', in *Cultural Feelings: Mood, Mediation and Cultural Politics*. London: Routledge, 93–118.
Hinds, D. (1966), *Journey to an Illusion: The West Indian in Britain*. Heinemann.
hooks, bell (1992), 'Eating the other: Desire and resistance', in *Black Looks: Race and Representation*. Boston: South End.
hooks, bell (1986), 'Sisterhood: Political solidarity between women', *Feminist Review*, 23, 125–38.
Hornaday, A. (2020), 'The unbreakable gaze of Steve McQueen: "I'm asking you, please, look"', *Washington Post*, 16 December, online at <https://www.washingtonpost.com/entertainment/steve-mcqueen-education-small-axe/2020/12/16/2b061d2c-3e23-11eb-8db8-395dedaaa036_story.html>.
Horlock, M. (1999), 'Steve McQueen', in M. Horlock, S. Rainbird and S. Wilson, *The Turner Prize 1999* [exhibition catalogue]. London: Tate Gallery Publishing Ltd, 7.
Howe, L. H. (2021), telephone interview with Thomas Austin, 15 November.
Hull, A. G., P. Bell-Scott and B. Smith (1982) (eds), *All the Women are White, All the Blacks are Men, But Some of Us Are Brave*. New York: The Feminist Press.
Hull, A. G. and B. Smith (1982), 'The Politics of Black Women's Studies', in A. G. Hull, P. Bell-Scott and B. Smith (eds), *All the Women are White, All the Blacks are Men, But Some of Us Are Brave*. New York: The Feminist Press.
Hunt, A. (2020), 'Steve McQueen: "Until things change, these stories will always be timely"', *Little White Lies*, 18 November <https://lwlies.com/interviews/steve-mcqueen-small-axe-ode-to-black-culture-and-resilience/> (last accessed 15 April 2022).
Iampolski, M. (1998), *The Memory of Tiresias: Intertextuality and Film*. Berkeley: University of California Press.
Ide, W. (2021), 'Emmys spotlight: Steve McQueen on achieving global impact', *Screen Daily*, 25 June <https://www.screendaily.com/features/emmys-spotlight-steve-mcqueen-on-achieving-global-impact-with-the-personal-black-british-stories-of-small-axe/5160811.article> (last accessed 15 April 2022).
Iwen, M. E. (2014), 'Shame, sexual addiction, and consumption in American culture', *Sexuality and Culture*, 19, 413–25.
Jacobs, H. (1861/2001), *Incidents in the Life of a Slave Girl*, edited by N. Y. McKay and F. S. Foster. Norton.
Jagernauth, K. (2013), 'James Franco thinks being a sex addict in "Shame" wasn't so bad, criticizes gay club sequence', *IndieWire*, 15 November <https://www.indiewire.com/2013/11/james-franco-thinks-being-a-sex-addict-in-shame-wasnt-so-bad-criticizes-gay-club-sequence-91584/>.
James, C. L. R. (1938/1963), *The Black Jacobins: Toussaint L'Ouverture and the San Domingo Revolution* [revised edition]. Vintage.
James, M. (2019), *Sonic Intimacy: Reggae Sound Systems, Jungle Pirate Radio and Grime Youtube Music Videos*. London and New York: Bloomsbury.
James, N. (2012), 'Sex and the City', *Sight and Sound*, 22: 2, (February), 34–8.
Jaramillo, D. (2013), 'Rescuing television from the "cinematic": The perils of dismissing television style', in J. Jacobs and S. Peacock (eds), *Television Aesthetics and Style*. London: Bloomsbury, 67–76.

Jefferson, T. (2012), 'Policing the riots: from Bristol and Brixton to Tottenham, via Toxteth, Handsworth etc.', available on the *Centre for Crime and Justice* website at <www.crimeandjustice.org.uk/publications/cjm/article/policing-riots-bristol-and-brixton-tottenham-toxteth-handsworth-etc> (last accessed 20 March 2022).

Jermyn, D. (2008), 'I ♥ NY: the rom com's love affair with New York City', in D. Jermyn and S. Abbott (eds), *Falling in Love Again: Romantic Comedy in Contemporary Cinema*. London: IB Tauris, 9–24.

John, C. (2006), 'The legacy of the Brixton riots', 5 April, available on the *BBC News* website at <http://news.bbc.co.uk/2/hi/uk_news/4854556.stm> (last accessed 20 March 2022).

Johnston, C. (1975), 'Femininity and the masquerade: "Anne of the Indies"', in C. Johnston and P. Willemen (eds), *Jacques Tourneur*. London: British Film Institute, 36–44.

Johnson, E. P. (2003), *Appropriating Blackness: Performance and the Politics of Authenticity*. Durham, NC: Duke University Press.

Johnson, W. (2013), *River of Dark Dreams: Slavery and Empire in the Cotton Kingdom*. Harvard University Press.

Johnson, W. (1999), *Soul by Soul: Life Inside the Antebellum Slave Market*. Harvard University Press.

Jonze, T. (2019), 'Tricky: "I've lost people before and bounced back. This is different"', *The Guardian*, 14 October, available online at <https://www.theguardian.com/music/2019/oct/14/tricky-interview> (last accessed 6 April 2022).

Joseph-Salisbury, R. and L. Connelly (2021), *Anti-racist Scholar-activism*. Manchester: Manchester University Press.

Kahn, P. W. (1999), *The Cultural Study of Law: Restructuring Legal Scholarship*. Chicago and London: University of Chicago Press.

Kaisary, P. (2014), *The Haitian Revolution in the Literary Imagination: Radical Horizons, Conservative Constraints*. University of Virginia Press.

Kaisary, P. (2017), 'The Slave narrative and filmic aesthetics: Steve McQueen, Solomon Northup, and colonial violence', *MELUS: The Society for the Study of the Multi-Ethnic Literature of the United States*, 42: 2, 94–114.

Kaisary, P. (2019), 'Black agency and aesthetic innovation in Sergio Giral's *El otro Francisco*', *PALARA*, 23, 22–32.

Kappelhoff, H. (2018), *Front Lines of Community. Hollywood between War and Democracy*. Berlin and Boston: De Gryuter.

Keeling, K. (2007), *The Witch's Flight: The Cinematic, The Black Femme, and the Image of Common Sense*. Durham, NC: Duke University Press.

Kew, T. (2021), 'Rebel music in the rebel city: the performance geography of the Nottingham "Blues Party", 1957-1987', in W. Henry and M. Worley (eds), *Narratives from Beyond the UK Reggae Bassline: The System is Sound*. Palgrave Macmillan.

Kilkenny, K. (2018), 'Widows: How art house director Steve McQueen went mainstream (sort of) with a $40 million heist movie about class disparity, racial inequality and sexism', *Hollywood Reporter*, 424: 38, 19 November, S52+.

Kim, C. (2020), 'On Steve McQueen', in C. Kim and F. Moran (eds), *Steve McQueen* [exhibition catalogue]. London: Tate Publishing, 9.

Kleinhans, M.-M. and R. A. Macdonald (1997), 'What is a critical legal pluralism?', *Canadian Journal of Law and Society*, 12: 2, 25–46.

Krutnik, F. (1990), 'The faint aroma of performing seals: The "nervous" romance and the comedy of the sexes', *The Velvet Light Trap*, 26, (Fall), 57–72.

Lansiquot, R. (2021), 'Circumventing the spectacle of black trauma in practice', in C. Nowonka and A. Saha (eds), *Black Film British Cinema II*. London: Goldsmiths Press, 91–106.

Latymer Foundation (2021), 'The making of *Small Axe*: A virtually speaking talk with Tracey Scoffield and Charles Wijeratna', 13 May <https://www.youtube.com/watch?v=4lZ9hBt4JLI> (last accessed 20 April 2022).

Laurier, J. (2013), '*12 Years a Slave* and other films', *World Socialist Web Site*, 22 September <www.wsws.org/en/articles/2013/09/23/tff2-s23.html> (last accessed 19 March 2017).

Lee, D. P. (2013), 'Where it hurts: Steve McQueen on why *12 Years a Slave* isn't just about slavery', *Vulture*, 8 December <www.vulture.com/2013/12/steve-mcqueentalks-12-years-a-slave.html> (last accessed 19 March 2017).

Lee, D. (2014), *The Heist Film: Stealing with Style*. New York: Wallflower Press.

Lichtenberg, P. A., S. E. MacNeill and B. T. Mast (2000), 'Environmental press and adaptation to disability in hospitalized live-alone older adults', *The Gerontologist*, 40: 5, 549–56.

Ley, D. (2012), *The Myth of Sex Addiction*. Plymouth: Rowman and Littlefield Publishers.

Li, S. (2014), '*12 Years a Slave* as a Neo-Slave narrative', *American Literary History*, 26: 2, 326–31.

Li, Y. (2014), 'Ethnic unemployment in Britain (1972–2012)', 15 January, available on the *Runnymede Trust* website at <https://www.runnymedetrust.org/blog/ethnic-unemployment-in-britain> (last accessed 20 March 2022).

Liarou, E. (2022), 'The Diverse spaces of Play for Today', *Journal of British Cinema and Television*, (April), 19: 2, 173–93.

Littlewood, R. and M. Lipsedge (1997), *Aliens and Alienists: Ethnic Minorities and Psychiatry*. Psychology Press.

Litwack, L. F. (1965), *North of Slavery: The Negro in the Free States, 1790–1860*. University of Chicago Press.

Lodge, G. (2018), '*Widows*: Why Steve McQueen's slick thriller is an art-pop triumph', *The Guardian*, 15 November <https://www.theguardian.com/culture/2018/nov/15/widows-steve-mcqueen-film-art-pop-triumph> (last accessed 22 March 2022).

'*Lovers Rock*: Sir Steve McQueen film wins film of the year award', *BBC News*, 11 December 2020 <https://www.bbc.co.uk/news/entertainment-arts-55271537>.

Lowndes, J. (2020), '*Small Axe* and the legacies of Black culture and resistance in the UK', Joe Lowndes, 6 December <https://www.joelowndes.org/post/small-axe-and-the-legacies-of-black-culture-and-resistance-in-the-uk> (last accessed 13 June 2022).

Lynskey, D. (2021), 'The story behind the song behind one of the great music scenes in movie history', *Los Angeles Times*, 13 January, online at <https://www.latimes.com/entertainment-arts/music/story/2021-01-13/small-axe-lovers-rock-silly-games-dennis-bovell-steve-mcqueen>.

MacNeil, W. P. (2003), '"You slay me!" Buffy as jurisprudence of desire', *Cardozo Law Review*, 24, 2421–40.

MacNeil, W. P. (2005), 'Precrime never pays! "Law and economics" in *Minority Report*', *Journal of Media and Cultural Studies*, 19: 2, 201–19.

Malik, S. (2021), 'Black Film British Cinema: In three acts', in C. Nwonka and A. Saha (eds), *Black Film British Cinema II*. London: Goldsmiths Press, 21–40.

Mallie, E. and D. McKittrick (1996), *The Fight for Peace: The Secret Story Behind the Irish Peace Process*. Oxford: Heinemann.

Manderson, D. (2004), 'In the tout court of Shakespeare: interdisciplinary pedagogy in law', *Journal of Legal Education*, 54: 283–301.

Manderson, D. and R. Mohr (2002), 'From Oxymoron to intersection: An epidemiology of legal research', *Law Text Culture*, 6: 1, 59–82.

Marks, L. U. (2000), *The Skin of the Film: Intercultural Cinema, Embodiment, and the Senses*. London and Durham, NC: Duke University Press.

Martin, K. (1995), 'Echo chamber odysseys', *The Wire*, (May), Issue 135.

Martin, R., C. J. Nwonka, O. Koksal and A. Clark (2021), 'Understanding Steve McQueen', in C. Nwonka and A. Saha (eds), *Black Film British Cinema II*. London: Goldsmiths Press, 81–90.

Maurice, A. (2013), *The Cinema and its Shadow: Race and Technology in Early Cinema*. Minneapolis: University of Minnesota Press.

Mayer, S. (2021), 'An invitation to enchantment: How exhibition and curation connect Black film and British cinema', in C. Nwonka and A. Saha (eds), *Black Film British Cinema II*. London: Goldsmiths Press, 109–23.

McCabe, J. and K. Akass (2008), 'It's not TV, it's HBO's original programming: Producing quality TV', in M. Leverette, B. L. Ott and C. L. Buckley, *It's Not TV: Watching HBO in the Post-Television Era*. New York and London: Routledge, 83–94.

McDonald, H. (2008), 'Anger as a new film of IRA hero Bobby Sands screens at Cannes', *The Observer*, 11 May <www.guardian.co.uk/film/2008/may/11/cannesfilmfestival.northernireland/print> (last accessed 29 June 2009).

McDonald, T. J. (2005), *When Harry Met Sally*. London: BFI.

McDonald, T. J. (2008), 'Homme-Com: Engendering change in contemporary romantic comedy', in D. Jermyn and S. Abbott (eds), *Falling in Love Again: Romantic Comedy in Contemporary Cinema*. London: IB Tauris, 146–59.

McEvilley, T. (2002), 'Documenta 11', *Frieze*, 9 September <frieze.com/article/documenta-11-1> (last accessed 19 March 2017).

McGill, H. (2020/21), 'Red, White and Blue', *Sight and Sound*, (Winter), 31: 1, 137–8.

McKay, S. (2008), *Bear in Mind These Dead*. London: Faber and Faber.

McKittrick, D. (1994), *Endgame: The Search for Peace in Northern Ireland*. Belfast: Blackstaff Press.

McNair, B. (2002), *Striptease Culture: Sex, Media and the Democratisation of Desire*. London: Routledge.

McNair, B. (2013), *Porno? Chic! How Pornography Changed the World and Made It a Better Place*. London: Routledge.

McNamee, E. (2004), 'Once more unto the breach', in L. Moran, E. Sandon, E. Loizidou and I. Christie (eds), *Law's Moving Image*. London: Cavendish, 17–29.

McQueen, S. (2019), in E. Balsom, S. Perks and L. Reynolds (eds), *Artists' Moving Image in Britain Since 1989*. London: Paul Mellon Centre for Studies in British Art, 396.

McQueen, S. (2013a), 'I want to be useful', interview by Rob Nelson, *Walker Magazine*, 9 November <www.walkerart.org/magazine/2013/steve-mcqueen-i-want-be-useful> (last accessed 19 March 2017).

McQueen, S. (2013b), 'Steve McQueen and Henry Louis Gates Jr. talk *12 Years a Slave*, Part 3', *The Root*, 26 December <www.theroot.com/steve-mcqueen-and-henry-louis-gates-jr-talk-12-years-a-1790899474> (last accessed 19 March 2017).

McQueen, S. (2020), interviewed by Dennis Lim for the New York Film Festival, October, online at <https://www.youtube.com/watch?v=WiHIgSZrs0c>.

McQueen, S. and S. Comer (2014), *Steve McQueen in Dialogue*, Walker Art Centre (public event). Available at <www.youtube.com/watch?v=-KM_5z9WvUc> (last accessed 30 May 2022).

McQueen, S and J. Riley (2018), *Steve McQueen on The Business*, SAG-AFTRA Foundation, Los Angeles (public event). Available at <www.youtube.com/watch?v=HthRkqPQfqo> (last accessed 21 May 2022).

Mercer, A. (2018), '*Widows* isn't the feminist triumph you think it is', *Vice*, 7 December <https://www.vice.com/en/article/mby57y/widows-isnt-the-feminist-triumph-you-think-it-is> (last accessed 22 March 2022).

Mercer, K. (1994), *Welcome to the Jungle: New Positions in Black Cultural Studies*. New York and London: Routledge.
Metz, C. (1974), *Language and Cinema*. The Hague: Mouton.
Meunier, J.-P. (2019), 'The Structures of the film experience', in J. Hanich and D. Fairfax (eds), *The Structures of the Film Experience by Jean-Pierre Meunier. Historical Assessments and Phenomenological Expansions*. Amsterdam: Amsterdam University Press, 32–156.
Mills, B. (2013), 'What does it mean to call television "cinematic"?', in J. Jacobs and S. Peacock (eds), *Television Aesthetics and Style*. London: Bloomsbury, 57–66.
Mishra, P. (2020), *Bland Fanatics: Liberals, Race and Empire*. London and New York: Verso.
Mitchell, G. (1999), *Making Peace: The Inside Story of the Making of the Good Friday Agreement*. Oxford: Heinemann.
Moakley, P. (2014), 'Behind the moving image: The cinematography of *12 Years a Slave*', *Time Magazine Lightbox*, 27 February <time.com/3807491/behind-the-movingimage-the-cinematography-of-12-years-a-slave/> (last accessed 19 March 2017).
Mondloch, K. (2010), *Screens: Viewing Media Installation Art*. Minneapolis: University of Minnesota Press.
Moran, L., E. Sandon, E. Loizidou and I. Christie (eds) (2004), *Law's Moving Image*. London: Cavendish.
Morgan, D. (2006), 'Rethinking Bazin: Ontology and realist aesthetics', *Critical Inquiry*, 32: 3, 443–81.
Morgan, J. (2021), 'Steve McQueen, James Rogan to direct BBC1 three-parter "Uprising"', *Realscreen*, 11 May <https://realscreen.com/2021/05/11/steve-mcqueen-james-rogan-to-direct-bbc1-three-parter-uprising/>.
Morrison, A. (2010), 'New fashioned computers and old fashioned romantic comedy: *You've Got Mail*'s futuristic nostalgia', *Canadian Journal of Film Studies*, 19: 1, 41–58.
Mortimer, C. (2010), *Romantic Comedy: Routledge Film Guidebooks*. London: Routledge.
Moten, F. (2018), *The Universal Machine, Consent not to be a single being, Vol. 3*. Durham, NC and London: Duke University Press.
Mottram, J. (2008), 'Steve McQueen on *Hunger*' <www.channel4.com/film/reviews/feature.jsp?id=166630> (last accessed 28 June 2009).
Mulcaire, T. (1998), '*Deadpan*: the film installations of Steve McQueen', *Nka: Journal of Contemporary African Art*, 8, 10–13.
Mullard, C. and A. Kirby (1973), *Black Britain*. London: Allen and Unwin.
Munby, J. (2017), 'Hollywood and the black stickup: Race and the meaning of the heist on the big white screen', in J. Sloniowsky and J. Leach (eds), *The Best Laid Plans: Interrogating the Heist Film*. Detroit: Wayne State University Press, 121–38.
Naidoo, R. (2021), '*Small Axe* and the big tree of 2020', *Soundings*, 77, 9–22.
National Film Theatre (NFT) Panel (2021), 'The making of *Small Axe*', 23 October. Personal notes.
Navas, E. (2014), *Remix Theory: The Aesthetics of Sampling*. Ambra Verlag.
Nesbitt, N. (2003), *Voicing Memory: History and Subjectivity in French Caribbean Literature*. University of Virginia Press.
Newman, M. (1999), in G. Van Noord, *Steve McQueen* [exhibition catalogue]. London/Zurich: Institute of Contemporary Art/Kunsthalle Zurich, 24.
Newman, M. Z. and E. Levine (2012), *Legitimating Television: Media Convergence and Cultural Status*. New York and London: Routledge.
Nietzsche, F. (2002), *Beyond Good and Evil: Prelude to a Philosophy of the Future* [1886], edited by R.-P. Horstmann, translated by Judith Norman. Cambridge: Cambridge University Press.
Ngai, S. (2005), *Ugly Feelings*. Cambridge, MA: Harvard University Press.

Nixon, R. (2013), *Slow Violence and the Environmentalism of the Poor*. Cambridge, MA: Harvard University Press.

Northup, S. (1853/2014), *Twelve Years a Slave*. Penguin.

Norton, M. (2014), '*12 Years a Slave*: What happened to slave rebellion?', *San Francisco Bay View National Black Newspaper*, 14 March <sfbayview.com/2014/03/12-years-a-slave-what-happened-to-slave-rebellion/> (last accessed 19 March 2017).

Nwonka, C. J. and A. Saha (2021), 'Film, culture and the politics of race: an introduction to *Black Film, British Cinema II*', in C. J. Nwonka and A. Saha (eds), *Black Film, British Cinema II*. London: Goldsmiths University Press, 1–18.

NYFF58 Talk (2020), 'The Making of *Small Axe*', 21 October <https://www.youtube.com/watch?v=lXkkNyq40aI> (last accessed 20 April 2022).

O'Hagan, S. (2008), 'McQueen and country', *The Observer*, 12 October <www.guardian.co.uk/film/2008/oct/12/2> (last accessed 28 June 2009).

O'Hagan, S. (2020a), 'Steve McQueen: "Black people are weirdly missing from the narrative"', *The Observer*, 15 November <https://www.theguardian.com/tv-and-radio/2020/nov/15/steve-mcqueen-black-people-are-weirdly-missing-from-the-narrative-small-axe-mangrove-viola-davis-idris-elba-bernardine-evaristo> (last accessed 17 March 2022).

O'Hagan, S. (2020b), 'Steve McQueen: "It's rebel music that moves me"', *The Observer*, 15 November <https://www.theguardian.com/culture/2020/nov/15/steve-mcqueen-its-rebel-music-that-moves-me-small-axe-lovers-rock> (last accessed 4 September 2022).

O'Rawe, R. (2005), *Blanketmen: An Untold Story of the H-Block Hunger-strike*. Dublin: New Island Books.

O'Toole, F. (2008), '*Hunger* fails to wrest the narrative from the hunger strikers', *The Irish Times*, 22 November <www.irishtimes.com/newspaper/weekend/2008/1122/1227288132671.html> (last accessed 28 June 2009).

Olusoga, D. (2020a), 'David Olusoga: his Edinburgh television festival speech in full', *The Guardian*, 24 August <https://www.theguardian.com/media/2020/aug/24/david-olusoga-his-edinburgh-television-festival-speech-in-full> (last accessed 20 April 2022).

Olusoga, D. (2020b), '"These are the untold stories that make up our nation": Steve McQueen on *Small Axe*', *Sight and Sound*, (December), 30: 10, 24–35.

Palmer, L. A. (2011), '"LADIES A YOUR TIME NOW!" Erotic politics, lovers' rock and resistance in the UK', *African and Black Diaspora: An International Journal*, 4: 2, 177–92.

Palmer, L. (2020), '*Small Axe*: What Steve McQueen got right and wrong about *Lovers Rock*', *The Conversation*, 30 November <https://theconversation.com/small-axe-what-steve-mcqueen-got-right-and-wrong-about-lovers-rock-151068>.

Palmer, R. W. (ed.) (1990), *In Search of a Better Life: Perspectives on Migration From the Caribbean*. Greenwood Publishing Group.

Palmer, T. S. (2017), '"What feels more than feeling?": Theorizing the unthinkability of black affect', *Critical Ethnic Studies*, 3: 2, 31–56.

Palmer, T. S. (2020), 'Otherwise than blackness: Feeling, world, sublimation', *Qui Parle: Critical Humanities and Social Sciences*, 29: 2, 247–83.

Paskin, S. (1987), '"We have to study you in order to survive": Horace Ové on black and white Britain', *Monthly Film Bulletin*, December <https://www.bfi.org.uk/sight-and-sound/interviews/horace-ove-interview-pressure-race-britain>.

Penman, I. (1995), 'Black secret tricknology', *The Wire*, March 1995, Issue 133.

Penman, I. (2001), 'KLANG! Garvey's ghost meets Heidegger's geist', in P. Brophy (ed.), *Experiencing the Soundtrack: Cinesonic*. Sydney: Allen and Unwin.

Power, N. (2011), 'Counter-media, migration, poetry: interview with John Akomfrah', *Film Quarterly*, 65: 2, 59–63.

Radner, H. (2010), *Neo-feminist Cinema: Girly Films, Chick Flicks and Consumer Culture*. London: Routledge.
Raengo, A. (2016), 'Blackness and the image of motility: a suspenseful critique', *Black Camera* 8: 1, 191–206.
Ramon, A. (2020), 'Mangrove', *Sight and Sound*, (December), 30: 10, 71.
Reay, B., N. Attwood and C. Gooder (2015), *Sex Addiction: A Critical History*. Cambridge: Polity Press.
Redmond, S. L. (2013), *Anthem: Social Movements and the Sound of Solidarity in the African Diaspora*. New York: NYU Press.
Redmond, S. L. (2020), *Everything Man: The Form and Function of Paul Robeson*. Durham, NC: Duke University Press.
Restivo, A. (2019), *Breaking Bad and Cinematic Television*. Durham, NC and London: Duke University Press.
Reynolds, S. (2012), *Retromania: Pop Culture's Addiction to its Own Past*. London: Faber.
Richards, R. W. (2021), *Cinematic TV: Serial Drama Goes to the Movies*. Oxford: Oxford University Press.
Riviere, J. (1929/1986), 'Womanliness as a masquerade', in V. Burgin, J. Donald and C. Kaplan (eds), *Formations of Fantasy*. London: Methuen, 35–44.
Robeson, P. (1978), *Paul Robeson Speaks: Writings, Speeches, Interviews, 1918–1974*, edited by Philip S. Foner. New York: Citadel Press.
Robinson, S. (2020), 'In *Small Axe*, food is so much more than just a meal', *Bustle* <https://www.bustle.com/entertainment/small-axe-food-mangrove>.
Rodowick, D. N. (2007a), 'An elegy for theory', *October*, 122, 91–109.
Rodowick, D. N. (2007b), *The Virtual Life of Film*. Cambridge, MA and London: Harvard University Press.
Roediger, D. R. (ed.) (1998), *Black on White: Black Writers on What it Means to Be White*. New York: Shocken Books.
Roediger, D. R. (1998), 'Introduction', in D. Roediger (ed.), *Black on White: Black Writers in What it Means to Be White*. New York: Shocken Books, 3–26.
Rony, F. T. (1996), *The Third Eye: Race, Cinema, and Ethnographic Spectacle*. Durham, NC: Duke University Press.
Rose, N. (1992), *Governing the Soul: The Shaping of the Private Self*. London: Routledge.
Rose, S. (2019), 'When the kissing stopped: Why did Britain turn its back on black TV?', *The Guardian*, 7 February <https://www.theguardian.com/tv-and-radio/2019/feb/07/britain-bfi-forgotten-black-tv-drama-> (last accessed 20 April 2022).
Ross, D. (2018), 'A heist plus everything', *National Review*, 70: 24, 31 December, 47.
rottentomatoes.com <https://www.rottentomatoes.com/m/shame_2011> (last accessed 2 April 2022).
Royal Television Society (RTS) London, *Small Axe* production focus, discussion livestreamed on 19 May 2021. Also available at <https://www.youtube.com/watch?v=xVLLWRIaeNo> (last accessed 17 April 2022).
Ryan, M. (2018), 'Steve McQueen on "Widows" and why he ignored a "warning" that an actor was "difficult" to work with', *Uproxx*, 11 September. Available at <https://uproxx.com/movies/steve-mcqueen-interview-widows-michelle-rodriguez/> (last accessed 17 March 2022).
Russell, C. (2019), 'Widows', *Cinéaste*, 44: 2, 49–51.
Russell, N. (2020/21), 'The year in black cinema', *Sight and Sound*, (Winter), 31: 1, 76–7.
Saha, A. (2017), 'Scheduling race', in S. Malik and D. M. Newton (eds), *Adjusting the Contrast: British Television and Constructs of Race*. Manchester: Manchester University Press, 50–70.
Said, E. W. (2000), *Reflections on Exile and Other Essays*. Cambridge, MA: Harvard University Press.

Saraiya, S. (2020), 'Lush and romantic, Steve McQueen's magnificent *Lovers Rock* simply rocks', *Vanity Fair* <https://www.vanityfair.com/hollywood/2020/11/small-axe-lovers-rock-steve-mcqueen-review> (last accessed 13 June 2022).

Schiller, B.-M. (2021), 'Siblings, sex, and shame: The film *Shame* (2011)', *The International Journal of Psychoanalysis*, 102: 3, 603–16.

Schulenberg, S. E. (2003), 'Psychotherapy and movies: On using films in clinical practice', *Journal of Contemporary Psychotherapy*, 33: 1, 35–48.

Scobie, E. (1972), *Black Britannia: A History of Blacks in Britain*. Johnson Publishing Company Inc.

Searle, A. (2007), 'Steve McQueen's tribute to Britain's war dead features stamps bearing the soldiers' faces. Why wouldn't the MoD help him?', *The Guardian*, 12 March <www.guardian.co.uk/politics/2007/mar/12/iraq.art> (last accessed 28 June 2009).

Searle, A. (2012), 'A conversation with Steve McQueen', in I. Friedli (ed.), *Steve McQueen Works* [exhibition catalogue]. Basel: Laurenz Foundation, Schaulager, 194–202.

Sekimoto, S. and C. Brown (2022), *Race and the Senses: The Felt Politics of Racial Embodiment*. London and New York: Routledge.

Sepinwall, A. (2020), '"It's about a certain kind of blackness": Steve McQueen on the making of *Small Axe*', *Rolling Stone*, 18 December <https://www.rollingstone.com/movies/movie-features/small-axe-steve-mcqueen-interview-1104952/> (last accessed 15 April 2022).

Shadow and Act staff (2011), 'Review – Steve McQueen's "Shame" (smack it up, flip it, rub it down, oh, no . . . !)', *Shadow and Act*, 2 December <https://shadowandact.com/review-steve-mcqueens-shame-smack-it-up-flip-it-rub-it-down-oh-no>.

Sharf, Z. (2018), 'Steve McQueen says cinema is a communal experience: "There's no point looking at a movie on your laptop at home"', *IndieWire*, 12 September. Available at <https://www.indiewire.com/2018/09/steve-mcqueen-theaters-streaming-netflix-laptops-1202003045/> (last accessed 17 March 2022).

Sharfstein, D. J. (2012), *The Invisible Line: A Secret History of Race in America*. Penguin.

Sharpe, C. (2016), *In the Wake: On Blackness and Being*. Durham, NC: Duke University Press.

Shaviro, S. (2010), *Post-Cinematic Affect*. Winchester: Zero Books.

Shearer, M. (2016), *New York City and the Hollywood Musical: Dancing in the Streets*. Basingstoke: Palgrave Macmillan.

Shone, T. (2014), '*Nymphomaniac, The Wolf of Wall Street* and cinema's bad sex renaissance', *The Guardian*, 19 March <http://www.theguardian.com/film/2014/mar/19/nymphomaniac-wolf-wall-street-cinemas-bad-sexrenaissance?CMP=fb_us> (last accessed 1 September 2016).

Simmons, W. J. (2019), 'On affect and criticality in Steve McQueen's *Widows*', *Jump Cut: A Review of Contemporary Media Jump Cut*, 59, Fall <https://www.ejumpcut.org/archive/jc59.2019/Simmons-Widows/text.html> (last accessed 22 March 2022).

Simmons, W. J. (2022), 'Steve McQueen "Sunshine State" Pirelli HangarBicocca/Milan', *Flash Art*, 26 July <https://flash---art.com/2022/07/steve-mcqueen/> (last accessed 2 September 2022).

Sinha-Roy, P. (2018), 'WIDOWS', *Entertainment Weekly*, 1524/1525, 17–24 August, 51.

Skvirsky, S. A. (2020), *The Process Genre: Cinema and the Aesthetics of Labor*. Durham, NC and London: Duke University Press.

Small Axe (nd) website at <https://www.bbc.co.uk/programmes/p08vxt33>.

Smits, K. (2015), 'The silencing of women's voices: Catherine Mackinnon's *Only Words*', in G. Kemp (ed.), *Censorship Moments: Reading Texts in the History of Censorship and Freedom of Expression*. London: Bloomsbury Academic, 165–71.

Snead, J. (1994), *White Screens/Black Images: Hollywood for the Dark Side*, edited by C. MacCabe and C. West. Abingdon and New York: Routledge.
Sobchack, V. (1992), *The Address of the Eye: A Phenomenology of Film Experience*. Princeton, NJ: Princeton University Press.
Stäheli, A. (2013), 'Wie eine offene Wunde. Steve McQueens Kinospielfilme und das Phänomen der somatischen Wahrnehmung', in *I Want the Screen to be a Massive Mirror: Lectures on Steve McQueen*. Schaulager Basel: Laurenz-Stiftung, 133–48.
Stephens, M. A. (2014), *Skin Acts: Race, Psychoanalysis, and the Black Male Performer*. Durham, NC: Duke University Press.
Stepien, A. (2014), 'Understanding male shame', *Masculinities: A Journal of Identity and Culture*, 1: 7–26.
'Steve McQueen and Dr. Cornel West on Paul Robeson, Art, and Politics' (2016). Whitney Museum of American Art, accessed December 5, 2022.
Steve McQueen, interviewed by Dennis Lim for the New York Film Festival, October 2020, online at <https://www.youtube.com/watch?v=WiHIgSZrsoc>.
'Steve McQueen: Year 3, a portrait of Britain's future' Guardian Live streamed discussion, 22 June 2022.
Stevens, D. (2013), '*12 Years a Slave*: A beautiful film about the ugliest of subjects', *Slate*, 17 October <www.slate.com/articles/arts/movies/2013/10/_12_years_a_slave_directed_by_steve_mcqueen_reviewed.html> (last accessed 19 March 2017).
Stoever, J. L. (2016), *The Sonic Color Line: Race and the Cultural Politics of Listening*. New York: New York University Press.
Stratton, J. and N. Zuberi (2014) (eds), *Black Popular Music in Britain Since 1945*. Farnham: Ashgate.
'Studio Q: Michael Fassbender and Steve McQueen Bring Shame to Studio Q' (2011) <https://www.youtube.com/watch?v=3dCD9977ARY> (last accessed 19 April 2022).
Sullivan, P. (2014), *Remixology: Tracing the Dub Diaspora*. London: Reaktion Books Ltd.
Sunday Times, extract, 1978, republished in *Pressure* DVD booklet, 2005.
Suzman, J. (2020), *Work: A History of How We Spend Our Time*. London: Bloomsbury Circus.
Tauss, A. (2012), 'Contextualizing the current crisis: Post-fordism, neoliberal restructuring, and financialization', *Colombia Internacional*, 76: 51–79.
Thompson, K. (1985), 'From primitive to classical', *The Classical Hollywood Cinema: Film Style and Mode of Production to 1960*. in D. Bordwell, J. Staiger and K. Thompson (eds.), London: Routledge, 246–64.
Thorpe, V. and S. O'Hagan (2020), 'Top director Steve McQueen attacks racism in British film and TV industry', *The Observer*, 20 June <https://www.theguardian.com/culture/2020/jun/20/steve-mcqueen-attacks-racism-british-film-indutsry> [sic] (last accessed 19 July 2020).
Tookey, C. (2008), '*Hunger* – More Terrorist Propaganda', *The Daily Mail*, 30 October <www.dailymail.co.uk/tvshowbiz/reviews/article-1081911/Hunger-More-pro-terrorist-propa-ganda.html> (last accessed 28 June 2009).
Travers, B. (2018), 'Steve McQueen does not like TV one bit, and he'd never make his 2015 HBO pilot today', *IndieWire*, 25 October, online at <https://www.indiewire.com/2018/10/steve-mcqueen-tv-is-bad-hbo-pilot-codes-of-conduct-1202015069/>.
Travers, B. (2021), 'Steve McQueen on 5 integral moments that connect his "Small Axe" series', *IndieWire*, 3 June, online at <https://www.indiewire.com/2021/06/small-axe-connections-series-steve-mcqueen-interview-1234641368/>.
'*12 Years a Slave*: An ALH Forum', *American Literary History*, 26: 2, 317–84.
Tudor, D. (2011), 'Twenty-first century neoliberal man', in J. Kapur and K. B. Wagner (eds), *Neoliberalism and Global Cinema: Capital, Culture, and Marxist Critique*. London: Routledge, 57–68.

United Families and Friends Campaign, available on the *United Family and Friends Campaign* website at <www.uffcampaign.org> (last accessed 30 March 2022).

Veal, M. (2013), *Dub: Soundscapes and Shattered Songs in Jamaican Reggae*. Middletown, CT: Wesleyan University Press.

Vidali, D. and K. Phillips (2020), 'Ethnographic installation and "the archive": Haunted relations and relocations', *Visual Anthropology Review*, 36: 1, (Spring), 56–89.

Walker, H. and S. McQueen (2020), 'Acts of looking', *Steve McQueen*, edited by C. Kim and F. Moran. London: Tate Publishing, 104–11.

Wanzo, R. (2021), 'How long, not long: A take on Black joy', *Film Quarterly*, 74: 4, 51–5.

Warner, K. J. (2019), 'It can't always be Nina: The battle between plasticity and specificity in *Widows*', *Adaptation*, 12: 2, 185–9.

Warner, M. (1999), *The Trouble with Normal: Sex, Politics and the Ethics of Queer Life*. Cambridge, MA: Harvard University Press.

Waterson, J. (2021), 'BBC director general welcomes proposals for "distinctly British" content', *The Guardian*, 21 September <https://www.theguardian.com/media/2021/sep/21/bbc-welcome-governments-distinctly-british-content-legislation> (last accessed 15 April 2022).

Weheliye, A. G. (2005), *Phonographies: Grooves in Sonic Afro-Modernity*. Durham, NC: Duke University Press.

White, N. (2022), 'Child Q: Hundreds protest against "disgusting" strip search outside London police station', *Independent* online at <www.independent.co.uk/news/uk/home-news/child-q-protest-london-police-b2039395.html> (last accessed 19 March 2022).

Whiteley, S. and S. Rambarran (2020), *The Oxford Handbook of Music and Virtuality*. Oxford: Oxford University Press.

Williams, E. (1962), *History of the People of Trinidad & Tobago*. PNM Publishing Company.

Williams, J. S. (2021), 'Redemption song: Performing Black history and masculinity', *Film Quarterly*, 74: 4, 56–61.

Williams, M. (2020), 'Editorial', *Sight and Sound*, (December), 30: 10, 5.

Williams, P., S. Bath, J. Arday and C. Lewis (2019), *The Broken Pipeline: Barriers to Black PhD Students Accessing Research Council Funding*. London: Leading Routes.

Wilson, T. and H. Donnan (2006), *The Anthology of Ireland*. Oxford: Berg Publishers.

'Winford Fagan in Handsworth, 1970', *The Guardian*, 11 September 2015, online at <https://www.theguardian.com/artanddesign/2015/sep/11/winford-fagan-handsworth-photograp-vanley-burke>.

Winfield, J. (2020), 'Axe to grind', *Drama Quarterly*, 13 November <https://dramaquarterly.com/axe-to-grind/> (last accessed 15 April 2022).

Whyman, T. (2021), 'The ghosts of our lives', *New Statesman*, 9 September <https://www.newstatesman.com/politics/2019/07/the-ghosts-of-our-lives> (last accessed 13 June 2022).

Wolf, S. (2006), '"We'll always be bosom buddies": Female duets and the queering of Broadway musical theater', *GLQ*, 1: 3, 351–76.

Wood, M. (2000), *Blind Memory: Visual Representations of Slavery in England and America, 1780–1865*. Manchester: Manchester University Press.

Wood, M. (2014), 'At the movies', *London Review of Books*, 6 February, 23.

Yamato, J. (2020), '*Small Axe* brings untold history to the screen', *Los Angeles Times*, 21 November <https://www.latimes.com/entertainment-arts/movies/story/2020-11-21/mangrove-small-axe-amazon-steve-mcqueen> (last accessed 20 April 2022).

Young, L. (1996), *Fear of the Dark: 'Race', Gender and Sexuality in the Cinema*. London and New York: Routledge.

Younge, G. (2020), 'Red, White and Blue', *Sight and Sound*, (December), 30: 10, 28.

Yusuff, A. (2021), 'The Women of the British Black Arts Movement', 20 August, online at <awarewomenartists.com/en/magazine/les-femmes-du-british-black-arts-movement> (accessed 27 March 2022).

Zaibi, L. (2014), 'Pocomania rituals and identity in Andrew Salkey's *A Quality of Violence* (1959)', *Global Journal of Human-Social Science*, 14: 1, online.

Index

Abbott, Diane, 173, 180, 184
Abdurraqib, Hanif, 77
Adams, Gerry, 53
aesthetics, 1, 6, 8–11, 20, 24, 26, 30–40, 43–4, 52–4, 66, 69, 87–90, 98–9, 103–8, 125, 129–34, 139, 142–3, 146, 150–4, 167–71, 185
affect, 3, 10, 31–3, 36, 43, 52, 129, 133–7
Aftab, Kaleem, 115
Akass, Kim, 138
Akomfrah, John, 5, 11, 121, 161, 169, 185, 187–8, 192
Alex Wheatle (2020), 7–8, 114–18, 126, 131, 139, 178–9, 193
All Day/I Feel Like That (2015), 28
Altman, Rick, 97–8
Amazing Grace (2006), 78
Amazon, 4, 5, 113, 119, 123, 127–8
American Civil War, 80
Amnesty International, 173
Amponsah, George, 5
Anderson, Melissa, 87
Andrews, Kehinde, 114, 116, 155
Ani, Ivie, 160–1
archive, 187, 189
Ashes (2002–15), 22
Ashley, Colin Patrick, 135
Asokan, Ratik, 188–9

The Asphalt Jungle (1950), 100
audience, 5, 8, 10, 13, 43, 137–40, 143, 191

Babylon (1980), 122
Bach, Johann Sebastian, 71–2
Baldwin, James, 7, 12, 189
Bernard, Jay, 114, 116–17, 155
Barrage (1998), 25
Bart, Helen, 123, 181
Baughan, Nikki, 115
Bazin, André, 38, 130
Bear (1993), 19–21, 24, 26, 29, 32, 44
Belafonte, Harry, 73
Bell, James, 115–16, 120
Belle (2013), 93, 120
Belton, John, 130–1
Benjamin, Walter, 137
Berlin, 97
Best, Khali, 139
Biggs, Barry, 146
Billies, Michelle, 135
Birmingham, 185–7
The Birth of a Nation (1915), 81
Black Audio Film Collective, 5, 11, 121, 167, 185, 187
Black Lives Matter, 4, 160, 182–4
Black Power: A British Story of Resistance (2021), 5, 6

Blackwood, Maureen, 5, 122, 182
Blame (2001), 2–3
Bleu de Chanel (2018), 28
Blue Collar (1978), 101
Bobbitt, Sean, 26, 34, 79, 88–9, 109
body, 2–3, 19–20, 26, 31–40, 49–51, 57, 79, 83, 102, 132–3, 145–7, 164, 170–1
Body and Soul (1925), 74
Bourdieu, Pierre, 6
Bovell, Dennis, 148, 155
Boy with Flag, Winford in Handsworth Park, 1970, 185, 187, 192
Boyce, Sonia, 182
Boyega, John, 29, 135, 191
Bradley, Rizvana, 39
Breaking Bad (2008–13), 133, 137
Brinkema, Eugenie, 133, 135, 137
British Academy of Film and Television Arts (BAFTA), 115, 123
British Broadcasting Corporation (BBC), 4, 5, 10, 113–16, 118–20, 122–8, 140–1, 184
Brown, Christopher, 3, 145
Brown, Kimberly Juanita, 39
Bryan, Beverley, 173
Buñuel, Luis, 1
Burke, Vanley, 5, 11, 185–9, 191–3
Burn! (1969), 93
Burning an Illusion (1981), 5, 121
The Butler (2013), 93

calypso, 158, 195
Campion, Jane, 129
Caribs' Leap (2002), 22, 25, 80, 92
Carty-Williams, Candice, 114
Catch (1997), 25, 152
Cavell, Stanley, 109
Chambers, Eddie, 183
Channel 4, 44, 120–1, 124, 140, 185
Charlotte (2004), 1–3, 22
Chicago, 101, 109
Child Q, 174
Clark, Ashley, 6, 143
class, 7, 91, 96, 100–1, 138, 146, 176, 194

Clifford, James, 166
Clover, Carol, 1
Coard, Bernard, 11–12, 194–8
Cobb, Jasmine Nicole, 91
Codes of Conduct (2016), 12, 125
Coel, Michaela, 116
Cold Breath (1999), 20, 22, 32
Cole, Sheyi, 139
Collier, Delinda, 152
Collins, Patricia Hill, 144
Connell, Kieran, 185
Conrad, Joseph, 93
Coomber, Saffron, 155
Corless, Kieron, 115–16, 120, 122
Covid-19 pandemic, 4, 113, 115, 128
Crichlow, Frank, 19, 139
de Cuir Jr., Greg, 115
Cumberbatch, Benedict, 85
Current (1999), 25

Dadzie, Stella, 173
Dahl, Roald, 7
Danticat, Edwidge, 88
Dassin, Jules, 102
Davie, Tim, 122
Davis, Viola, 24, 96
Davy, Gary, 123
Dawes, Kwame, 166
Deadpan (1997), 8, 20–2, 25–6, 31, 33, 43, 152
Dean, Tacita, 18
Deleuze, Gilles, 167
Deller, Nadine, 114, 144, 160–1
Demos, T. J., 34, 36, 150, 152, 156
Derrida, Jacques, 170
Desai, Jayaben, 176
Dixon, Ivan, 101
Django Unchained (2012), 78, 93–4
Doherty, Thomas, 80, 83
Douglass, Frederick, 81
Drumroll (1998), 22, 25, 37, 44
Du Bois, W. E. B., 187
dub, 11, 132, 158–71
Duvall, Robert, 28, 98
Dyer, Richard, 68, 72

Eames-Bradley Commission, 46–8, 54
Education (2020), 5, 12, 115, 118, 125–6, 131, 134, 175, 179, 181, 194–8
Eisenstein, Sergei, 130
El-Enany, Nadine, 4
Ellis, John, 141
The Emperor Jones (1933), 74
English, Darby, 3, 153, 156
End Credits (2012), 73, 76
Enwezor, Okwui, 25, 33, 35, 156, 168
Erivo, Cynthia, 102
Eshun, Kodwo, 163, 169
Esquire magazine, 181
Empire Windrush, 184
excess, 32
Everard, Sarah, 173
Exodus (1992–7), 26–8

Fagan, Winford, 186–8
Fanon, Frantz, 166, 171, 188, 192
Farred, Grant, 39
Farrell, Colin, 28, 98
Faulkner, William, 85
Federal Bureau of Investigation (FBI), 73
feminism, 64,
Fassbender, Michael, 22, 59–60, 62, 68, 85, 94, 153
Fincher, David, 129
Fintoni, Laurent, 161
Fisher, Jean, 1, 6, 40
Fisher, Mark, 163, 167
Five Easy Pieces (1995), 20, 23, 37
Fleetwood, Nicole, 32
Floyd, George, 4
food, 3, 12, 145, 148, 160, 178
Fox, Alistair, 60, 62
Fox, Frankie, 154
Francis-Swaby, Daniel, 155

gallery space, 21–2, 36, 132
Gates, Henry Louis Jr., 8
gender, 5, 8, 13, 32–3, 35, 59, 64, 96, 99, 101, 103–9, 138, 144–57, 172–84
genre, 59, 63–5, 67–9, 72, 73, 81–3, 92, 96–109, 191

George, Ellis, 155
Gerstle, Gary, 70
Gillespie, Michael Boyce, 107, 132
Gilroy, Paul, 13, 80, 161, 163
Girls, Tricky (2001), 9, 25, 30–40
Gledhill, Christine, 99–100
Glennon, Mike, 168–9
Glover, Danny, 87
Gooding, Ena, 2
Gooding, Denise, 2
Goodman, Steve, 164
Gorton, Kristyn, 133
Goya, Francisco, 88
Graham, Stuart, 153
Grandin, Greg, 92
Gravesend (2007), 80, 92–3
Gray, F. Gary, 101
Green Book (2018), 77
Greenlee, Sam, 101
Grenfell (2019), 13
Grenfell Tower, 13
Griffith, D. W., 81
Guillén, Nicolas, 76

Haley, Alex, 163
Hall, Stuart, 192–3
Hamilton, Shem, 139
Hammonds, Evelynn, 192
Handsworth Songs (1986), 5, 11, 122, 161, 169, 187–93
Hanssen, Tina Rigby, 132
Hassan Howe, Leila, 13, 156
Haynes, Wayne, 2
Heart of Darkness, 93
The Help (2011), 93
Henry, Bibaa, 173
Henry, Brian Tyree, 105
Highmore, Ben, 188
Hiller, Arthur, 101
Himid, Lubaina, 180–3
A Hole in Babylon (1979), 121
hooks, bell, 172
How to Steal a Million (1966), 101
How the West Indian Child is Made Educationally Sub-normal in the British School System, 194–6

Hunger (2008), 3, 9, 20–1, 23, 26, 41–58, 73, 96, 150, 152–4, 156
Hunt, Aaron, 125
Hull, Akasha, 173
Huston, John, 100

I Am Not Your Negro (2016), 189, 192
I May Destroy You (2020), 116
Iampolski, Mikhail, 151
Ide, Wendy, 119
Illuminer (2002), 152
intertextuality, 20–2, 25–6, 31, 33, 150–1, 153, 156, 185, 187–92
Iraq, 45
Irish Republican Army (IRA), 9, 41, 55, 58, 153
Irwin, Brett, 2

Jackson, Samuel L., 189
Jacobs, Harriet, 81
Jacobs, Jason, 130
Jafa, Arthur, 109
James, C. L. R., 85
Jamarillo, Deborah, 130
Jermyn, Deborah, 63
Johnson, Linton Kwesi, 169, 193
Johnson, Walter, 84
Jones, Claudia, 176, 184
Julien, Isaac, 5, 121, 183
Just Above My Head (1996), 11, 20, 32, 150–4, 156

Kaluuya, Daniel, 98, 100
Kay, Janet, 145, 148, 167, 180
Keaton, Buster, 8, 22, 31–2, 43–4, 152
Kew, Tom, 171
Kidao, Sinéad, 123
The Killing (1956), 104
Kirchner, Shabier, 114, 117, 127, 131, 146
Kubrick, Stanley, 104
Kunz, Molly, 103

La Plante, Lynda, 101
Lamming, George, 158
Lansiquot, Rabz, 147
Laurier, Joanne, 90–1

Lee, Daryl, 98
Lee, Spike, 13
legal studies, 41–2, 56
Li, Stephanie, 79, 86
Li, Yaojun, 174
Lincoln (2012), 78
Logan, Leroy, 29, 121, 123–4, 135, 153–4, 179, 187, 191
London, 4, 93, 144, 175,
London Film Festival, 117
Lord Kitchener, 195
Louisiana, 88, 91
L'Ouverture, Toussaint, 87
Love is the Message, the Message is Death (2017), 109
Lovers Rock (2020), 8, 11, 39, 111–18, 121, 126, 131–2, 139, 144–71, 175, 179, 181

Malik, Sarita, 139–41, 143
Mangrove (2020), 19, 22–3, 114–16, 118, 121, 125–6, 131, 139, 141, 156, 178, 181, 183, 193
Mann, Michael, 100
Manderlay (2005), 92–4
Marian Goodman Gallery, 18
Marks, Laura U., 37
Marsh-Edwards, Nadine, 122
Maurice, Alice, 32, 145–6
McCabe, Janet, 138
McDonald, Tamar Jeffers, 64
McEvilley, Thomas, 89
McGill, Hannah, 115
memory, 42–4, 45–8, 54–5, 78, 162–71, 187
Mercer, Kobena, 141, 182
Metropolitan Police, 173, 175, 178, 191
Metz, Christian, 130, 143
Michaeux, Oscar, 74
Mighty Sparrow, 195
Mill, Jon Michael, 102
Mills, Brett, 130
Morris, Olive, 176, 184
Moten, Fred, 107
Mr Burberry (2016), 28
Mulcaire, Thomas, 152
Mullard, Chris, 159

Müller, Robby, 25
Mulligan, Carey, 22, 59
My Beautiful Laundrette (1985), 120

Naidoo, Roshni, 139–41, 149
National Film Theatre, 120–1
National Front, 174
Neeson, Liam, 102
Nietzsche, Firedrich, 109
neoliberalism, 61, 67, 69–70, 81
Nesbitt, Nick, 88
Netflix, 131
Nevill, Noski, 26
New Cross Fire, 2–3, 12
New Orleans, 86, 92
New York, 59, 63, 67–8, 71–2, 86
New York Film Festival (NYFF), 117
New York, New York (1977), 59, 68
Newland, Courttia, 114, 123, 157, 181
Ngai, Sianne, 145
The Nine Muses (2010), 189
Northern Ireland, 42–58
Northup, Solomon, 9–10, 78–94
Norton, Marc, 86
Nwonka, Clive James, 129, 138–9, 141
Nyong'o, Lupita, 9

Ocean's Eleven (2001), 104
Odds Against Tomorrow (1959), 101
Okwok, Shaniqua, 144
Olusoga, David, 4, 6, 12, 114, 121–3, 141, 146, 156
O'Neill, Eugene, 74
O'Toole, Fintan, 52–4
Ové, Horace, 5, 13–14, 117, 121

Parkes, Shaun, 19, 139
Palmer, Lisa Amanda, 147–8
Palmer, Tyrone, 135
Pablo, Augustus, 162–3
Peacock, Steven, 130
Peck, Raoul, 189
Peel, Robert, 191
Penelope (1966), 101
Penman, Ian, 163, 166, 171
Perry, Lee 'Scratch', 155, 162, 165–6

Phullar, Kulraj, 120
Pink Nails (1999), 25
Piper, Keith, 182
Plomley, Roy, 7
Pontecorvo, Gillo, 93
Poole, Tom, 117, 127
Powell, Enoch, 175
Pressure (1975), 5, 13, 121
Prey (1999), 37
Pursuit (2005), 22

Queen and Country (2007–9), 45

race and racialisation, 3–8, 17, 20–1, 28–9, 31–5, 37–40, 44, 66, 72, 73–5, 79–95, 96, 99, 101–9, 135–98
Raengo, Alessandra, 31–2, 38
Ramon, Alex, 114, 116
Rampling, Charlotte, 1
Ramsay, Kadeem, 146
Red, White and Blue (2020), 5, 11, 29, 114, 118, 123–4, 131, 135, 150, 153–4, 178–9, 181, 185–7, 190–2
Redmond, Shana L., 160
reggae, 8, 11, 144–9, 156, 161–71, 180
Regnault, Félix, 32
Restivo, Angelo, 133, 135, 137
Revivalism, 165–6
The Revolutionaries, 161, 163
Richards, Rashna Wadia, 130
Du Rififi chez les hommes (1955), 102, 104
Rigg, Marcia, 184
Rigg, Sean, 184
Robeson, Paul, 9, 73–7
Rodriguez, Michelle, 99
Rodowick, D. N., 130
Roediger, David, 7
Rogan, James, 2, 5, 13
Rogan, Soleta, 5
Rogan Productions, 5
Rony, Fatimah Tobing, 32
Roots, 163
Rossi, Franco, 122
Rouget, Gilbert, 166
Royal Television Society, 115
Ruddock, Sandra, 2

Ruddock, Osbourne 'King Tubby', 162
Russell, Nicholas, 115
Ryan, Mike, 131

Sagar, Anjalika, 169
Saha, Anamik, 138–9, 141
Said, Edward, 166
Sanders of the River (1935), 74
Sands, Bobby, 9, 24, 41, 44–5, 48, 51, 53–8, 153
Sandy, Kenyah, 134, 198
Sankofa Film and Video Collective, 5, 121, 182
Saraiya, Sonia, 167
Scafe, Suzanne, 173
Schnabel, Julian, 18
Schrader, Paul, 101
Scoffield, Tracey, 5, 10, 114, 121, 123–7, 131, 141, 143
Scorsese, Martin, 68, 129
Sekimoto, Sachi, 3, 145
Set It Off (1995), 101
7th November (2001), 25
Sex and the City (1998–2004), 59, 67
sexuality, 59–72, 147, 149
Shabazz, Melenik, 5, 117, 121
Shame (2011), 5, 7, 8, 9, 22–3, 59–72, 96, 161
Shannon, Lyttanya, 5, 197
Shapiro, Stephen, 92
Shaviro, Steven, 135
Sharfstein, Daniel, 80
Show Boat (1936), 74
Siddons, Alastair, 114, 123, 181
Sight and Sound magazine, 10, 113–16, 120–3, 132, 155–6
Simone, Nina, 96
slavery, 9–10, 78–95, 146–7, 198
Small Axe (2020), 3–8, 10–12, 19, 22, 28, 29, 39, 75, 113–98
Smallman, Mina, 173
Smallman, Nicole, 173
Smits, Katherine, 172
Snead, James, 32
Soane, Echo, System I (1999), 25

Soane, Echo, System II (1999), 25
Sobchack, Vivian, 36–7
Soderbergh, Steven, 104
Something Old, Something New, Something Borrowed, Something Blue (1998), 20, 25
Song of Freedom (1936), 74
La Sortie de l'usine Lumière à Lyon, 102
sound, 34, 38, 132–4,
Spitulnik, Debra Vidali, 169
The Spook Who Sat by the Door (1972), 101
Spruell, Sam, 139
St. Aubyn, Amarah-Jae, 144, 165
Stage (1996), 20
Static (2009), 22
Steamboat Bill Jr. (1928), 8, 22, 31, 152
Stephens, Michelle Ann, 32–3
Stevens, Dana, 90
Stoever, Jennifer Lynn, 10
The Story of Lovers Rock (2011), 121
Stowe, Harriet Beecher, 79, 94
Stuart, Moira, 180
Subnormal: A British Scandal (2021), 5, 6, 12, 194, 196–8
Sullivan, Paul, 163–4, 169
Sunshine State (2022), 6, 13

Tarantino, Quentin, 78, 94
Taylor, Clyde, 76
technology, 31–3, 35, 37–9,
television, 4–5, 10, 17, 113–27, 128–44, 187–9, 191
Thatcher, Margaret, 174–6
Thief (1980), 100
Thomas Dane Gallery, 18
Thompson, Errol 'Errol T.', 162
Thompson, Shirley, 181
Titanic (1997), 150
Touissant, Steven, 154
Travers, Ben, 120
von Trier, Lars, 93
Tricky, 30–40
Tremé (2010–13), 92
Turbine Studios, 5, 124
Turner Prize, 4, 17, 43, 56, 121

12 Years a Slave (2013), 4, 5, 8, 9–10, 22, 39, 78–95, 96, 124, 146, 155, 161

Un Chien Andalou (1929), 1
Uncle Tom's Cabin (1852), 79–80
United Families and Friends, 183–4
unemployment, 174
Untitled-Wall (1998), 25
Uprising (2021), 2–3, 5, 6, 156

Veal, Michael E., 162, 165–6, 168, 171
voice, 31, 38, 157, 165, 172

de Waal, Kit, 114, 155
Walker, Hamza, 30
Walsh, Enda, 41, 48, 57
Wanzo, Rebecca, 132
Ward, Michael, 145, 165
Weber, Max, 6
Weheliye, Alexander, 171
West, Cornel, 75
Western Deep (2002), 24–6, 34–6, 80, 89, 92, 132

Wheatle, Alex, 7–8, 13, 123, 160, 181, 193
White Elephant (1998), 25
White Water Circle (1994), 23
Widows (1983–5), 8, 101
Widows (2018), 5, 7, 8, 10, 22, 24, 28, 96–109, 120, 124
Williams, Eric, 159, 198
Windrush Generation, 160
Winfield, John, 118
Winterbottom, Michael, 26
Wise, Robert, 101
Wonderland (1999), 26
Wood, Marcus, 90
World in Action, 175
Wright, Letitia, 123

Year Three (2019), 13
Younge, Gary, 114, 155
Yusuff, Aurella, 180

Zaibi, Lamia, 166
Zephaniah, Benjamin, 12
Zimmer, Hans, 81, 105

EU representative:
Easy Access System Europe
Mustamäe tee 50, 10621 Tallinn, Estonia
Gpsr.requests@easproject.com

www.ingramcontent.com/pod-product-compliance
Lightning Source LLC
Chambersburg PA
CBHW070348240426
43671CB00013BA/2440